Y0-CAH-956

The Server+ Cram Sheet

This Cram Sheet contains the distilled, key facts about the Server+ exam. Review this information last thing before entering the test room, paying special attention to those areas where you feel you need the most review. You can transfer any of the facts onto a blank piece of paper before beginning the exam.

SERVER ENVIRONMENT

1. Temperature—The temperature in a server will be approximately 20 to 30 degrees (Fahrenheit) higher than the temperature in the room. Room temperature above 80 and server temperature above 110 can cause damage.

2. Electricity—It is essential that proper electricity, including battery backup, is provided in a server room.

3. Humidity—Humidity above 20 to 30 percent could cause short circuits, and below this amount could cause circuit boards to become brittle.

UPGRADE

4. BIOS—Upgrading or flashing the BIOS requires a boot floppy disk that can usually be downloaded from the customer support link on the particular manufacturer's Web site. Once the floppy is booted, it will automatically run the BIOS upgrade process. A reboot thereafter is necessary.

5. SNMP/RMON—SNMP and RMON alerts might be in place to indicate network utilization, processor utilization, and so on. Network utilization lower than 60 percent is not a concern. SNMP and RMON traps can also be changed to report different thresholds, and the management application can be changed to notify you at different ranges.

HARDWARE UPGRADE AND INSTALLATION

6. Memory
   - Server motherboards have a limit on how much RAM they can support and the maximum supported memory in a single SIMM.
   - Many servers have problems with different SIMMs being on the same machine or on the same memory bank. Some systems require that the same memory speeds be on the system; others require that identical capacity SIMMs be in place, and still others require that everything be identical including the manufacturer.

7. CPU—Adding a CPU will require a BIOS upgrade

8. SCSI
   - When anything goes wrong, check termination and LUN.
   - HVD is not compatible with LVD or SE.
   - LVD and SE devices are compatible with each other but will run at the slower SE bus speeds
   - 8-bit (SCSI, Fast, Ultra, and Ultra2) SCSI internal devices are male; cables are female

- RAID 1 offers mirroring or duplexing, has 50 percent available disk space, is slower than RAID 0, and is also slower than a single drive.
- RAID 5 offers striping with parity, has available disk space equal to the capacity of the disks minus one, and is faster than RAID 1 but slower than RAID 0.
- Hardware-based RAID array configuration supports hot swapping and hot plugging and is configured using a RAID BIOS. Changing the order in which the hard drives are configured in an array requires reconfiguration, during which all data will be lost. Hardware-based RAID has a separate processor and is not CPU intensive.
- Software-based RAID does not support hot swapping or hot plugging and is configured using the NOS or supported application. Drive replacement occurs by taking down the server. Software-based RAID is CPU intensive.

TROUBLESHOOTING

9. Baselines should cover pertinent server usage information over a period of several days or a week. The same data should be gathered again and compared with the baselines during the troubleshooting process.

- High memory utilization can indicate bad or failing RAM.
- High CPU utilization may indicate software-based RAID or a failing CPU.
- High pages/second can indicate that there is not enough RAM or that the RAM is failing.
- High hard disk utilization might point to insufficient drive space, a failing hard drive, or a paging problem (for paging problems, refer to the previous bulleted item).

20. Services and daemons are primarily software issues, but because services and daemons work closely with drivers, they can be hardware related. When a service or daemon fails, restart the daemon. If it fails again, reboot the server. If it fails yet again, disable or remove other services by using a process of elimination.

21. Antivirus software can be configured to automatically update from the Web. Communications for this usually occur via FTP. If the update fails, check to ensure that the FTP site is available, and also check to ensure that outbound communications are intact.

base volume is called "sys." NetWare services/daemons are called NetWare Loadable Modules (NLMs). Server shutdown occurs using the command **down** followed by **exit**, which will exit to a DOS prompt. Typing **server** reinitializes the server.

- Windows NT/2000 is both an OS and an NOS that uses hard disks formatted with the NTFS format but also supports FAT32 formats. Daemons/NLMs for Windows NT/2000 are called services. Server shutdown occurs by either pressing Ctrl+Alt+Del followed by clicking the Shutdown button or by selecting Start menu | Shutdown and then choosing Shutdown or Restart.

- Unix and Linux are both OSs and NOSs that use hard disks formatted with the NIS or NFS file system. Services or NLMs for Unix and Linux are called daemons. Server shutdown occurs by using the command **shutdown now -g -0**.

DISASTER RECOVERY AND FAULT TOLERANCE

16. Disaster Protection
    - Data Loss
        - RAID 1 offers mirroring (one drive controller) or duplexing (two drive controllers), and 50 percent of the overall disk space is available for data storage. RAID 5 offers striping with parity, and the available disk space is one less than the number of drives installed on the stripe set.
        - Tape backup and rotation schemes can include a GFS rotation method. A full backup occurs once a month (grandfather), a full backup occurs once a week (father), and an incremental or differential backup occurs once a day. Remember that tape backups can also be used for archiving for long periods of time.
    - Fire/flood/complete destruction—Protection from fire is provided when storing tape backups in a fireproof safe on the premises. Protection from flood and complete destruction requires offsite backup storage.

- Power loss requires a UPS unit. UPSs can be installed with management software that can perform remote notification and automatic system shutdown.

17. Data Center Destruction
    - Hot sites are available for use within 48 hours. Most, if not all, equipment is onsite.
    - Cold sites are available for use within a few weeks. None of the necessary equipment is onsite, and building, structure, or office modifications may be necessary.
    - Offsite tape storage is required to recover from any full destruction situation.

18. Fault Tolerance
    - Technologies
        - Hot swap occurs when a failed component can be replaced without taking down the server.
        - Hot plug is a feature whereby a spare component is installed and automatically comes online when an identical component fails. This occurs without taking down the server.
    - Hardware
        - Dual PCI buses are used to help prevent a single bus from becoming flooded with traffic. The second bus is usually used for RAID controller cards.
        - Dual network cards are used to reduce problems with a single NIC, cable, or hub/switch port.
        - Dual CPUs are primarily used for additional power; however, failover procedures can allow a system to boot from a different CPU if the first one fails. For this reason, a BIOS upgrade is necessary when installing a second CPU.
        - Fault-tolerant cooling fans and power supplies are simply hot-swappable devices found in servers.
        - RAID 0 is not fault tolerant, but it is fast and has 100 percent available disk space.

- 16-bit (Wide, Fast Wide, Wide Ultra, Wide Ultra2, Ultra3, Ultra160/160+/320) internal devices are female; cables are male.
- External devices are female; connectors are male.
- Rule of thumb—50-pin connectors go with 8-bit SCSI standards, and 68-pin connectors are for 16-bit SCSI. Table 1 lists the SCSI standards.

. RAID

- Software-based RAID relies on the CPU for processing the RAID algorithms. If server performance decreases immediately after a RAID installation, it is due to the software-based RAID. The solution is to either change to hardware-based RAID or upgrade the CPU.
- Hardware-based RAID enables features such as hot swapping, which allows a replacement drive to be installed without taking down the server.

. I/O bus—ISA is slower than MCI, which is proprietary. EISA was developed to compete with MCI and is backward compatible. EISA device installation requires that the EISA CONFIG application be run to properly identify and configure the server. PCI came along and basically replaced all previous bus types because it is faster and has plug-and-play features, but it is not backward compatible with anything. AGP is not really an I/O bus, but a port.

. External connections—SCSI is the fastest standard. IEEE 1394 (Firewire) is second fastest.

NETWORKING AND CONNECTIVITY

12. Cabling
- Crossover cables are used to connect two servers to each other and two hubs to each other without a crossover port. On one side of the cable, wires are labeled 1, 2, 3, 4, 5, 6, 7, 8. On the other side of the cable, wires are crossed over to be 3, 6, 1, 4, 5, 2, 7, 8.
- Straight cables are used to connect servers to hubs/switches and hubs to other hubs or switches, providing the connection is through a crossover port.

14. Connectivity—Check connectivity if someone is unable to log in, connect, or access another system or the Web.
- Use Windows Explorer (if applicable) to ensure that the computer is accessible.
- Use the PING 127.0.0.1 command to first check that the IP protocol is bound to the local computer network card.
- PING the address of the server in question. Also use TRACERT to see if there are any breaks in communication between you and the server in question.
- Use IPCONFIG/IFCONFIG to check your current TCP/IP configuration and also to reconfigure DHCP client information.

15. Network Operating Systems
- Novell NetWare is strictly an NOS that configures hard disks as volumes and still uses DOS as its base operating system. The

ble 1   SCSI standards.

fining Standard	Transfer Mode	Bandwidth	Connector	Bus	Termination Method
SI-1	SCSI (SCSI-1)	5	50 pin	8-bit	Passive 32 Ohm
SI-2	Wide SCSI	10	68 pin	16-bit	Passive 110 Ohm
SI-2	Fast SCSI	10	50 pin	8-bit	Passive 110 Ohm
SI-2	Fast Wide SCSI	20	68 pin	16-bit	Passive 110 Ohm
SI-3/SPI-1	Ultra SCSI	20	50 pin	8-bit	Active 110 Ohm
SI-3/SPI-1	Wide Ultra SCSI	40	68 pin	16-bit	Active 110 Ohm
SI-3/SPI-2	Ultra2 SCSI	40	50 pin	8-bit	Active 110 Ohm
SI-3/SPI-2	Wide Ultra2 SCSI	80	68 pin	16-bit	Active 110 Ohm
SI-3/SPI-3	Ultra3 SCSI	160	68 pin	16-bit	Active 110 Ohm
I-3/SPI-3	Ultra160(/m) SCSI	160	68 pin	16-bit	Active 110 Ohm
I-3/SPI-3	Ultra160+ SCSI	160	68 pin	16-bit	Active 110 Ohm
-3/SPI-4	Ultra320 SCSI	320	68 pin	16-bit	Active 110 Ohm

Server+

Deborah Haralson
Jeff Haralson

Server+ Exam Cram

Limits of Liability and Disclaimer of Warranty

Trademarks

The Coriolis Group, LLC
14455 N. Hayden Road
Suite 220
Scottsdale, Arizona 85260

(480)483-0192
FAX (480)483-0193
www.coriolis.com

Library of Congress Cataloging-in-Publication Data
Haralson, Deborah.
    Server+ / by Deborah Haralson and Jeff Haralson.
       p. cm. -- (Exam cram)
    Includes bibliographical references and index.
    ISBN 1-58880-106-3
    1. Electronic data processing personnel--Certification. 2.
Client/server computing--Certification--Study guides. 3. Web
servers--Certification--Study guides. I. Haralson, Jeff. II. Title.
III. Series.
QA76.3 .H365 2001
004.36--dc21
                               2001047222
                                 CIP

President and CEO
Roland Elgey

Publisher
Steve Sayre

Associate Publisher
Katherine Hartlove

Acquisitions Editor
Hilary Long

Product Marketing Manager
Jeff Johnson

Project Editor
Sybil Ihrig,
Helios Productions

Technical Reviewer
Steven Maxon

Production Coordinator
Sybil Ihrig,
Helios Productions

Cover Designer
Laura Wellander

Layout Designer
April Nielsen

Printed in the United States of America
10 9 8 7 6 5 4 3 2 1

The Coriolis Group, LLC • 14455 North Hayden Road, Suite 220 • Scottsdale, Arizona 85260

A Note from Coriolis

Our goal has always been to provide you with the best study tools on the planet to help you achieve your certification in record time. Time is so valuable these days that none of us can afford to waste a second of it, especially when it comes to exam preparation.

Over the past few years, we've created an extensive line of *Exam Cram* and *Exam Prep* study guides, practice exams, and interactive training. To help you study even better, we have now created an e-learning and certification destination called **ExamCram.com**. (You can access the site at **www.examcram.com**.) Now, with every study product you purchase from us, you'll be connected to a large community of people like yourself who are actively studying for their certifications, developing their careers, seeking advice, and sharing their insights and stories.

We believe that the future is all about collaborative learning. Our **ExamCram.com** destination is our approach to creating a highly interactive, easily accessible collaborative environment, where you can take practice exams and discuss your experiences with others, sign up for features like "Questions of the Day," plan your certifications using our interactive planners, create your own personal study pages, and keep up with all of the latest study tips and techniques.

We hope that whatever study products you purchase from us—*Exam Cram* or *Exam Prep* study guides, *Personal Trainers, Personal Test Centers*, or one of our interactive Web courses—will make your studying fun and productive. Our commitment is to build the kind of learning tools that will allow you to study the way you want to, whenever you want to.

Visit ExamCram.com now to enhance your study program.

Help us continue to provide the very best certification study materials possible. Write us or email us at **learn@examcram.com** and let us know how our study products have helped you study. Tell us about new features that you'd like us to add. Send us a story about how we've helped you. We're listening!

Good luck with your certification exam and your career. Thank you for allowing us to help you achieve your goals.

ExamCram.com Connects You to the Ultimate Study Center!

Look for these other products from The Coriolis Group:

Server+ Exam Prep
By Drew Bird and Mike Harwood

Server+ Exam Cram Personal Test Center
By Drew Bird and Mike Harwood

MCSE SQL Server 2000 Database Design Exam Cram
By Richard Alan McMahon, Sr. and Sean Chase

MCSE SQL 2000 Administration Exam Cram
By Kalani Kirk Hausman

Linux+ Exam Prep
By Emmett Dulaney

Also recently published
by Coriolis Certification Insider Press:

MCSE Exchange 2000 Design Exam Prep
By Michael Shannon and Dennis Suhanovs

Java 2 Exam Prep, Second Edition
By Bill Brogden

CCSA Exam Cram
By Tony Piltzecker

CISSP Exam Cram
By Mandy Andress

For our boys: Raymond, Johnathan, Steven, and Michael

About the Authors

Deborah Haralson (MCSE, MCP+I, Server+) has been a computer geek since elementary school, learning Basic programming on her father's Commodore VIC20. While earning her engineering degree, she discovered that her true passion was IT and began working for Windows, DOS, and Macintosh network clients, quickly graduating to network servers and WAN technologies. With more than ten years of IT experience, she has worked for companies such as Honeywell, MicroAge, Moon Valley Software, and Mastering Computers. Along the way she has become proficient in a wide array of hardware, software applications, operating systems, and both Windows and Novell networking technologies. Apart from an occasional stint as a PBX and ACD administrative coordinator, DBA, trainer, Webmaster, and application programmer, Deborah is currently working as an independent consultant in the IT industry.

Jeff Haralson was born in in Germany to American parents while his father served in the United States Air Force. He started his career working at Honeywell as a systems programmer and administrator. Jeff quickly established himself as an accomplished hardware programmer, working on projects such as the MD-11 aircraft, Space Shuttle, Hubble Space Telescope, and Space Station Freedom. With this background, Jeff is uniquely qualified to speak and teach on the topics of PC and server evolution and hardware. Jeff eventually moved on as a consultant, programming business applications for companies such as Blue Cross/Blue Shield, Motorola, and the US Army's Electronic Proving Grounds. Jeff's passion and talents remain in hardware, and he currently works for ConsultNet at Prolink. Jeff can be reached at **jeff.haralson@bigfoot.com**.

Acknowledgments

Thanks go to Anne Marie Walker, our copyeditor, for making everything look and sound proper, and to our technical reviewer, Steven Maxon, for working so diligently to ensure that our content was correct and valid and that we got the point across. Thank you so very much to Chris Ward and Doug Bassett for helping out when we were in a crunch. We are very grateful to Jeff Milburn and Gary Martz at Intel for hosting the Train-the-Trainer event where so many questions were made clear. Thanks also to Intel for providing the photographs in this book. Thank you to Jonathan Thatcher and Jim Vanne at CompTIA for putting the entire Server+ project together and being so open and available to questions and inquiries.

On a more personal level, thanks go to our kids, Johnathan and Raymond, for allowing mommy and daddy time to write this book. Thanks to our parents for encouraging and supporting us all our lives. Thanks to Michael and Steven, who kept asking how the book was coming along. Finally, we can say, "It's finished!"

And finally—humble gratitude and love to our Father in Heaven, for the ability to write, for the blessing and the challenge of writing this book, and for both the trials and the blessings received during the writing of this book.

Contents at a Glance

Table of Contents

Introduction

Welcome to *Server+ Exam Cram!* This introduction is very much like the "Quick Setup" reference section for a software application, and we use it to give you some important insights into the exam. The purpose of this book is to get you ready to take—and pass—the Server+ certification exam. In the following pages, we've outlined the CompTIA Server+ certification in general, and we talk about how this *Exam Cram* can optimize your knowledge of servers and help you focus on critical exam topics.

New job listings often require applicants to be Server+ certified, and many individuals who complete the program qualify for increases in pay and/or responsibility. If the job requirements don't require an existing Server+ certification, many corporations require that you complete the certification process within 90 days of being hired.

This book is aimed strictly at exam preparation and review. It will *not* teach you everything you need to know about a topic. Instead, it will present and dissect the question topics that you're probably going to see on the exam. We've drawn on material from CompTIA's own listing of requirements and from the exams themselves. We've also drawn from our own experience with microcomputers and servers going all the way back to the Altair. Our aim is to bring together as much information as possible about the Server+ certification exam.

Our explicit purpose in writing this book is to stuff as many facts and technical answers about computers as possible into your brain before you begin the test. The Server+ exam makes a basic assumption that you already have a *very* strong background of experience with servers, hardware, and network operating systems. On the other hand, we think that technology changes so fast that no one can be a total expert. We believe this book is the most up-to-date analysis of the Server+ exam on the market.

Depending on your experience in the industry, we recommend that you begin your studies with some classroom training or visit the CompTIA Web site (www.comptia.org) for a definition of what it means to be Server+ certified. We *strongly* recommend that you install, configure, and generally "fool around" with the Windows NT, Windows 2000, NetWare, and OS/2 networking environments that you'll be tested on. Nothing beats hands-on experience and familiarity when it comes to understanding the questions you're likely to encounter. Book learning is essential, but hands-on experience is the best teacher of all!

A quick way for you to determine where you stand in relation to the current certification process is to turn to the end of the book and examine the Sample Test (Chapter 12). This is a highly accurate representation of both the test format and the types of questions you will encounter.

The New CompTIA Certification Path

At the time of this writing, CompTIA offers six different certifications. Each one is targeted for a specific type of job in the marketplace. The important thing to remember with many of these tests is that there is some overlap in technical content from one to another, just as there is some overlap from job to job within an IT organization. Many companies will use these certifications not only as milestones for employee development, but also as prerequisites for promotion and employment. CompTIA has recommendations for which exams should be taken first for what types of jobs; however, there are still choices to be made. Figure 1 illustrates the job roles and the order in which to take the exams that we believe will yield the highest chance of your success, and therefore the greatest improvement to your career potential. Keep in mind that no single exam is required in order to pass another exam. Experienced IT personnel might consider taking only the exam that best meets their current career goals. If you're an established server administrator, you might consider taking just the Network+ exam rather than possibly wasting time on the Server+ exam, which might not further your career. When you consider taking any CompTIA exam, it is important to look at all of these exams, how they fit together, and how they might be able to further your career.

A+

The A+ exam was the first CompTIA exam created. This exam is for an entry-level computer technician with anywhere from one month to one year's worth of practical experience in maintaining and servicing microcomputers (PCs). CompTIA recommends at least six months of experience.

The A+ exam is the only certification that actually requires taking two tests: A+ Core Hardware and Operating Systems Technologies. The A+ Core Hardware exam concentrates on basic PC hardware architecture, configuration, and troubleshooting. The Operating Systems Technologies test is exactly that: It tests you on basic DOS, Windows 9x, Windows ME, Windows NT, and Windows 2000 installation, functionality, file management, memory management, and troubleshooting.

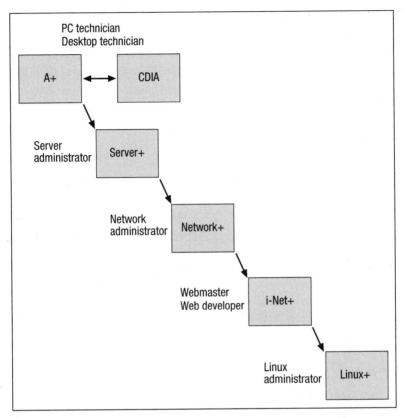

Figure 1   Career paths and the suggested order of taking the CompTIA exams.

Network+

The Network+ exam covers networking technology and practices and the OSI networking model in depth. This exam includes information about a great deal of theory and infrastructure, and not much about hardware or hands-on information that is useful in day-to-day operations. This is perhaps why the Server+ certification was created. The Network+ certification is tailored for administrators with 18 months to two years' experience in networking personal computers.

CDIA (Certified Document Imaging Architech)

CDIA is a second-level exam, recommended to be taken after the A+ or Network+ exams. It is not necessary to take both exams, and it is certainly not required either. It is recommended, however, because of the advanced nature of the content of this exam. The CDIA exam is a unique test specifically created for the precision job of an image architech. Yes—that is the correct word, architech being a new term for a technical designer/builder. Corporations such as Xerox, Canon, and Ricoh (just to name a few) have sponsored this exam.

What is the need for a Certified Document Imaging Architech? Here's one example: When the government chose to convert all of its military specifications into digital format, they needed an expert in document imaging, not only to transfer the information from paper onto disk, but also to develop an appropriate means of searching, retrieving, and accessing that data after it had been scanned. A CDIA-certified person would be ideal for that job. Keep in mind that, as shown in Figure 2, content for the CDIA exam does have some overlap with A+ and Network+.

Server+

The Server+ exam, another second-level exam, is recommended to be taken after the A+ exam and either before or after the Network+ exam. Because this exam covers advanced PC hardware, network operating systems (NOSs), and limited networking technologies, our personal recommendation is that this exam be taken *before* Network+ in order to better bridge the gap between the PC and networking worlds. Also, do not underestimate the value of this certification for your career: Desktop support personnel go around fixing user issues, rolling out new software, and fixing hardware problems. Network administrators deal primarily with server hardware, software, security, and network access. *This certification is the turning point to get you from desktop support to network administration.* Trust us, the jump in pay is worth the effort.

The Server+ exam content covers seven major topics: installation, configuration, upgrading, proactive maintenance, environment, troubleshooting, and disaster recovery. As with all CompTIA exams, one of the reasons the Server+ exam was created was to essentially prequalify personnel for real jobs in the real world.

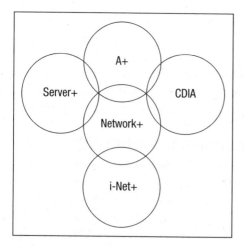

Figure 2 How exam objectives overlap between tests.

Evidence of this reality-based commitment is seen in the fact that the trouble-shooting questions in the exam command a whopping 27 percent of the entire question base. Installation covers 17 percent of the exam, while configuration covers 18 percent. Upgrading and disaster recovery both handle 12 percent of the exam, and proactive maintenance and environment deal with 9 percent and 5 percent of the exam, respectively. Consider these relative emphases as you study for the Server+ exam.

i-Net+

A second-level exam, the i-Net+ exam is the only CompTIA exam that blurs the job role description somewhat, in that it combines both Internet administration basics (such as administering an intranet and configuring clients to access the Web) and the foundations of Web site development. The reasoning behind this is valid and practical: As a Webmaster, quite often you are required to administer IIS or Apache. As an IT person, sometimes you are called upon to modify and update Web content running within the organization. You can easily see that knowledge of and familiarity with both roles would be an asset for a well-rounded Internet guru. When charting your career path, it's recommended that you take the i-Net+ exam after passing the Network+ test.

Linux+

Considering the increase in corporate Linux usage, along with the broad array of available Linux flavors, it is wise to establish a standard by which to measure administrative and technical capabilities. The irony here is that this exam and the content it covers could very well be the only "standardized" element of the entire Linux platform. If we were to hazard a guess, we'd probably consider taking this exam after the i-Net+ test in view of the huge demand for the Linux Apache Web Server in the marketplace.

Taking a Certification Exam

Unfortunately, testing isn't free. The exam costs $190 for nonmembers—defined as individuals who are not employed by a company that is a CompTIA member. The cost is lower if you are employed by a company that *is* a CompTIA member. In the United States and Canada, tests are administered by either Prometric or VUE. Prometric can be reached at 1-800-776-4276 or on the Web at **www.2test.com**. VUE can be reached at 1-952-995-8800 or on the Web at **www.vue.com**.

To schedule an exam, you must call at least one day in advance. To cancel or reschedule an exam, you must call at least 12 hours before the scheduled test time or you may be charged. When calling either service, please have the following information ready for the sales representative who handles your call:

➤ Your name, organization, and mailing address

➤ The name of the exam(s) you wish to take (Server+)

➤ A method of payment

The most convenient payment method is to provide a valid credit card number with sufficient available credit. Otherwise, payments by check, money order, or purchase order must be *received* before a test can be scheduled. If you choose one of these latter methods, ask your sales representative for more details.

Keep in mind that if you choose to pay for your exam by a method that involves the postal service and banking system (check, purchase order, and so on), you'll have to call to schedule your exam much earlier than one day in advance.

Arriving at the Exam Site

On the day of your exam, try to arrive at least 15 minutes before the scheduled time slot. You must bring *two* forms of identification, one of which *must* be a photo ID. Typically, a driver's license and credit card are valid forms of identification. Insurance cards, birth certificates, state ID cards, employee identification cards, or any other legal identification can also be used. If you're not sure whether your identification is acceptable, ask the person with whom you schedule your exam.

You will be given a user ID code as an identification number for your test, which you enter in the computer at the time you begin your exam(s). The exam is fully computer-based, and it is all multiple choice. Ordinarily, your ID number is the same as your Social Security number, though it may be different. Your ID number will be used to track your session.

In the Exam Room

All exams are completely closed book. In fact, you will not be permitted to take anything with you into the testing area other than a blank sheet of paper and a pencil provided by the exam proctors. We suggest that you *immediately write down the most critical information* about the test you're taking on the blank sheet of paper you're given. *Exam Cram* books provide a brief reference that lists essential information from the book in distilled form. This reference is The Cram Sheet, a tear-out card located in the front of the book. You need to master this information (by brute force, if necessary) so you can dump the information out of your head onto a piece of paper before answering any exam questions. You need to remember the information only long enough to write it down when you walk into the test room. You might even want to look at The Cram Sheet in the car or in the lobby of the testing center just before you walk in to take the exam.

Each question offers you an opportunity to mark that question for later review. We strongly suggest that you mark any questions about which you have any doubt regarding the answers. Each exam gives you an ample amount of time to complete the questions, and by marking questions for review, you can go back without the pressure of worrying whether you'll have time to complete the whole exam.

The amount of time you take to answer each question is not factored into scoring your test. Your answers can be changed at any time before you terminate the session, and the review option is not tracked for scoring. Many terms and words are easy to mix up, so take time to review your work.

When you complete the exam, the software will tell you whether you've passed or failed. Even if you fail, we suggest that you ask for (and keep) the detailed report that the test administrator prints out for you. You can use the report to help you prepare for another go-round, if necessary. If you need to retake an exam, you must call one of the testing services, schedule a new test date, and pay another exam fee.

Certification

When you've passed the Server+ certification exam, you will be Server+ certified. It's a good idea to save the test results you are given at the conclusion of the test, because they are your immediate proof. Official certification normally takes anywhere from four to six weeks, so don't expect to get your credentials overnight. When the package arrives, it will include a Welcome Kit, a certificate (suitable for framing), and an identification lapel pin.

As an official recognition of hard work and broad-based knowledge, Server+ certification is also a badge of honor. Many organizations view certification as a necessary foundation for a career in the IT industry.

How to Prepare for an Exam

The Server+ exam can be loosely divided into two courses: server hardware and server software, with a sprinkling of networking technologies to bind the two together. You will be quizzed on specific functions falling within seven different categories. Keep in mind that although the exam is primarily tuned toward server hardware, you could encounter questions related to client machines. This is because one of the goals is to ensure that you are an effective *advanced* PC hardware technician. In the same way that the A+ exam covers entry-level PC hardware generally found on end-user desktops, the Server+ exam covers advanced PC hardware generally found in a server room. There is no hard-and-fast rule that says you will not be administering a desktop that has RAID and its own UPS. This is also why the A+ exam is recommended (though not required) prior to taking this exam. In this manner, employers can be assured that you are capable of handling literally *any* PC hardware issue.

By using this book in your preparation efforts, you'll be able to concentrate your efforts on the areas considered to be the most important in understanding server systems. We've "been there, done that," so to speak, and we'll point you in the right direction for your studies.

At a minimum, preparing for the Server+ exam requires a good test guide (this book) and detailed reference materials addressing the information covered on the exams. We've attempted to make no assumptions whatsoever about your current knowledge and to cram between the covers of the book as much information as possible about servers. However, our main focus is to get you through the exam. Using the self-study method, you might consider us as virtual tutors, coming to your site at your convenience and stuffing the facts between your ears.

Past certification candidates have used many individual reference books which, taken together, cover most of the required material on the exam. A good professional should always have a solid reference library as a matter of course. See the "Need to Know More?" sections at the end of each chapter for our lists of recommended references.

If you like a little more structure, there are several good programs available in both self-paced and classroom formats. Consider too that the cost of structured class instruction is significantly higher than the price of this book.

The Server+ certification exam will be updated over time to reflect the ever-evolving developments in the technology industry. The best source of current exam information is CompTIA's Web site: **www.comptia.org**. If you don't have access to the Internet, you can call or write CompTIA directly at:

Computing Technology Industry Association
450 East 22nd Street, Suite 230
Lombard, IL 60134-6158
Phone: (630) 268-1818

In addition, you'll probably find any or all of the following materials useful in your quest for Server+ expertise:

➤ *Study guides*—The Coriolis Group certification series includes the following:

   ➤ *The Exam Cram series*—These books give you information about the material you need to know to pass the tests.

➤ *The Exam Prep series*—These books provide a greater level of detail than the *Exam Cram* books and are designed to teach you everything you need to know from an exam perspective. Each book comes with a CD that contains interactive practice exams in a variety of testing formats.

Together, the two series make a perfect pair.

➤ *Multimedia*—These Coriolis Group materials are designed to support learners of all types—whether you learn best by reading or doing:

➤ *The Exam Cram Personal Trainer*—Offers a unique, personalized self-paced training course based on the exam.

➤ *The Exam Cram Personal Test Center*—Features multiple test options that simulate the actual exam, including Fixed-Length, Random, Review, and Test All. Explanations of correct and incorrect answers reinforce concepts learned.

About This Book

Each *Exam Cram* chapter follows a regular structure, along with graphical cues about especially important or useful material. The structure of a typical chapter includes:

➤ *Opening hotlists*—Each chapter begins with lists of the terms you'll need to understand and the concepts or techniques you'll need to master before you can be fully conversant with the chapter's subject matter. We follow the hotlists with a few introductory paragraphs to set the stage for the rest of the chapter.

➤ *Topical coverage*—After the opening hotlists, each chapter covers a series of topics related to the chapter's subject title. Throughout this section, we highlight topics or concepts likely to appear on the exam by using a special Exam Alert layout that looks like this:

 This is what an Exam Alert looks like. An Exam Alert stresses concepts, terms, software, or activities that will most likely appear in one or more certification exam questions. For that reason, we think any information found offset in Exam Alert format is worthy of extra attentiveness on your part.

Even if material isn't flagged as an Exam Alert, *all* the content in this book is in some way test related. The book is focused on high-speed test preparation. You'll find that what appears in the meat of each chapter is critical knowledge.

➤ *Notes*—Notes throughout the text dip into nearly every aspect of working with and configuring PCs and networks. Where a body of knowledge is far deeper than the scope of the book, we use Notes to indicate areas of concern or specialty training.

Note: Cramming for an exam will get you through a test, but it won't make you a competent IT professional. Although you can memorize just the facts you need to become certified, your daily work in the IT field will rapidly put you in water over your head if you don't know the underlying principles of computers.

➤ *Tips*—We provide Tips that will help you build a solid foundation of knowledge. Although the specific information in a given Tip might not be on the exam, it is highly relevant and will help you become a better test-taker.

 This is how Tips are formatted. Here's an example of a Tip: You should always choose the Custom or Advanced option, if the setup routine offers one. In every case we've ever seen, there is a default setting for any steps in the program where you're given a choice. In situations where you don't know what you're looking at, you can choose the default. However, in places where you do know what you're looking at, you might often disagree with what some faraway programmer has decided to do to your system.

➤ *Practice questions*—This section presents a series of mock test questions and explanations of both correct and incorrect answers. Each chapter has a number of practice questions that highlight the areas we found to be most important on the exam.

➤ *Details and resources*—Every chapter ends with a section titled "Need to Know More?" This section provides direct pointers to resources that offer further details on the chapter's subject matter. In addition, this section tries to rate the quality and thoroughness of each topic's coverage. If you find a resource you like in this collection, use it, but don't feel compelled to use all these resources. On the other hand, we recommend only resources that we have used on a regular basis, so none of the recommendations will be a waste of your time or money.

The bulk of the book follows this chapter structure, but there are a few other elements that we would like to point out:

➤ *Sample Test and Answer Key*—A very close approximation of the Server+ exam is found in Chapter 12. Chapter 13 presents the answers to the sample test, as well as explanations of the correct and incorrect answers.

➤ *Glossary*—An extensive glossary of acronyms and key terms.

➤ *The Cram Sheet*—A tear-away card inside the front cover of this *Exam Cram* book, this is a valuable tool that represents a condensed and compiled collection of facts and numbers that we think you should memorize before taking the test.

Using This Book

If you're preparing for the Server+ certification exam for the first time, we've structured the topics in this book to build upon one another. The topics covered in later chapters will make more sense after you've read earlier chapters. In our opinion, many computer manuals and reference books are essentially a list of facts. Rather than simply list raw facts about each topic on the exam, we've tried to paint an integrated landscape in your imagination, where each topic and exam fact takes on a landmark status.

We suggest you read this book from front to back for your initial test preparation. You won't be wasting your time, because everything we've written pertains to the exam. If you need to brush up on a topic or you have to bone up for a second try, use the index or table of contents to go straight to the topics and questions that you need to study. After taking the test, we think you'll find this book useful as a tightly focused reference and as an essential foundation of microcomputer knowledge.

We've done our best to create a real-world tool that you can use to prepare for and pass the Server+ exam. We're definitely interested in any feedback you would care to share about the book, especially if you have ideas about how we can improve it for future test-takers.

We'd like to know if you found this book to be helpful in your preparation efforts. We'd also like to know how you felt about your chances of passing the exam *before* you read the book and then *after* you read the book. Of course, we'd love to hear that you passed the exam, and even if you just want to share your triumph, we'd be happy to hear from you.

Send your questions or comments to Coriolis at **learn@examcram.com**. Please remember to include the title of the book in your message. Also, be sure to check out the Web pages at **www.examcram.com**, where you'll find information updates, commentary, and certification information.

Thanks for choosing us as your personal trainers, and enjoy the book!

Self-Assessment

The reason we included a Self-Assessment in this *Exam Cram* book is to help you evaluate your readiness to tackle Server+ certification. But before you tackle this Self-Assessment, let's talk about concerns you may face when pursuing Server+ certification and what an ideal candidate might look like.

CompTIA Certified Computer Technicians in the Real World

In the next section, we describe an ideal Server+-certified candidate. Many people will take the two modules of the Server+ certification exam in order to serve as an advanced PC technician in the server hardware and software repair field. Others may see these tests as a great starting point for gaining the basic PC knowledge that can be used in many other fields.

Many people are already certified, so it's obviously an attainable goal. You can get all the real-world motivation you need from knowing that many others have gone before, so you'll be able to follow in their footsteps. If you're willing to tackle the process seriously and do what it takes to obtain the necessary experience and knowledge, you can take—and pass—the certification modules involved in obtaining Server+ certification. In fact, *Exam Crams*, and the companion *Exam Preps*, are designed to make it as easy as possible for you to prepare for certification exams. But prepare you must!

The same, of course, is true for other CompTIA certifications, including the following:

➤ CompTIA's Certified Document Imaging Architech (CDIA) certification is a nationally recognized credential acknowledging competency and professionalism in the document imaging industry. CDIA candidates possess critical knowledge of all major areas and technologies used to plan, design, and specify an imaging system.

➤ Network+ certifies the knowledge of networking technicians with 18 to 24 months of experience in the IT industry.

➤ i-Net+ certification is designed specifically for any individual interested in demonstrating baseline technical knowledge that would allow him or her to pursue a variety of Internet-related careers.

➤ A+ certification is designed for the IT desktop technician with approximately sixth months or more of recent experience. The A+ certification consists of two exams: A+ Core and A+ OS (operating systems). Whereas the A+ exam focuses on general PC hardware, the Server+ exam focuses on advanced PC and server hardware.

➤ Linux+ certification, as with all CompTIA exams, is a vendor-neutral exam. The Linux+ exam focuses on Linux concepts and functions that are appropriate for somene with at least six months of Linux experience.

Put Yourself to the Test

The following series of questions and observations is designed to help you determine how much work you must do to pursue Server+ certification and the kinds of resources you can consult on your quest. Be absolutely honest in your answers; otherwise you'll end up wasting money on exams you're not yet ready to take. There are no right or wrong answers, only steps along the path to certification. Only you can decide where you really belong in the broad spectrum of aspiring candidates.

Two things should be clear from the outset, however:

➤ Even a modest background in computer science will be helpful.

➤ Hands-on experience with personal computers is an essential ingredient of certification success.

Educational Background

1. Have you ever taken any computer-related classes? [Yes or No]

   ➤ If Yes, proceed to question 2; if No, proceed to question 4.

2. Have you taken any classes on computer operating systems? [Yes or No]

   ➤ If Yes, you'll probably be able to handle operating system architecture and system component discussions. If you're rusty, brush up on basic operating system concepts, especially virtual memory, multitasking regimes, user-mode versus kernel-mode operation, and general computer security topics.

➤ If No, consider some basic reading in this area. We strongly recommend a good general operating systems book, such as *Operating System Concepts*, by Abraham Silberschatz and Peter Baer Galvin (Addison-Wesley, 1997, ISBN 0-201-59113-8). If this title doesn't appeal to you, check out reviews for other, similar titles at your favorite online bookstore.

3. Have you taken any networking concepts or technologies classes? [Yes or No]

➤ If Yes, you'll probably be able to handle the Server+ certification networking terminology, concepts, and technologies. If you're rusty, *A+ Exam Prep, Third Edition*, by Scott Reeves et al. (The Coriolis Group, 2001, ISBN 1-57610-699-3) will help you brush up on basic networking concepts and terminology, especially networking media, transmission types, the OSI Reference Model, and networking technologies such as Ethernet, Token Ring, FDDI, and WAN links.

➤ If No, you might want to supplement the material available in this book with other good works. The three best books that we know of are *Computer Networks, 3rd Edition*, by Andrew S. Tanenbaum (Prentice-Hall, 1996, ISBN 0-133-49945-6), *Computer Networks and Internets*, by Douglas E. Comer (Prentice-Hall, 1997, ISBN 0-132-39070-1), and *Encyclopedia of Networking*, by Tom Sheldon (Osborne/McGraw-Hill, 1998, ISBN 0-07-882333-1).

Skip to the next section, "Hands-on Experience."

4. Have you done any reading on operating systems or networks? [Yes or No]

➤ If Yes, review the requirements stated in the first paragraphs after questions 2 and 3. If you meet those requirements, move on to the next section, "Hands-on Experience."

➤ If No, you'll find the real-world projects of *A+ Exam Prep, Third Edition* to be most helpful.

Hands-on Experience

The most important key to success on all the CompTIA tests is hands-on experience, especially with basic server hardware, as well as Windows NT, Windows 2000, Novell NetWare, and IBM OS/2. If we leave you with only one realization after taking this Self-Assessment, it should be that there's no substitute for time spent installing, configuring, and using server hardware and network operating systems.

Before you even think about taking any exam, make sure you've spent enough time with the related hardware and software to understand how it is installed and configured, how to maintain such an installation, and how to troubleshoot when things go wrong. This will help you in the exam, and in real life.

Testing Your Exam-Readiness

Whether you get ready for an exam by attending a formal class on a specific topic or use written materials to study on your own, some preparation for the Server+ certification exam is essential. At $190—pass or fail—you want to do everything you can to pass on your first try. That's where studying comes in.

For any given subject, consider taking a class if you've studied on your own but failed the test. The opportunity to interact with an instructor and fellow students can make all the difference in the world, if you can afford that privilege. For information about CompTIA classes, visit the CompTIA Web site at **www.comptia.org** (follow the certification link to find training).

If you can't afford to take a class, visit the Web page anyway, because it also includes a detailed breakdown of the objectives for the Server+ certification exam. This will serve as a good roadmap for your studies. Even if you can't afford to spend much at all, you should still invest in some low-cost practice exams from commercial vendors. Practice exams can help you assess your readiness to pass a test better than any other tool. The CompTIA Web site lists sources for additional study material.

5. Have you taken a practice exam on your chosen test subject? [Yes or No]

   ➤ If Yes, and you scored 75 percent or better, you're probably ready to tackle the real thing. If your score isn't above that crucial threshold, keep at it until you break that barrier.

   ➤ If No, obtain all the free and low-budget practice tests you can find and get to work. Keep at it until you can break the passing threshold comfortably.

 When it comes to assessing your test readiness, there's no better way than to take a good-quality practice exam and pass with a score of 75 percent or better. When we're preparing ourselves, we shoot for more than 80 percent, just to leave room for the "weirdness factor" that sometimes shows up on exams.

One last note. We can't stress enough the importance of hands-on experience in the context of the Server+ certification exam. As you review the material for that exam, you'll realize that hands-on experience with basic PC hardware, operating system commands, tools, and utilities is invaluable.

Onward, through the Fog!

Once you've assessed your readiness, undertaken the right background studies, obtained the hands-on experience that will help you understand the products and technologies at work, and reviewed the many sources of information to help you prepare for a test, you'll be ready to take a round of practice tests. When your scores come back positive enough to get you through the exam, you're ready to go after the real thing. If you follow our assessment regime, you'll know what you need to study, as well as when you're ready to make a test date at Prometric or VUE. Good luck!

Server+ Certification

. . . .

Terms you'll need to understand:

✓ Exhibit
✓ Multiple-choice question formats
✓ Traditional vs. adaptive testing
✓ Careful reading
✓ Strategy

Techniques you'll need to master:

✓ Preparing to take a certification exam
✓ Budgeting your time
✓ Marking for review
✓ Using one question to figure out another question
✓ Analyzing responses logically
✓ Guessing (as a last resort)

As experiences go, test-taking isn't something most people eagerly anticipate, no matter how well they're prepared. In most cases, familiarity reduces exam anxiety. You probably wouldn't be as nervous if you had to take a second Server+ certification exam as you will be taking your first one. We've taken a lot of exams, and this book is partly about helping you to reduce your test-taking anxiety. This chapter explains what you can expect to see in the exam room itself.

Whether it's your first or your tenth exam, understanding the exam particulars (how much time to spend on each question, the setting you'll be in, and so on) and the testing software will help you concentrate on the material rather than on the environment. Likewise, mastering a few basic test-taking skills should help you recognize—and perhaps even outfox—some of the tricks and "gotchas" you're bound to find in Server+ exam questions.

The Test Site

When you arrive at your scheduled testing center, you'll be required to sign in with a test coordinator. He or she will ask you to produce two forms of identification, one of which must be a photo ID. After you've signed in and your time slot arrives, you'll be asked to deposit any books, bags, or other items you brought with you, and then you'll be escorted into a closed room.

Typically, the testing room will be furnished with anywhere from one to six computers. Each workstation will be separated from the others by dividers designed to keep you from seeing what's happening on someone else's computer.

When you sign in, the exam administrators will furnish you with a pen or pencil and a blank sheet of paper, or, in some cases, an erasable plastic sheet and an erasable felt-tip pen. You're allowed to write down any information you want on both sides of this sheet. As mentioned in the Introduction, you should memorize as much of the material that appears on The Cram Sheet (inside the front cover of this book) as you can, then write down that information on the blank sheet as soon as you are seated at the computer. You can refer to your rendition of The Cram Sheet anytime you like during the test, but you'll have to surrender the sheet when you leave the room.

Most exam rooms feature a wall with a large picture window. This permits the test coordinator to monitor the room and to observe anything out of the ordinary, and to prevent test-takers from talking to one another. The exam coordinator will have preloaded the Server+ certification test, and you'll be permitted to start as soon as you're seated in front of the computer.

Server+ certification exams are designed with 80 questions to be answered within a 90-minute period with a passing score of 75 percent or better. A countdown timer on the computer screen will show you the time remaining. In our opinion, the amount of time is fair and generous, and it offers ample time for reviewing your responses.

The Server+ certification exam is computer generated and uses a multiple-choice format. Although this may sound easy, the questions are constructed to check your mastery of basic facts and figures, as well as to test your ability to evaluate one or more sets of circumstances or requirements.

A question might ask you to select the best or most effective solution to a problem from a range of choices, all of which technically are correct. A question might ask you to select the best choice from a graphic image. A question might have a series of blanks representing a list of terms used to complete a sentence. All in all, it's quite an adventure, involving some real thinking. This book shows you what to expect and how to deal with the problems, puzzles, and predicaments you're likely to find on the test.

The sample test in Chapter 12 is a very close approximation of the Server+ exam. As you'll see, we've included a sample of every type of question, as well as mimicked the phrasing style of the overall exam. (You can find detailed answers to these questions in Chapter 13.)

Knowledge breeds confidence, and confidence breeds success. If you study the materials in this book carefully, review the practice questions at the end of each chapter, and take the sample test in Chapter 12, you will be aware of all the areas where additional studying is required.

Test Layout and Design

As mentioned earlier, the questions on the Server+ exam are multiple choice. Depending upon the success of the soon-to-be-released A+ adaptive exam, the Server+ exam could be converted to adaptive format by mid-2003.

Note: Adaptive tests work by evaluating the test-taker's most recent answer. A correct answer leads to a more difficult question because the test software's estimate of the test-taker's knowledge and ability level is raised. An incorrect answer leads to a less difficult question because the test software's estimate of the test-taker's knowledge and ability level is lowered. This process continues until the test targets the test-taker's true ability level.

The test screen will display each question one at a time. Along the top of the screen is the countdown timer so you will always know how much time is left in the whole test. The text of the question displays near the top of the screen. Some questions will provide the information in paragraph format, and others will provide an exhibit (line drawing) and ask you to identify specific components. If a question includes a graphic exhibit, a button links to the graphic. *Paying careful attention* is the key to success! Be prepared to toggle between a picture and a question as you work. Often, both are complex enough that you might not be able to remember all of either one.

The response choices are listed below the question. To select a response you click on the adjacent button or checkbox to turn it black. You can change your selection at any time while you are still within the question window, and you can mark questions for review by clicking on the review checkbox at the bottom of the window. Some questions indicate that more than one answer is correct, in which case you should choose the number of answers specified. The time you take to respond and the number of times you change a response are not factored into the scoring process.

Review Responses

If you take the traditional test format (before the conversion to an all adaptive format), when you complete the last question of the exam and press the Next button, a final screen will offer you the option to review your responses and any questions that you specifically marked for review. A listing of all the question numbers, along with your chosen response letter, shows on the screen, and the marked questions have a graphic indicator. When you highlight a marked question and choose Review, the test displays the selected question.

Note: If the Server+ exam is adaptive by the time you take the exam, you will not have the option to review questions.

When you review a question, you'll see a window displaying the original question and your response. You can use the window to change or verify your answer. When you're satisfied with your response, you can unmark the question by clicking on the Mark For Review checkbox, or you can proceed to the next review question. At the bottom of the screen, you'll see a Review Next button, which will take you to your next marked question (bypassing unmarked questions). The number of questions you choose to review is not factored into the scoring process.

Take Your Test Seriously

The most important advice we can give you about taking any test is this: *Read each question carefully!* Some questions are deliberately ambiguous, offering several responses that could be correct, depending on your reading of the question. Other questions use terminology in very precise ways. We use Exam Alerts and Tips throughout this book to point out where you might run into these types of questions.

We've taken numerous practice and real tests, and in nearly every case, we've missed at least one question because we didn't read it closely or carefully enough. For example, the use of the word *requires* commonly causes test-takers to answer incorrectly. Consider the following sample question.

Sample Question 1

> Windows 95 requires the WIN.INI and SYSTEM.INI files during the startup process in order to load device drivers and user options.
>
> ○ a. True
>
> ○ b. False

The correct answer is b, false, because the WIN.INI file isn't *required*.

Here are some suggestions for dealing with the tendency to select an answer too quickly:

➤ Read every word in the question! If you find yourself jumping ahead impatiently, go back and start over on the question.

➤ Schedule your exam on a day when you don't have a lot of other appointments and errands. This should help you feel a little more relaxed.

➤ As you read, try to rephrase the question in your own terms.

➤ When returning to a question you had earlier marked for review, reread every word again—otherwise, you might fall into a rut. Sometimes, seeing a question fresh after turning your attention elsewhere enables you to catch something you missed earlier. This is where the review option comes in handy.

➤ If you return to a question more than twice, try to explain to yourself what you don't understand about the question, why the answers don't appear to make sense, or what appears to be missing. If you ponder the subject for a while, your subconscious might provide the details you're looking for, or you might notice a "trick" that will point to the right answer.

Finally, try to deal with each question by thinking through what you know about hardware and software systems. By reviewing what you know (and what you've written down on your Cram Sheet), you'll often recall or understand concepts sufficiently to determine the correct answer.

Question-Handling Strategies

Based on the tests we've taken, we've noticed a couple of interesting trends in exam question responses. Usually, some responses will be obviously incorrect, and two of the remaining answers will be plausible. Remember that only one response can be correct. If the answer leaps out at you, reread the question to look for a trick—just in case. Our best advice regarding guessing is to rely on your intuition. None of the exam topics should come as a surprise to you if you've read this book and taken the sample test.

Unfamiliar Terms

If you see a response that's totally unfamiliar, chances are good that it's a made-up word. Recognizing unfamiliar terms can help narrow down the possible correct answers for a question. For example, the following sample question shows how you can use the process of eliminating unfamiliar terms to arrive at the correct answer.

Sample Question 2

Which is the most useful tool for analyzing network traffic?

◯ a. Differentiometer

◯ b. Benchmark analyzer

◯ c. SMTP Monitor

◯ d. Integrity meter

The correct answer is c. Chances are that you've at least heard of an *SMTP Monitor* before, thereby enabling you to take an educated guess at this question.

Last-Minute Guesses

As you work your way through the test, the traditional exam format indicates the number of questions completed and questions outstanding. Under the adaptive format model, you will not be given information on how many questions are left. The adaptive testing engine will determine when you are through. If you are taking the traditional format test, budget your time by making sure that you've completed one-fourth of the questions one-quarter of the way through the test period. Check again three-quarters of the way through. If you're not finished with the test at the five-minute mark, use the last five minutes to *guess* your way through the remaining questions.

Guesses are more valuable than blank answers, because blanks are *always* wrong. A guess has a 25 percent (one in four) chance of being right. If you don't have a clue regarding the remaining questions, pick answers at random, or choose all A's, B's, and so on. The important thing is to submit a test for scoring that has *an answer for every question.*

Additional Resources

By far, the best source of information about Server+ certification tests comes from CompTIA. Because products and technologies, and the tests that go with them, change frequently, the best resource for obtaining exam-related information is the Internet. If you haven't already visited the CompTIA Web site, do so at **www.comptia.org**.

There's *always* a way to find what you want on the Web, if you're willing to invest some time and energy. As long as you can get to the CompTIA site (and we're pretty sure that it will stay at **www.comptia.org** for a long while yet), you have a good jump on finding what you need.

The Server Room

Terms you'll need to understand:

✓ KVM

✓ UPS/SPS

✓ Raised flooring

✓ Ambient room temperature

✓ Environmental controls

✓ Cable ducts

✓ Server cabinets

✓ U-racks

Techniques you'll need to master:

✓ Planning proper KVM placement

✓ Using uninterruptible power sources

✓ Controlling the environment

✓ Devising cabling strategies

✓ Securing the servers

✓ Developing physical and logical documentation

To some people, the server room is the holy shrine of the IT world, which contains racks of equipment humming along and glowing monitors dutifully showing that all is well with your network. Unfortunately this is not always the case. I'm sure most of you have experienced the cluttered closet of equipment with cabling running all over the place. A properly planned server room or closet can make your life as a network administrator so much easier. On the Server+ exam, you will be expected to know how to create this utopian environment.

Many issues you will face as an administrator deal with the placement of equipment, cables, and power. Other topics deal with documentation, security, and the room environment. The goal of this chapter is to help you become aware of your equipment's home.

Layout

When planning for server placement, there are several components that need addressing: keyboard, video, and mouse device placement (KVM), uninterruptible power supplies (UPSs), raised floors or cabling ducts, environmental controls, and of course the location of cables. With proper layout, troubleshooting and disaster recovery becomes much easier to accomplish.

KVM

When working at your desk, you usually place your monitor, keyboard, and mouse in a convenient place. In server rooms containing many servers, there might not be enough room for convenience or comfort. As you might know if you have seen servers, it is possible to stack two to three servers in the same space in which you can store a monitor. If you have the luxury of space, placing the monitors and keyboards away from the server racks or tables is helpful. This gives you more room to breathe. The Server+ exam assumes space is at a minimum, so you will need to plan accordingly.

In situations where multiple PC servers are used, KVM switches are a necessity when faced with small amounts of space. With a KVM switch, you can use a single keyboard, monitor, and mouse to control the servers. This reduces the cost of having multiple monitors, keyboards, and mice. KVM switches also reduce your energy consumption and air conditioning costs, and they save valuable space. Some KVMs can handle up to 64 servers, and others can be chained together to allow multiple KVMs to use the same keyboard, video, and mouse as shown in Figure 2.1. KVMs can also have on-screen displays that help you identify which server you are working on.

Most KVM switches are located inside the server cabinet, so you need to allocate enough room for the equipment and cables. Remember that you should label

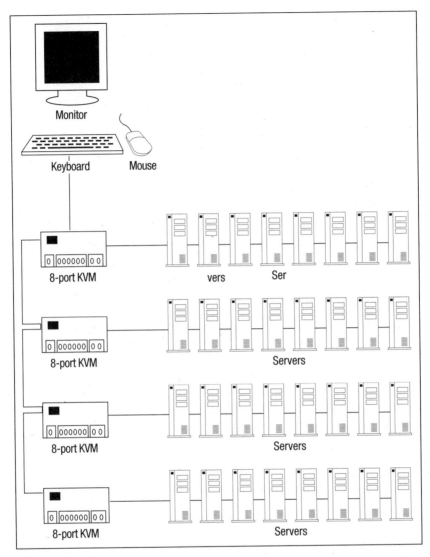

Figure 2.1 Daisy-chained KVMs.

everything accurately. If you have several servers in the cabinet, you will most likely be using a single KVM setup for all of those machines. You will want to label the switch box correctly so that you know you are configuring the right server. Nothing can be more frustrating than spending an hour entering the TCP/IP configuration of what you think is the Exchange server, only to find out that it is your file server. Label the cables that lead to the switch box as well.

KVM setups have three cables that connect from each switch port. These cables have connectors that attach to the monitor, keyboard, and mouse connections on your servers. It is a good idea to bind the cables together, label them for each server, and label the port they are on. When you wrap the cables together, it will be easier to match the appropriate connections with the server.

 KVMs are usually mounted towards the top of the cabinets. Make sure you take this into consideration when estimating cable lengths.

The exam focuses on the preplanning aspect of cabinet setup. So remember that planning the device placement is key to the success of your KVM setup.

UPS

The equipment in your server room is vital to the integrity of your network. This means that you definitely need to have some form of backup. As of this writing, the state of California is undergoing rolling blackouts, brownouts, and other power issues. Without a UPS system in place to keep the system up and running long enough to shut down properly, you might have a disaster on your hands. Computers are not very robust when it comes to abrupt shutdowns. You definitely must have some UPSs in your server room.

To make electrical equipment work, you need electricity. We could spend volumes discussing electrical power, but for this exam it comes down to how your systems are powered and what happens if the power goes out?

Electricity comes in two forms:

➤ Alternating current (AC)

➤ Direct current (DC)

AC power is the electricity that runs through the walls from the power stations. The reason it is called alternating current is because it is constantly switching directions. If you look at it on an oscilloscope, you would see a sine wave. Because it is constantly cycling up and down, this frequency is measured in hertz or Hz. In North America, the frequency runs at 60 Hz. For most of the rest of the world, it runs at 50 Hz.

DC power is the type of electricity that comes from batteries. This power is local power and is stored. This type of current also creates much more heat than AC power. Regardless, it is important to be careful around all types of electricity. Do not believe people who tell you that DC electric cannot hurt you. If it is powerful enough, it will harm you as much as AC.

Unfortunately, computers and electrical appliances run on DC power. DC power looks like a straight line on an oscilloscope. The electricity runs in one direction. Because AC power needs to be converted into DC power to run computers, a power supply is used. The power supply "switches" the AC power to DC power. This allows the computer equipment to work.

However, a power supply requires constant electricity to convert. If there is a power outage, electricity ceases, and problems occur because computers will not be shut down properly. UPSs are used as backup power systems. There used to be standby power sources (SPS), but these days a UPS is used to describe both types of systems. An SPS takes current from the wall and converts it to DC battery power. Once a battery is charged, it then monitors the AC current running through the line. If the current stops at any point, the SPS quickly switches to its batteries, converts the DC back to AC, and sends it out. A UPS, on the other hand, is always operating from its battery. A voltage inverter continuously converts the DC power to AC for your PC while charging the batteries from the wall. If the power fails, no switching takes place. The batteries just continue to convert to AC until there is no power left.

Note: Because of the switching that would take place, SPSs were generally frowned upon in the past. However, with more robust power supplies and faster switching, SPSs are making a comeback with their lower cost. To tell if a unit is an SPS, look for the words "switch time" anywhere in its documentation or box. If the unit switches, it is not a true UPS.

UPSs come in many forms. They can come in small boxes, large trunk size boxes, room size installations, and even in horizontal mounted styles. Some UPSs merely provide battery backup in the event of a power outage. Other UPSs are intelligent and are able to shut down your server carefully. These intelligent UPSs are generally much more expensive, but they are worth it. If you are not on-site when a power failure occurs, the 15 minutes of extra power you have will not help you. An intelligent or "smart" UPS utilizes a software solution that integrates with your servers. The software also helps you with battery management. The batteries in the UPS will more than likely need to be changed at some point in the future. With intelligent battery management, you will know when it is time to change the batteries. With the addition of Hot Swap batteries, you can keep your systems up and running very efficiently without having to take your servers down to change the batteries on the UPS.

Because of the differences in size and mounting styles, you need to plan for UPS placement in your server cabinets or on your server tables. Remember to place them conveniently for your equipment to plug into. Power cables are very bulky and harder to bend than CAT 5 cable. So make your power cable runs cleaner by placing the equipment closer to the UPS. Also, do not coil power cords. This creates a greater magnetic field, which creates heat in the cords.

Another consideration is the amount of power you need to keep your systems up and running. The more equipment you need, the bigger the UPS solution. Keep in mind that the bigger the UPS, the more power it outputs. So if you are running two or three cabinets of servers, routers, and switches, make sure you have the power necessary to keep them up for awhile in the event of a power failure. A UPS generally has its maximum output load on the side of the server (i.e., 1600 VA). When planning for power allocation for your servers, add the wattage and multiply by 1.4. This will give you the volt-amperage necessary to cover your power needs on an on-going basis. However, you will still need to take into consideration the load over time factor. If your load is 50 percent, you will have more battery time than a load of 75 percent.

 Do not plug a laser printer or copier into a UPS. UPS power should be reserved for mission-critical equipment.

Raised Floors

Back when computers were the size of buildings, some bright fellow figured out that it would be easier to run cabling underneath a raised floor. This would allow access to the cabling versus placing it in a wall that you would need to break into. By using raised flooring, you can place cables into half tubes and not clutter your clean server room.

A raised floor also gives you the ability to access the cabling in case you need to troubleshoot a bad wire. If the cabling is behind walls, you have to pull the cable out of the wall and use a snake to replace it.

Be careful when laying cable. Cables can get pinched in between the floor panels causing issues with your network. If you are using a raised floor, take your time and make sure everything is under the floor and not caught between the panels. Also, consider that raised floors make lazy cable layers. Because the cable is out of sight, installers tend to be a bit more careless with their work. This can cause major problems when trying to follow a cable from its source to its destination. We'll cover that in more detail later in the "Cabling" section of this chapter. Although raised floors can protect from some water damage in case of a leak, remember that you need to check under the floor on occasion to make sure you catch any problems before they get out of hand. It could turn into a flood, and then you will have to implement your disaster recovery plan.

One method of monitoring water and flooding issues is to place a water sensor underneath the raised floors. You can run this sensor to the rest of your environment controls and have alarms in place in case water appears. It is important that you monitor all of the elements under your raised floors.

When designing the layout of your server room, determine where you will be placing your cabinets and where you want to run the cabling. This will allow you to have much of the cabling in place before you hook up the first computer.

Note: Some organizations use cable trays or tracks in the ceiling to make it easier to run cable through the building or rooms. The term "cable drop" originated from these ceiling tracks, as the cabling would run on these "trellises" and be dropped behind the walls. Some telephone companies actually refuse to use raised floors. They would rather bolt the racks into the flooring and run the cabling above.

Temperature

When running or exercising, our bodies get warmed up. So it is with any computer equipment. Because components are running electricity through silicone chips, these chips get hot. The CPUs in today's servers use fans or heat sinks to dissipate the heat from the motherboards. The bottom line is that the server room can quickly become very hot.

Although this is a good thing in a sauna, heat is an equipment killer. Computer equipment likes a cool environment. Typically anywhere from 65–70 degrees Fahrenheit is where you want the ambient temperature to be in your server room. Hot equipment does not perform well and can quickly damage valuable resources.

Whether your equipment is hot or cold is not your only environmental concern. Humidity can also damage equipment. As the air gets cooler around the equipment, the moisture in the air can begin to form condensation on the metal cases. Water and electrical equipment do not mix well. You also need to remember that when the chips and motherboards were created, there was a certain amount of humidity in the room. If your server room gets too dry, it will dry out the boards and silicone chips. They can become brittle and break when you take them out for maintenance or upgrading. On the other side of the equation, dry, hot air can produce static electricity, which can rapidly destroy your computer's circuitry.

Take note of your outside environment. If you live in Phoenix, Arizona, you will want to add humidity to your server room. If you live in New Orleans, Louisiana or Houston, Texas, you might want to utilize a dehumidifier. The optimal humidity for your server room is between 30–45 percent.

To help maintain this environment, several companies offer smart thermostats that will monitor the relative humidity and temperature of your server room. These thermostats take constant readings and can be programmed to activate an alarm if either of the readings are out of alignment. Some of these thermostats, like those made by Liebert, have a serial port that allows you to integrate its readings into your monitoring solution. If the temperature gets too hot, it triggers an alarm and perhaps shuts down the server before it melts.

With the amount of equipment that you normally encounter in a data center or server room, you will definitely want to invest heavily in air-conditioning units. Pay careful attention to how much cold air it can produce. Make sure that you have separation between your cabinets, or utilize open-air racks. This space allows the air to flow freely and not get trapped by the racks closest to the air conditioning. Don't forget that the ambient room temperature is not the same as the temperature inside the case. It can be 80 degrees in the room, but the inside of the server could be running closer to 120 degrees.

 Know the difference between ambient room temperature and equipment operating temperatures.

Cabling

When it comes to cabling, most network administrators cringe and start talking about the weather. They know how vital it is, but it is definitely an odious task. When you work with equipment that communicates with each other, you obviously need some form of cabling. Given that you have to run cables of multiple sorts and varieties to any number of pieces of equipment, it can quickly become confusing and messy. The server room is generally the heart of the network, which means that eventually many end-user data requests end up here when users attempt to access resources, send mail, surf the Web, and so on. Because of all the equipment and resources located in the server room, you will have numerous cables running throughout the room.

As mentioned earlier in the chapter, there is a limited amount of space in the typical server room or closet. Because cable installation is very expensive, you will want to install cables right the first time. But once the cables are installed and ready to be hooked up, your battle is only half done.

There is beauty to a well laid out server room. With cables neatly laid out and labeled correctly, your job as an administrator becomes even easier. If you think about it, you can have 10–20 cables coming from the back of each server. When you have more than five computers, routers, switches, and so on, it can become an issue when trying to track down connections. To make things easier on administrators, most of the server cabinets have cable ducts that allow you to run cables in an orderly fashion along the left side and up through the top or down through the bottom. It is generally a good idea to wrap together the cables that lead to the same piece of equipment. Give enough lead on the cabling so that you can tug on and spot each cable. When you do this, however, make sure that you make the cables with screw on or clip connectors shorter. This will prevent you from pulling serial and other nonattaching cables out of the server inadvertently. If you are trying to track down a particular grouping and give a good tug, you could possibly disconnect a universal serial bus (USB), serial, or other cable.

For example, one day we were attempting to find the cable grouping that led to the back up file server. After tugging on a few groups, I found the cables I was looking for. I disconnected the cables from the file server, pulled it out and installed the memory upgrade. I plugged all the cables back in and fired up the file server to check for any errors. Everything was great. A little later, a colleague, who was also along on the job, called to see what I had done to the Exchange server. He was unable to get the keyboard to type. After troubleshooting the keyboard and other items, it dawned on me that I had been pulling on a set of wires that led to the Exchange server. I had accidentally unplugged the keyboard connector wire. If I had given it a little more leeway, I would merely have pulled on the attached monitor cable instead. So remember to plan accordingly as you lay the cables.

There are several different types of cabling that are used in networks, and you are likely to encounter most of them in your server room. Knowing the different types of cables will also help in planning the layout of these cables. Table 2.1 lists the common types of networking cables used.

Remember to check all your cabling and connections before you wrap them up in the ducts to make sure they are in good shape. Confirm that the cable is firmly

Table 2.1 Types of cable used in networks.		
Type of Cable	**Maximum Length**	**Flexibility**
Unshielded twisted pair (UTP), AKA CAT 3-5	100 meters	Fairly good
Fiberoptic	2,000 meters (2 kilometers)	Very stiff (bending too much can cause breaks in the fibers)
Thinnet – Coaxial	185 meters	Fair
Thicknet – Coaxial	500 meters	Stiff

connected to the server and that connectors are not frayed or weakly attached. This is vital for coaxial cables.

When laying network or KVM cables, plan on keeping them away from power cords. Even with shielding, electromagnetic interference (EMI) can affect your signaling if electric power is placed too close to the network cables. Many server cabinets have power strips on the right side and the cabling is run up the left side. Fiber-optic cables are immune to this effect, so you are free to place them in proximity to each other. If you are using cable trellises, you will more than likely run the power below the data cables.

The most important aspect is labeling. This is where you will save yourself and others incredible amounts of time troubleshooting and replacing equipment. If you have equipment and cables labeled correctly, replacing a file server with an off-line backup is a snap. Proper labeling allows you to install the new one quickly and be up and running in no time. Labeling also allows for quicker cable trouble-shooting. If you seem to have issues with one of your network cables, you can use a time domain reflectometer (TDR) to test the cable. But you will have to find both ends of the cable to complete the test. By labeling your cables you will make your job quite a bit easier. The following suggestions will help you properly label all of your cabling:

➤ Use permanent markers on the cables.

➤ Label the cables every three feet or so.

➤ Use a label maker to label ports and cable ends.

➤ Label the sleeves if you run cables inside.

➤ List each cable that is included in the sleeve.

There is one other aspect of cabling that you need to be aware of with regards to the Server+ exam. We briefly mentioned earlier that many vendors prefer to run cables in the ceiling rather than through the floor for several reasons. This would not be the case if an innovation had not come along that allowed false ceilings to be dropped lower than the regular standard ceilings. United States laws require that any cabling that goes through the ceilings must be made with a specialized fire-resistant casing called plenum. As you can imagine, plenum is somewhat expensive, so one of the workarounds to decrease this expense and still cooperate with the law is to essentially create a drop-down false ceiling that is only strong enough to hold lighting and cabling. This false ceiling is suspended from the true ceiling using heavy-gauge wires or metal rods.

If/when the exam mentions ceilings, it assumes standard or regular ceilings and is surely referring to plenum.

Racks and Cabinets

Placing equipment in racks and server cabinets greatly reduces the space taken by the equipment. Not only does it free up space, but cabinets and racks also help with organizing cabling. There are several different types of racks:

➤ Open racks

➤ Cabinets

➤ Rolling cabinets

Open racks are generally mounted to the floor and ceiling, and the equipment is placed out where you can see it. From a security standpoint, this might not be the best solution. However, it does allow for easy access to the equipment from both front and back.

When purchasing a rack, you need to make sure that the bolt holes on each side are aligned. The best way to do this is to ensure that each hole is spaced evenly from each other. Newer rackmount equipment has been made specifically to fit the industry standard bolt hole units, which are called a "U." Not even the experts can reach back to antiquity to determine what a U really stands for other than units. For the exam, you need to know that both racks and rackmount equipment are usually made to fit this U-based standard where one U represents a height of 1.75 inches or 4.45 centimeters.

One U is 1.75 inches or 4.45 cm.

Cabinets are like the open racks, but they also give you the option of locking the front and back access. This is good for security reasons. Because they are not in the open air, some cabinets have built-in fans to help cool the equipment. When placing servers in these cabinets, be sure to leave some space in between each component to allow air to flow through the cabinet.

Some cabinets can be rolled around the server room. Personally, we think it is a great time saver, but also a potential hazard. The important fact concerning racks is that they allow you to conserve valuable space.

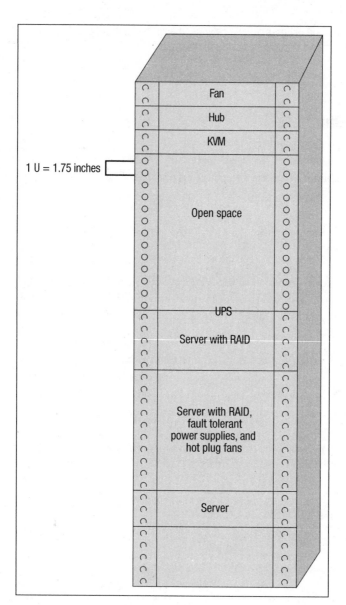

1 U = 1.75 inches

Fan

Hub

KVM

Open space

UPS

Server with RAID

Server with RAID, fault tolerant power supplies, and hot plug fans

Server

Figure 2.2 A typical cabinet configuration.

Equipment is mounted by machine screws into the racks. Figure 2.2 shows the vertical spacing between the bolt holes or Us. Each U is 1.75 inches. All equipment is measured vertically by Us. This makes it easier to plan how much equipment can fit in your racks or cabinets. If you have a 3U piece of equipment, it is 5.25 inches tall. If you have a server that is not U-mountable, there are U-mounted shelves that you can place the equipment on. Some shelves and equipment will even slide out, allowing you to work on the equipment without removing it from the rack. For this reason, you will want to place your cabinets at least three feet away from the wall in back and six feet in the front to allow you to open doors and work on equipment.

When placing components on the shelves, make sure that you put the heavy items on the bottom and the lighter equipment, such as KVMs, on top. This will help center the gravity of the cabinet or rack.

Many cabinets are also equipped with their own ventilation fans. This is to optimize air circulation in a small space that may contain many servers running at full capacity. Each fan in a cabinet or rack is designed and placed specifically for that particular cabinet. Additional ventilation holes can usually be found all around the cabinet to assist the fan in its job. When purchasing cabinets, make sure that a fan comes with the package, and that there is abundant ventilation in the cabinet by itself. Generally, cabinet fans are located in either the top or bottom of the cabinet, and multiple fans can be purchased to provide cabinet circulation. By and large, you can check with the cabinet manufacturer for recommendations on air circulation improvement. If multiple fans are an option, the manufacturer will also have recommendations on how many servers or pieces of equipment a single fan can support within the specified cabinet.

 Although it is possible to add fans to servers and computers, adding a fan to a server from within a cabinet will not improve overall circulation. Cabinet temperature in an "overheated" situation will only improve with additional cabinet fans.

Security

You hear all about the security holes in Windows 2000 or viruses that are spread by malicious hackers, but one of the biggest security threats to your organization is the unlocked, unmonitored server room. It's like putting in the most complex security system in the world, yet leaving the door wide open.

Sometimes people forget that the most obvious thing they can do to keep their equipment safe is to simply lock the door. This will suffice for some people, but you should also make sure you monitor access to the server room as well.

When others have access to your server room, they are given the keys to the kingdom. Your file servers, mail servers, Web servers, routers, backbone switches, and so on are all contained in one place. When planning the server room, you should take into consideration the physical security of your equipment and resources.

Physical Security

Most hackers look for backdoors to crack into your network. However, internal employees have easier access when you leave a server room unlocked and unmonitored. They don't need a back door; they can come right in the front door. Sometimes it is not even an intruder who causes problems. Peter Norton of Norton Software tells the story of troubleshooting a server that kept rebooting itself between midnight and 2:00 A.M. As the administrators kept watch one evening, they found that the janitor would unplug the server in that area and plug in his vacuum cleaner. Obviously, this person was not intent on bringing down the network in a fit of rage or revenge, but nonetheless, the janitor was definitely bringing down the network.

There are several ways to lock components in your server rooms. Passkeys, badge scanners, locked cabinets, and even a deadbolt can keep unwanted visitors from accessing equipment or entering your server room. The following list contains additional guidelines for keeping your equipment safe:

➤ Use passkeys and security badges to help audit access to the room.

➤ Integrate the passkey system into your building security, but try to keep the server room on a separate system or circuit.

➤ Purchase server cabinets with locks on the doors.

➤ Lock down the server with a passcode.

➤ Secure access to the power as well.

Many people might love to access your data directly from the source, so make sure you protect yourself and your company by taking the time to lock it up. If you cannot lock the room, then at least lock up the equipment inside it. The more layers of protection you have, the more likely you are to not have to recover from a physical attack on your server room. Believe it or not, the majority of physical attacks on servers come from internal personnel. You can prevent much of these attacks with a good security policy.

Security Policy

All security policies should be defined for employees regarding access to the server room and the server resources. Make sure that the policy is clear and to the point. This will alleviate many accidental security breaches. It is a good idea to consider all aspects of the security of your network when you are creating this policy:

➤ Have people threatened to cause harm to your environment?

➤ How much access should employees have to the equipment?

➤ Do you monitor the room with cameras and other recording devices?

➤ How often should you test your security policies?

➤ Are there different levels of security needed to accommodate different groups?

These are questions that will be answered by your security policy. The bottom line is to allow access only to those who need it. This rule of thumb is not only useful for the exam, but also for your real world situation.

Other Security Measures

If someone does get into the server room and steals a server, the intruder still has to have administrator rights to access the server data. However, most electronic thieves know that they can take the server home, reload the operating system, and access the resources on the computer. This is a common scenario with corporate theft, which is rampant around the globe. Although, there is a new feature in Windows 2000 that will help keep this from occurring.

Be sure to sign up for security alert emails from the major security firms. Although you do not have the time to constantly research all of the security holes in your network, there are companies that provide this service 24/7. Utilize their manpower to make your server environment as secure as it can be.

In addition, use seals on equipment so that you can spot any tampering with the equipment. If the seal is broken, you know that someone has either attempted or gained access to your equipment.

The Cost of Downtime

If you do have a break-in, you will quickly discover the penalties of being lax in your security. Loss of resources, replacing equipment, recreating lost documents, and restoring backups will consume your time as an administrator for weeks if not months. It has been said many times in many ways: downtime is death to a company.

Consider having a special security team that specializes in recovery from this particular type of incident. Make sure you have a plan that lists very detailed procedures that will aid in the recovery of data or replacement of equipment.

Documentation

The three "Ds" of network administration are document, document, and document. When looking at all of the components in your server room, it makes sense that you will need to have some form of documentation to help make sense of it all. With documentation, you can track service on equipment, troubleshooting calls, audits, cabling, new equipment, and so on. All of this documentation is vital to an organized server room.

If you have more than one person working in the server room, documentation takes on even more meaning. You cannot always count on being able to talk to your coworkers about what work they did the past few days. If you were facing a critical stop on your servers and had management breathing down your neck, think about how much calmer you would be with some documentation to help you out. The exam expects you to know what to document, so make sure you are aware of this information.

Physical Documentation

When you have more than one computer, router, switch, or hub in your network, it becomes difficult to remember all the physical aspects of the network.

Keep electronic copies of your documentation handy, but always have a hard copy available. Print the documents and organize them in a binder that remains in the server room. Having this documentation available will make it easier to access if the server room has a problem, and you cannot access your local or networked copy.

What should you include in your binder? The basics should come first and include the type of equipment you have and all of the internal components, which are the foundation of your network.

Each server contains:

➤ CPU

➤ Power supply

➤ Fan

➤ Basic Input/Output Service (BIOS)

➤ Memory

➤ Video card

➤ Network card

➤ Hard drives

➤ Other peripherals

Create a document that lists these for each of the servers in your server room. You should also do this for other pieces of equipment, such as routers, switches, and so on. However, the exam concentrates on the server/PC aspect. It is particularly important for you to track which items are fault tolerant within a server so that you can react properly during a failure. Quite often, fault-tolerant systems not only remain running when components fail, but also do not require shutting down the server to fix the problem.

From the list of internal server components, fault-tolerant components can include the CPU, memory, network cards, hard drives, power supplies, and fans.

Next, you should keep careful maintenance logs. By knowing what work has been done or needs to be done, you will be solving many problems before they even occur. Make sure you cover when, who, and what.

➤ *When*—For example, knowing when the last defragmentation occurred will help determine whether the slowdown on your drives is an access problem or fragmentation. An access problem would require some major troubleshooting, whereas fragmentation is easy to fix. Timing is an integral part of figuring out what needs to be updated or upgraded. As mentioned earlier, certain equipment contains parts that start to deteriorate over time. It might be time to replace those surge protectors, or time to clean the dirt and dust off the motherboards.

➤ *Who*—It is vital to know who performed the maintenance on your equipment. If you have to work with or fix something that was built or configured by someone else, it would be important to contact this person. This information will also help to track down any errors that might occur after any maintenance work. Whoever the last person was to touch the equipment can help you troubleshoot. Answers to questions—was a patch installed, were the cards reseated correctly, were all the appropriate cables reattached—can reduce your follow up time.

➤ *What*—Record items such as what was replaced and which one of the servers was fixed. If you just use a checkbox labeled "maintenance" next to each server, you won't have much information to go on when problems arise.

Warranty information should also be documented. At home, we have a file cabinet that contains the instruction manuals and warranty information for each appliance, computer, and electronic device that we own. Having all this information in one place makes it easier for me to replace my equipment. This is especially true for you as a network administrator. When you have thousands of dollars of equipment, you'll definitely want to have all of your warranty information in one place. Keep track of the following information for each device:

➤ Vendor

➤ Date of purchase

➤ Parts covered

➤ Telephone number for warranty service

➤ Serial number of the device

With this vital information, you will make it much easier to replace or repair components in an expeditious fashion. Equipment that is down costs you money.

Additionally, you'll want to keep good records of the configuration you have in place on each server. If you have a SCSI RAID array (See Chapter 3 for more information on SCSI and RAID technologies) on a server, make sure that the configuration is written down. We cannot tell you how many times we have done some work or maintenance on a component and have then had to reconfigure it from memory. Configuring a device from memory can be hit or miss. Most likely, you will miss rather than hit. With the configuration recorded, you won't have to rely on the "gray matter recall" method.

Part of the configuration should include the TCP/IP or other network protocol configuration. Let's use TCP/IP for illustration purposes. However, the details would be the same for Internetwork Packet Exchange/Sequence Packet Exchange (IPX/SPX), AppleTalk, and so on. Most servers utilize static IP addresses, and it is important to know which machine is where. For example, if you have a domain name service (DNS) server, you will want to keep that IP address the same no matter what. When the workstations need to access the Internet or a directory service like Active Directory in Windows 2000, they need to resolve the host name to the IP address they are looking for. This means they send a query to a DNS server. If you change the IP address of the DNS server, this query will fail. Therefore, it is important to keep track of this type of configuration as well.

Speaking of DNS, you will also want to keep track of each server's role in the enterprise. Knowing that server1 is the Dynamic Host Configuration Protocol (DHCP) server, server2 is the Remote Access server, and server3 handles the Windows Internet Naming System (WINS), and DNS will make it easier to troubleshoot specific problems that might arise. Make sure that you identify each server and the role that it plays in your network. Do not forget that some servers might play multiple roles. Whether it is a file server, Web server, or email server, you'll want to know which is which.

By keeping good records of the physical aspects of your server room, you will make your life a lot easier when it comes to troubleshooting your network.

Software Documentation

It is also a good idea to keep a copy of the software documentation in the server room as well. When you are monitoring your servers, you will also want to keep copies of the logs handy. Logs contain information the operating system and all its applications put on file.

Anytime a program or application does something, it usually logs the information. Having this information helps you to troubleshoot the situation or send the information to your customer support person. In your server room, you should keep information about:

➤ Your network operating system

➤ The different services running on the equipment

➤ Latest driver information

➤ Latest patch applied

➤ A snapshot of the network when it is running at peak efficiency

The network operating system you are using is one of the vital pieces of information that most people forget to place in their documentation. Make note of which version of the network operating system (NOS) you are running, license information, and technical support information.

Similar to the roles that a server might have, you should also record the different services that are running on each machine. If you use a print server, document the print spooler. If you have a DNS machine, record the Berkeley Internet Name Domain (BIND) version are you running. All important items should be written down.

Device drivers are an absolute necessity to operate your equipment and services on your network servers. Unfortunately, with the constant change of software, operating systems, and equipment, these drivers can become outdated, unnecessary, and even dangerous to your network. Keep track of the drivers you have installed on the servers for all of the peripheral and internal devices. It is almost impossible to keep track of the software drivers, but that is where software patches come into play. We also include BIOS updates in this area of the documentation. Remember to keep track of which version of the BIOS you are running. As more and more "hardware-aware" software becomes available, you will want to make sure your BIOS is updated.

Software updates or "patches" will never cease. Like death, taxes, and the surprise visit from your mother-in-law, you can never outrun these little bundles of "joy." To make software available to the market, it sometimes needs to be pushed out the door as fast as possible. This means that coders are not always able to check all the little details. With millions of lines of code in some of the major operating systems, there is no end to the possibilities of random errors. Software publishers have to wait for someone to find something wrong, and then fix it with a patch. A patch is generally a "hot fix" that can be downloaded from a Web site or FTP site in order for users and administrators to fix the problem. An update generally consists of many patches and additional accessories that are provided as downloads and are also made available on disk or CD-ROM.

Note: You should investigate updates or upgrades carefully before installing them on your network. Make sure you do some testing on machines that are not linked to your intranet to watch for any atypical behavior. For example, the odd-numbered service packs for Windows NT 4.0 are supposedly more stable than the even-numbered service packs.

Chapter 7 discusses logs and how they can provide tools to monitor the condition of your network. To utilize logs effectively, you need a baseline. A baseline is a "snapshot" of your network operating at peak efficiency. By knowing what your network looks like in a working situation, it is easier to know when something is wrong. By having a snapshot of a "healthy" network, you will quickly recognize when the network is having problems and in need of repair. Baselines are also discussed in Chapter 7.

Practice Questions

Question 1

KVMs can handle a maximum of how many systems?

○ a. 8

○ b. 16

○ c. 32

○ d. 64

Answer d is correct. No more than 64 systems can be chained together with KVMs without causing signal degradation. Although a single KVM can handle 8 servers as in answer a, and subsequent KVMs can be chained together for 16 and 32 servers for answers c and d, this is not the maximum capability; therefore answers a, c, and d are incorrect.

Question 2

Servers use what type of power?

○ a. AC

○ b. MHz

○ c. DC

○ d. Amps

Answer c is correct. Servers use DC (direct current) power. Answer a is incorrect because AC (alternating current) power is used to transmit power across large distances. Answers b and d are incorrect because MHz is a unit of frequency, and Amps is a unit of amplitude, not power.

Question 3

> The ideal ambient operating temperature in a server room is:
>
> ○ a. 60–65 degrees Fahrenheit
>
> ○ b. 65–70 degrees Fahrenheit
>
> ○ c. 70–75 degrees Fahrenheit
>
> ○ d. 75–80 degrees Fahrenheit

Answer b is correct. The ideal ambient operating temperature in a server room is 65–70 degrees Fahrenheit. Answer a is incorrect because you do not want the temperature to be so cold that humans are uncomfortable or mechanical parts in a server malfunction. Remember that the internal server temperature can be up to 30 degrees higher than the ambient temperature in a room, and answers c and d are incorrect because of this fact.

Question 4

> The optimal humidity levels in a server room should be:
>
> ○ a. 15–30 percent
>
> ○ b. 30–45 percent
>
> ○ c. 45–60 percent
>
> ○ d. 60–75 percent

Answer b is correct. The optimal humidity levels in a server room should be 30–45 percent. It is important to maintain some levels of humidity in a server room in order to prevent parts from becoming brittle. Answer a is incorrect because 15–30 percent is still a very dry environment. Answers c and d are incorrect because it is also important to reduce humidity in wet areas in order to prevent short circuits from happening when water condenses on equipment.

Question 5

> The maximum length for CAT 5 cables is:
>
> ○ a. 2000 meters
>
> ○ b. 200 meters
>
> ○ c. 185 meters
>
> ○ d. 100 meters

Answer d is correct. A single CAT 5 cable will carry signals without degradation for 100 meters. Answer a is incorrect because 2000 meters is the length for fiber-optic cables. Answer c is incorrect because it is the length for thinnet, and answer b is incorrect because it is the length for thicknet. Both thinnet and thicknet are coaxial cable types that have shielding, which reduces interference and increases the length that signals can travel without degradation.

Question 6

> You need to figure out how many servers can fit into your rackmount server cabinet. The cabinet specifications show the cabinet as being 40-U high. What is a U?
>
> ○ a. 15 mm
>
> ○ b. 2 cm
>
> ○ c. 1.75 inches
>
> ○ d. 2.25 inches

Answer c is correct. A U is 1.75 inches, which is the equivalent of 4.45 centimeters. Answers a, b, and d are incorrect because they are not the standard length for Us.

Question 7

> Plenum is used for which type of cables?
>
> ○ a. Raised floor cables
>
> ○ b. Network cables
>
> ○ c. Ceiling cables
>
> ○ d. Power cables

Answer c is correct. U.S. fire code requires that ceiling cables be shielded with plenum. Answer a is incorrect because raised floor cables have no such restrictions usually because they are not exposed to additional heat that you find in roofs, attics, ducts, and crawlspaces. Answers b and d are incorrect because network and power cables are both types of cables that are available with plenum shielding in order to conform to fire code, but plenum is not specific to these types of cables.

Question 8

When installing equipment into a server rack or cabinet, what should be placed on the bottom?

- ○ a. KVM
- ○ b. Servers
- ○ c. UPS
- ○ d. Hub

Answer c is correct. A UPS should be placed on the bottom because it is most likely to be the single heaviest component in the rack. As a rule of thumb, all heavy components should be placed lower on the rack in order to prevent the rack from becoming top-heavy and tipping over. Answers a and d are incorrect because KVMs and hubs should be placed at the top of the rack. Answer b is incorrect as servers should be placed just above the UPS because they are still heavy, yet weigh less than a UPS.

Question 9

Which of the following is not capable of being fault tolerant in a server?

- ○ a. Fan
- ○ b. Power supply
- ○ c. BIOS
- ○ d. CPU

Answer c is correct. The BIOS is not fault tolerant. Fans, power supplies, and CPUs can all be fault tolerant. Therefore, answers a, b, and d are incorrect.

Need to Know More?

 Reeves, Scott, Kalinda Reeves, Stephen Weese, and Christopher S. Geyer. *A+ Exam Prep 3rd Edition.* The Coriolis Group, LLC, Scottsdale, AZ, 2001. ISBN 1-57610-699-3. Basic UPS technical information and information on how UPSs work.

 Zacker, Craig and Paul Doyle. *Upgrading and Repairing Networks.* Que Corporation, Indianapolis, IN, 1996. ISBN 0-78970181-2.

 www.pcguide.com. This site, run by Charles M. Kozierok and similar to TechRepublic, contains a wealth of information on many IT topics.

 www.support.intel.com is a great reference for server hardware information.

Data Storage

Terms you'll need to understand:

✓ SCSI

✓ ATA/ATAPI

✓ IDE/EIDE

✓ HVD

✓ LVD

✓ SE

✓ PIO

✓ DMA

✓ UltraDMA

✓ CHS

✓ LBA

✓ BIOS

✓ IEEE 1394

✓ USB

✓ SAN

✓ Fault tolerance

✓ RAID

✓ Striping

✓ Parity

✓ Mirroring

✓ Duplexing

✓ Array

✓ Hot swap/Hot plug/Hot spare

✓ NAS

Techniques you'll need to master:

✓ Selecting proper data storage methods for your company

✓ Choosing proper RAID levels based upon given criteria

✓ Installing and configuring RAID systems

✓ Installing and configuring SCSI drives & controllers

✓ Installing and configuring ATA/ATAPI drives & controllers

Drive Types

In this chapter we will discuss primary data storage, the means by which the computer stores or remembers information between reboots. Only one method is used to implement this type of memory: the hard drive.

Two types of computing interfaces between a hard driveand the computer are currently in common use: Small Computer Systems Interface (SCSI) and AT Attachment (known variously as ATA, ATAPI, or IDE). Other interfaces, such as Universal Serial Bus (USB) and IEEE 1394 (FireWire), hold promise for the future, but these are not yet capable of serving as primary storage because they are not fast enough and not bootable. These interfaces and others are covered in Chapter 6.

There are several reasons for choosing an IDE drive for a server:

➤ ATA drives are cheaper than SCSI drives.

➤ An ATA interface is already installed on most computers.

➤ ATA drives are easier to setup than SCSI drives.

➤ ATA speeds are on a par with SCSI when a server uses only one or two drives.

➤ ATA drives have limited RAID capability (an advantage only when a server does not require RAID capability).

➤ ATA drives are a good choice when the redundancy and fault tolerance features of hot swap and hot spare are not important.

There are also several reasons for choosing a SCSI drive:

➤ SCSI supports RAID.

➤ SCSI works with external drives or arrays.

➤ SCSI is significantly faster if you have multiple drives.

These competing standards are maintained by the same organization, the American National Standards Institute (ANSI), which is a consortium of industry and government agencies working together to create voluntary standards. ANSI committees have responsibility for specific categories of hardware standards within the IT industry. The committee with responsibility for SCSI and ATA standards is the National Committee on Information Technology Standards (NCITS). NCITS is further divided into technical committees. The technical committee responsible for SCSI is called T10 and the Committee responsible for ATA is called T13. Both of these committees maintain Web sites that contain their working documents, **www.t10.org** and **www.t13.org**.

Small Computer Systems Interface (SCSI)

This standard was invented in the mid-1980s, when a small computer was approximately the size of a refrigerator. It was designed to connect mainframes to midsize and minicomputers such as a DEC PDP-11 or a Data General. It gained popularity when Apple included it as the primary device attachment bus in the original MacIntosh. It has evolved since then into a conglomeration of standards that range from the standard parallel interface to fiber channel and even ATAPI (IDE).

The general structure of SCSI has five protocol layers:

➤ Common Access Method

➤ SCSI Device-Type Specific Command Sets

➤ Shared Command Set

➤ Transport Protocol

➤ Physical Interconnect

With its layered structure, the SCSI bus is flexible while still providing a single access point and a method that allows the host to communicate with many different types of devices over many different types of media. A SCSI bus also makes adding new technology easy; just insert a new variant of a layer at the appropriate level, and you are up and running. This is exactly how SCSI evolved to SCSI-2 and how SCSI-2 evolved to SCSI-3.

The Shared Command Set is aptly named. There are only two variants of this layer: one for SCSI-2 and one for SCSI-3. The Common Access Method layer has the same attributes, two variants, and involves the way a host talks to the bus regardless of what is connected to it. The SCSI Device-Type Specific Command Sets layer has eight variants and allows the bus to talk to various devices such as hard drives, CD-ROMs, DVDs, and scanners, each of which has different features that warrant extra commands. The Transport Protocol changes depending upon the type of media, such as parallel, fiber, and serial. The Physical Interconnect layer defines electrical and timing characteristics of the bus—a feature that most people notice easily. This layer is responsible for transforming an old SCSI-1 to an Ultra320.

The SCSI Controller

The SCSI controller, sometimes referred to as a SCSI host adapter, is another device on the SCSI bus. Distinguish the computer from the controller this way: the host computer is really the device, and the controller is how it talks to the bus. The SCSI standard provides a mechanism to set priority among competing devices and usually assigns the highest priority to the host. In the case of two devices with the same priority, a fairness algorithm comes into play.

You can have multiple hosts on a SCSI bus. The hosts can communicate with each other and share resources on the bus. Several types of host clustering operate in this way. The majority of multihost installations involve providing redundant paths to resources such as RAID storage devices.

The SCSI Bus

The SCSI standard is a set of rules that allows devices to interoperate. These rules define mechanical, electrical, timing, and protocols characteristics of the bus.

Each device on the bus is assigned a unique address. Depending on the version of SCSI you are using, there can be 8 or 16 devices on a bus. Because the host is just another device on the bus, it follows that you must assign it one of the addresses. By convention, it is usually assigned address 0. This leaves 7 or 15 device addresses to assign to other devices.

Devices are attached to the bus via a daisy chain. Each end of the bus must be terminated. This termination is either passive or active based on the version of SCSI in use.

SCSI devices are not limited to being dumb devices, unlike a hard drive that can initiate no action on its own and must be told everything to do. Any device on a SCSI bus can initiate a conversation with any other device on the bus. In actual practice, though, most devices in common use are of the dumb variety.

The host can initiate a conversation between two SCSI devices, then sit back and let the devices complete their conversation without further intervention. This might occur between two hard drives, for example. Once the host sets up a file transfer, the drives can transfer the file without further instructions from the host, freeing the host to proceed to other tasks. These features allow you to use a SCSI bus in a variety of roles.

HVD, LVD, SE

There are two methods by which logic signals are transmitted over a cable. The first, called single-ended (SE), applies a positive voltage to a signal line. The current flows down the signal line to the receiver and returns through a common ground. This technique is less expensive to implement, but its limitations are that the signal cannot be transmitted over long distances or quickly. SE is the SCSI standard, and viable cable lengths range from 1.5 meters to 3 meters.

The second method of transmitting logic signals is to assign two conductors to a signal. At the same time a positive voltage is applied to one conductor, a negative voltage is applied to the other. This creates an instantaneous voltage differential at the receiver and has the advantage of being capable of traveling much further than is possible with the SE method.

SCSI implemented this second technique in two ways: through the high voltage differential (HVD) and low voltage differential (LVD) methods. HVD was first implemented in the SCSI-2 standard. It required extra circuitry not natively present in hosts or SCSI devices to power signals through the bus. It allowed cable length up to 25 meters but was expensive to implement and was not widely used. LVD was introduced with the SCSI-3 standard and uses lower voltages already present in the host and devices. The use of lower voltages simplifies the circuits required to support it and lowers the cost, but not to the level of an SE device. LVD interfaces are capable of cable lengths up to 12 meters.

 HVD devices are not compatible with LVD or SE devices and should never be attached to the same bus. LVD and SE devices are mutually compatable, but the presence of an SE device will cause the bus to run at the slower SE speed and reduce the cable length limit to that allowed by the SE device.

SCSI-1

The SCSI-1 standard provided for seven devices and a controller that had a limited command set and was basically only good for attaching hard drives. The termination here was passive and used a 132 ohm resistor. The allowable cable length was up to 6 meters.

SCSI-2

The SCSI-2 standard changed the termination requirements to an active terminator that better matched the cable impedance and improved signal quality. It added support for more types of devices and increased the speed to 10MB per second, but the maximum cable length was reduced to 1.5 meters, a little more than 5 feet. This might seem like a long cable, but if you try to attach 15 devices within this length, you are allowed less than 4 inches between devices. In the HVD version of SCSI-2, you could reach a total cable length of 25 meters, but due to the expense involved, not many HVD devices were in use.

Here are the chief variants of the SCSI-2 standard:

➤ Wide SCSI is a SCSI-2 standard that supports a 16-bit bus with data running at 5 MHz and with a throughput of 10 megabytes per second (Mbps). The connector has 68 pins. Wide SCSI can connect a maximum of 16 devices and allows a maximum cable length of either 1.5 or 25 meters, depending upon whether an SE or HVD device is attached to the bus.

➤ Fast SCSI is a SCSI-2 standard that supports an 8-bit bus with data running at 10 MHz and with a throughput of 10Mbps. The connector has 50 pins with a maximum of 8 devices and a maximum cable length of either 3 or 25 meters depending upon whether an SE or HVD device is attached to the bus.

➤ Fast Wide SCSI is a SCSI-2 standard that supports a 16-bit bus with data running at 10 MHz and with a throughput of 20Mbps. The connector has 68 pins. A maximum of 16 devices can be connected, and the maximum viable cable length is either 3 or 25 meters depending upon whether an SE or HVD device is attached to the bus.

SCSI-3

When SCSI-3 became available, the T-10 committee decided that there would never be a SCSI-4 standard, only further revisions of the SCSI-3 standard. The result is that whenever a change is made to one of the five protocol layers previously listed, a new SCSI Parallel Interface (SPI) revision number is generated. The SPI is currently at version 3, or SPI-3, with SPI-4 on the way. At the same time, the committee decided that creativity was out of the question with regard to naming the SCSI variants, and they simply conjugated prior SCSI names for the newer versions. Hence we have a legacy of confusion about SCSI variants.

➤ Ultra SCSI is a SCSI-3 standard that supports an 8-bit bus, with data running at 20 MHz and with a throughput of 20Mbps. The connector has 50 pins and can support a maximum of 8 devices depending upon cable length. Maximum cable length is either 3 or 25 meters depending upon whether an SE or HVD device is attached to the bus.

➤ Wide Ultra SCSI is a SCSI-3 standard that supports a 16-bit bus width, with data running at 20 MHz and with a throughput of 40Mbps. The connector has 68 pins and can support a maximum of 16 devices depending upon cable length. The maximum cable length is either 3 or 25 meters depending upon whether an SE or HVD device is attached to the bus. All SCSI-3 devices developed after the Wide Ultra SCSI variant was introduced no longer support SE signaling, which has since been replaced by LVD signaling.

➤ Ultra2 SCSI is a SCSI-3 SPI-2 standard that supports an 8-bit bus width, with data running at 40 MHz and with a throughput of 40Mbps. The connector has 50 pins and supports a maximum of 8 or 2 devices, depending upon cable length combined with LVD or HVD devices. Maximum cable length can be either 12 or 25 meters, depending again upon whether an LVD or HVD device is attached.

➤ Wide Ultra2 SCSI is a SCSI-3 SPI-2 standard that supports a 16-bit bus width, with data running at 40 MHz and with a throughput of 80Mbps. The connector has 68 pins and supports a maximum of 16 or 2 devices, depending upon cable length combined with LVD or HVD devices. Maximum cable length can be either 12 or 25 meters, depending again upon whether an LVD or HVD device is attached.

➤ Ultra3 SCSI is a SCSI-3 SPI-3 standard that supports a 16-bit bus width, with data running at 40 MHz (double clocked) and with a throughput of 160Mbps. The connector has 68 pins and supports a maximum of 2 devices when cable length is up to 25 meters; it supports up to 16 devices when the cable length is limited to 12 meters. This variant supports only LVD-terminated devices.

➤ Ultra160 SCSI is a SCSI-3 standard that supports a 16-bit bus width, with data running at 40 MHz (double clocked) and with a throughput of 160Mbps. The connector has 68 pins and supports a maximum of 2 devices when cable length is up to 25 meters; it supports up to16 devices when cable length is limited to 12 meters. This variant supports only LVD-terminated devices.

➤ Ultra320 SCSI is a SCSI-3 standard that supports a 16-bit bus width, with data running at 80 MHz (double clocked) and with a throughput of 320Mbps. The connector has 68 pins and supports a maximum of 2 devices when cable length is up to 25 meters; it supports up to 16 devices when cable length is limited to 12 meters. This variant supports only LVD-terminated devices.

SCSI devices do follow some fairly standardized cabling methods that might help you sort things out on the exam:

➤ 8-bit internal SCSI devices are all male, and cables are all female.

➤ 16-bit internal devices are all female, and cables are all male.

➤ All external devices are female, and the connectors are male.

➤ 50-pin connectors are used with 8-bit SCSI standards (SCSI, Fast SCSI, Ultra SCSI, Ultra2 SCSI).

➤ 68-pin connectors are used with 16-bit SCSI standards (everything else).

Aside from the HVD/LVD/SE incompatibility issue, newer SCSI controllers and devices are backward compatible with older SCSI controllers and devices. Keep in mind, however, that any SCSI chain is only as good as its bus speed. Table 3.1 lists SCSI standards from oldest to newest.

The bandwidth of the SCSI bus is intentionally designed to be approximately four times faster than the fastest device attached to it. This is by design to optimize performance for multiple attached devices. If you have only one device attached to an Ultra320 controller, you will not be using the full bandwidth of the bus and will have paid a premium for speed you cannot take full advantage of.

Table 3.1	The generations of SCSI.				
Defining Standard	**Transfer Mode**	**Bandwidth**	**Connector**	**Bus**	**Termination Method**
SCSI-1	SCSI (SCSI-1)	5	50-pin	8-bit	Passive 32 Ohm
SCSI-2	Wide SCSI	10	68-pin	16-bit	Passive 110 Ohm
SCSI-2	Fast SCSI	10	50-pin	8-bit	Passive 110 Ohm
SCSI-2	Fast Wide SCSI	20	68-pin	16-bit	Passive 110 Ohm
SCSI-3 / SPI	Ultra SCSI	20	50-pin	8-bit	Active 110 Ohm
SCSI-3 / SPI	Wide Ultra SCSI	40	68-pin	16-bit	Active. 110 Ohm
SCSI-3 / SPI-2	Ultra2 SCSI	40	50-pin	8-bit	Active 110 Ohm
SCSI-3 / SPI-2	Wide Ultra2 SCSI	80	68-pin	16-bit	Active 110 Ohm
SCSI-3 / SPI-3	Ultra3 SCSI	160	68-pin	16-bit	Active 110 Ohm
SCSI-3 / SPI-3	Ultra160(/m) SCSI	160	68-pin	16-bit	Active 110 Ohm
SCSI-3 / SPI-3	Ultra160+ SCSI	160	68-pin	16-bit	Active 110 Ohm
SCSI-3 / SPI-4	Ultra320 SCSI	320	68-pin	16-bit	Active 110 Ohm

ATA (AT Attachment)

The history of AT Attachment (ATA) is long and full of marketing hype. The following is a very brief synopsis. The ATA interface is a descendant of the MFM ST506 hard drive controller interface found in the original IBM PC-XT (circa 1984). It is, in fact, a clone of that controller. The original ATA specification grew out of the efforts of a group of clone manufacturers to achieve some amount of interoperability once the new 3.5-inch hard drive had been introduced. The original specification was called Common Access Method Committee (CAM) ATA. Members of this group were instrumental in approaching the ANSI peripheral interface committees, and the first ANSI ATA standard was born. The voluntary standard allowed interoperability of different vendor drives on the same hard drive bus. ATA defined a bus interface between disk drives and host processors.

This bus provided for a common electrical and command environment for system manufactures and suppliers of peripheral devices. The progression of processor speed and the development of alternate forms of data storage, such as CD-ROMs and DVDs, have prompted the standard to evolve to its current approved incarnation, ATA/ATAPI-5.

No history is complete without also discussing the acronym IDE. IDE stands alternately for IBM Disc Electronics or Integrated Drive Electronics and has been used as a nickname for this interface since its inception. It was used by Compaq, Western Digital, and Conner Peripherals as a marketing term for their (then) latest and greatest drive technologies. However, to some ANSI members the term was objectionable or not descriptive enough (depending on your choice of definition). It has never shown up in any official specification but is used interchangeably with ATA to describe ATA/ATAPI devices and interfaces. IDE is still widely used as a nickname to refer to ATA/ATAPI standard equipment.

The ATA standard (ATA-1) was formally withdrawn as an ANSI standard in 1999. The currently approved standard is ATA/ATAPI-5. The merging of the ATA standard and the ATAPI standard occurred with ATA/ATAPI-4. ATAPI added many features, including support for CD-ROM and DVD drives. Currently, the T-13 committee is working on the ATA/ATAPI-6 standard.

Physical Layer

The distinguishing characteristic of an ATA controller is its limit of two devices attached to the bus, a master and a slave. This is probably ATA's biggest drawback. Most computers built today bypass this problem by installing two controllers, allowing up to four peripherals. This flexibility does not come without a cost: you must allocate system resources to both controllers. Allocating system resources to them removes them from the pool of available resources for other interfaces (such as serial ports or video cards), thus limiting the number of other devices you can install in your computer. Some manufactures allow you to disable the second interface if it is not used, returning those resources to the pool. Because of the resources required, there is a practical limit of four controllers in a system. This limits the total number of ATA peripherals to eight. Table 3.2 shows the resources commonly used by ATA controllers.

 When building any server system, keep in mind that IDE is not optimally appropriate for servers because of its multiple drive speed capabilities and its limited or nonexistent RAID and fault tolerance capabilities.

Table 3.2	Resources commonly used by ATA controllers.	
Controller	**I/O Port Address**	**IRQ Number**
1	01F0h–01F7h	14
	03F6h–03F6h	
2	0170h–0177h	15
	0376h–0376h	
3	01E8h–01EFh	12 or 11
	03EEh–03EEh	
4	0168h–016Fh	10 or 9
	036Eh–036Eh	

Because both devices on an ATA bus are fully capable (meet the standard), you must tell one of them that it is the master and the other that it is the slave. There are two ways to do this. The first method, by far the most widely used, but also the most prone to mistakes, is to set device jumpers. It is easy to miss this step during installation, an error that can lead to minutes or even hours of debugging. Additionally, some drives designated as the master device require a third setting to inform them that a slave device is present. This is an easy step to miss when adding a second peripheral to the bus.

The second method of designating master and slave devices, provided by the ATA standard but rarely used in practice, is to set the jumpers on both devices to cable select (CSEL). This is not typically documented in most device installation instructions, but you can often find the setting by inspecting the drive and looking for pins labeled CS. The cable in such cases is constructed in a way that provides continuity to pin 28 on the connector for the master and no continuity to pin 28 for the slave. The ATA standard also requires that the master (Drive 0) be closest to the host on the cable and that the slave (Drive 1) be further away. For ribbon cables, the way to accomplish this is to remove pin 28 from the slave connector before assembling the cable. No one seems to pay any attention to this method in the field; we have never seen a cable assembly configured this way.

Note: The most recently introduced standard, ATA/ATAPI-5, uses the CSEL method of designating master and slave devices and requires that the new 80-conductor cable conform to the standard. It changes the orientation of the connectors for master and slave so that the master is the furthest from the host and the slave is the intermediate. It also provides for manually designating the devices as master and slave.

Protocol Layer

The standard provides two ways to send commands to devices. The addition of the ATAPI standard provided for a PACKET mode of command. These packets are SCSI commands and are defined in the SCSI-3 standard. Essentially, the bus uses SCSI commands over the ATA bus, which adds overhead. The PACKET mode is most commonly used to talk to CD-ROM, DVD, and tape devices. It was added to allow CDs to coexist with hard drives on the same bus. When a device does not support the PACKET mode—as is true of of most hard drives—the commands are written to command registers on the device.

The general flow of how commands are executed is:

1. The host CPU sets up the command on the controller.

2. The host CPU tells the device to execute the command.

3. The device executes the command.

4. The device sends an interrupt to the host CPU telling the host the command has been executed.

5. The host CPU checks the status of the command and performs any necessary cleanup.

For each sector of data, these five steps must occur. To optimize this process, PIO and DMA modes were devised.

PIO and DMA Modes

PIO stands for programmed input/output. In this scenario, the host sets up a list of sectors it wants from the disk. As part of the command to the disk, it sends a request for all of these sectors. The sectors are sent back to the controller, and the host then moves them to memory. This process speeds the transfer of data by moving it in blocks instead of one sector at a time, but the CPU still must get involved in moving the data to main memory from the controller.

All computers have a specialized device called the Direct Memory Access (DMA) controller. The DMA controller can be thought of as a mini-CPU that specializes in moving blocks of memory from one place to another very quickly. To use the DMA controller, the host first sets up a DMA channel. Once again it provides a list of sectors it wants, but this time the DMA controller is tasked with copying them directly to memory from the controller, eliminating the much slower method of moving them via the host CPU. Use of the DMA controller has the double benefit of moving the data faster and freeing the CPU for other tasks.

UltraDMA

At this point in the evolution of the ATA bus, computers were reaching the limit of what could be tweaked out of the hardware using existing methods. If speed was going to increase further, processes would have to become more complex. Enter UltraDMA. UltraDMA uses several techniques to dramatically increase the data transfer speed:

➤ It changes the protocol to allow for data to be transferred in a series of bursts.

➤ It uses double edge clocking to allow data to be transferred on the leading and trailing edge of the clock.

➤ In addition, changes to the termination and controlled slew rate techniques (slew rate refers to the time it takes for a signal to move from 0 to 1 or from 1 to 0 and is very important to bus timing and bus speed) allow the transfer rate to increase to 33 MBps.

To raise the transfer rate even higher than the foregoing advances permitted, a new 80-conductor cable was introduced. This cable places a ground wire between each of the signal lines, thus reducing crosstalk and controlling impedance. To support the transfer rates shown in Table 3.3, all UltraDMA modes greater than 2 require the new cable.

Note that a drive is often named according to its transfer rate, so it is not unusual to see a drive labeled as ATA/33 or ATA/66, which are equivalent to UltraDMA mode 2 or 4, respectively.

With so many different modes available, the question arises: is it possible to hook up an ATA/100 drive (the commercially popular term for UltraDMA mode 5) drive to a normal ATA controller without the 80-conductor cable? The answer is yes, it will work, but you will not derive the full benefit of the mode 5 technology. The drive will hum along at the speed of the lowest common denominator, which in this case is probably that of the controller. If the controller can manage a mode 5 speed, then the 40-conductor cable will limit you to mode 2. The specification

Table 3.3 UltraDMA modes.	
UltraDMA Mode	**Maximum Transfer Rate (megabytes per second)**
0	16.7
1	25
2	33.3
3	44.4
4	66.7
5	100

provides a method for detecting the 80-conductor cable, and the controller accordingly will operate at the slower speed. The moral of the story is: don't plug a CD-ROM into the same interface as a spiffy new ATA/100 drive; the CD-ROM will slow down the entire system operation. Plug the CD into another interface and get the new cable.

 Newer ATA devices are backward compatible with older ATA controllers and vice versa, with the caveat that the entire system of controller and devices is limited to the speed of its oldest/slowest member.

CHS vs. LBA

Historically, we can thank IBM for inserting a time bomb in everyone's BIOS. The hard disk controller selects a specific sector by telling the hard drive where it is located according to its cylinder, head, and sector numbers. The original IBM bios limited the physical characteristics of a drive to 1,024 cylinders, 16 heads, and 63 sectors (referred to as CHS for Cylinder, head, sector). With a sector size of 512 bytes, the maximum disk size was limited to 528,482,304 bytes, or 528MB. (Seems a bit puny now, doesn't it? It seemed huge when we were using a 20MB drive in our original PC.) In a feat of major overkill, the T-13 committee provided two solutions to this problem. The first was to provide an interface through the BIOS Int13h call. This interface permitted the use of a complicated three-tiered translation method, based on size of the drive, to convert the CHS coordinates to the actual coordinates on the drive. This solution is bogus because the drive does a further translation to its own internal coordinate system in any event. For quite some time, there have been no drives that have a fixed number of sectors per cylinder (track), as CHS would assume. Suffice to say that this is the most complicated way to solve the problem.

The second solution to the drive size limitation is called logical block address (LBA). This method numbers the sectors from 1 to n, where n is the maximum sector and allows for direct access by specifying the sector number. Currently in ATA-5, there is a 28-bit limit to this number—268,435,456 sectors (512 bytes/sector equals 137,438,953,472 bytes, or 137GB). We seem to be approaching another limit—T-13 committee to the rescue again. The draft ATA-6 specification in progress provides for a 48-bit address. This will provide 144,115,188,075,855,872 bytes or 144 Petabytes. (Peta is the next higher magnitude after tera—we looked it up!) The limit seems huge, but remember the 528MB limit of yore? It seemed huge at the time.

Note: One more little hiccup before we close the book on this subject. The draft ATA-6 standard removes all reference to CHS translation, effectively doing away with this technological solution in all new devices. Saying good-bye to CHS translation would be great if not for one little problem: all operating systems boot in CHS mode, then switch to LBA later if they are going to do so. Until someone comes up with a solution for this problem, you will not be able to boot on a new ATA-6-compliant device.

Other Storage Device Standards

There are a number of other storage device standards available, including IEEE 1394, Universal Serial Bus (USB), and Storage Area Networks (SAN).

IEEE 1394 (FireWire)

IEEE 1394 is a standard that was created several years ago to support external devices that require extremely fast data throughput. Apple adopted the standard into the Macintosh product cycle and called it FireWire. IEEE 1394 is plug-and-play compliant and supports hot plugging—the ability to install and configure hardware without downing the server. The IEEE 1394 specification supports uep to 63 devices at speeds up to 400Mbps. Not too long ago, IEEE 1394 devices were pricy, but with the advent of USB, prices have been driven down.

Note: Some translation is in order here: 8 bits equals 1 byte, 1,000 bytes equals 1 kilobyte (KB), 1,000KB equals 1 megabyte (MB). Realistically, 400Mbps is 50MB per second, which is still a high speed when compared with USB, seria, and parallel rates. When referring to storage, 1MB is not 1,000KB, but rather 1,048,576 bytes. When referring to data transfer rates, 1,000KB equals 1MB.

 Don't forget that SCSI devices can be internal or external and support up to 320 megabytes per second data transfer rates. When choosing between SCSI, IEEE 1394, and USB, SCSI will always win based upon speed, and quite often in price too.

Universal Serial Bus (USB)

USB was originally implemented in 1996 but did not gain widespread acceptance until the advent of the iMac in 1998 and of Windows 98 in 1999. USB looks and behaves much like IEEE 1394, with similar connectors and device types. Converters are also available to enable 1394 devices to run from USB connections. Just like IEEE 1394, USB is plug-and-play compatible and supports hot plugging. The biggest differences between the two types of interfaces lie in the fact that USB can support up to 127 devices per port at speeds up to 12 million bits per second.

It is useful to compare the features of the USB and IEEE 1394 standards. USB requires a master/slave relationship in which only one master can exist. IEEE 1394, on the other hand, can support a peer-to-peer relationship, which allows traditionally peripheral devices to talk to one another and achieve a useful function. For example, an IEEE 1394 camera can record directly to an IEEE 1394 hard drive without the intervention of a host. This is not possible with USB. USB devices must have a host to mediate and control the transfer. USB version 2.0 (available some time in 2001 or 2002) will have a much faster data transfer rate, achieving speeds close to those of the IEEE 1394 standard.

Storage Area Network (SAN)

Often confused with NAS (described in a later section) SANs are really their own technology-based entities. Administrators, hear ye: imagine a world where all data is stored in one place, isolated from extraneous network traffic, faster, always available, not tied to a specific server or network operating system, and infinitely scaleable. This is SAN. It evolved on two different fronts, based upon the need to support multiplatform interoperability and the need to recycle old mainframe storage. SAN has evolved into an effective storage solution that lives on its own high-speed network with centralized backup capability and extraordinary reliability. This high-speed network itself usually consists of gigabit Ethernet across fiber channel lines, and it is separated from the rest of the LAN/WAN by specialized hubs. This is why the biggest single disadvantage of SAN is its cost. Even when recycling mainframe storage, SAN startup costs limit its implementation to large enterprise and corporate networks.

Fault Tolerance—RAID

When analyzing a network or mission-critical system, it is important to pay particular attention to any system or component that can become a single point of failure. A single point of failure is any component or piece of a critical system or process that would cause immediate failure of the whole system should that component or piece fail. Fault tolerance is simply any component or process that is designed to eliminate a given single point of failure. Although fault tolerance is a technical term, the concept comes from the business world, where cross-training, documentation, and process development are the norms.

When looking for a single point of failure in a server system, it is important to consider components that are prone to wear and tear and natural failure more often than others. In particular, items with mechanical parts, such as hard disk drives and CPU fans, are far more likely to fail under normal working conditions than are other components. This is not to say that controller cards and CPUs do not fail, but failure of such components is more often a result of environmental factors or human mistakes such as humidity or electrostatic discharge (ESD) events. Because this chapter concerns data storage, we will discuss fault-tolerant disk storage here and consider other methods of fault tolerance and disaster recovery in Chapter 11.

RAID (Redundant Array of Inexpensive Disks) is a suite of fault-tolerant specifications specifically designed for hard disk drives. Depending upon the level and type of RAID implemented, RAID can provide any combination of the following features:

➤ Increased read/write speeds

➤ Replacement of a failed drive without powering down the server (called hot plugging or hot swapping)

➤ Automatic cutover to a standby drive (called a hot spare) when a drive fails

➤ Regeneration of data lost from a failed drive

➤ Recovery from multiple drive failures

➤ Automated performance of any or all administrative tasks (including the foregoing) with little or no downtime

This is not to say that there are no downsides to consider when choosing a RAID solution. We will discuss these as we consider the various RAID levels.

RAID Levels

Once upon a time, RAID was an administrative joke because disk drives were anything but inexpensive, and an array consisting of more than 2 drives was laughable for a company on a tight budget. With today's computer market, RAID solutions have become cheaper and more realistic for the small- to midsize company to implement and are now an absolute requirement in a large organization. RAID has been created with several different configurations that were designed to handle specific needs for different applications. There are six basic levels of RAID; however, levels 2, 3, and 4 are rarely used today, for reasons that we will discuss shortly. Figure 3.1 illustrates how RAID 0, 1, and 5 differ in practice.

RAID 0—Striping

Striping is the only RAID level that is not fault tolerant. Its true intent is to increase read/write performance. The concept is simple. Imagine that it takes one person an hour to lay bricks on the sidewalk. If you get six people to lay bricks on the sidewalk, the job will be completed in 10 minutes. The same idea applies for RAID 0 because many different drives lay down data. This works because the slowest part of a hard drive is not its controller or its "thinking" parts, but rather its motor and drive heads—the parts that actually encode the disk platters with data, analogous to people laying down bricks. If we have more than one drive working on the same task, the job will get done much faster.

Drive 1	Drive 2	Drive 3	Drive 4
Oh	beautiful	for	spacious
skies,	for	amber	waves
of	grain!	For	purple
mountain	majesties	above	the
fruited	plain!		

RAID 0

Drive 1	Drive 2
Oh beautiful for spacious skies, for amber waves of grain! For purple mountain majesties above the fruited plain!	Oh beautiful for spacious skies, for amber waves of grain! For purple mountain majesties above the fruited plain!

RAID 1

Drive 1	Drive 2	Drive 3	Drive 4
Oh	beautiful	for	OBF parity
spacious	skies,	SSF parity	for
amber	AWC parity	waves	of
GFO parity	grain!	For	purple
mountain	majesties	above	MMA parity
the	fruited	IFP parity	plain!

RAID 5

Figure 3.1 Examples of how "America the Beautiful" might be written in RAID 0, 1, and 5.

Because striping is not fault tolerant, you will not see it often in the real world, but it is an appropriate solution for companies that require a lot of temporary file space with as much speed as possible. Examples of the need for temporary file space include temporary files created by printing high-resolution graphics, or temp files created by rendering applications.

RAID 1—Mirroring and Duplexing

Mirroring is a process whereby changes to a primary hard drive are implemented to a secondary hard drive at the same time. Duplexing is similar, with the exception that the secondary hard disk drive is attached to a redundant drive controller as an additional level of fault tolerance.

Mirroring and duplexing tend to read data from disk at the same rates as if RAID were not in use. The data write time, however, will be slightly slower because data needs to be written to two devices before moving on. A miniscule performance advantage exists for duplexed systems here, because separate controllers would be responsible for passing instructions to their respective drives, rather than a single controller passing instructions to multiple drives.

RAID 2—Striping with Error Correction

RAID 2, also known as Striping with error correction, is a proprietary form of RAID that was created for hard disk drives that do not support error correction. Today's RAID is usually implemented with SCSI drives, which have error correction built-in, so RAID 2 is infrequently found in the field, and may not be available any longer.

RAID 3—Striping with a Parity Drive (Byte Level)

Byte level striping with a parity drive is also known as RAID 3. Understanding when this should be implemented requires some knowledge of how data is packaged. Without going too in-depth, let us just say that like matter, data comes in small packages that are put together to form larger packages, and so on. In the same way that atoms come together to form molecules and molecules come together to form cells, data bits come together to form bytes, and bytes come together to form blocks. In just the same way as RAID 0, RAID 3 lays the data bricks across several different drives. The difference is that RAID 3 has parity. Parity is a fault-tolerant process where pieces of data are compared with other data in such a manner that in the event of a single drive failure, the missing data can be regenerated automatically. This is called an automatic rebuild process. Because the parity is stored on its own separate drive, any other drive can fail and the data can be automatically rebuilt; however, if the parity drive fails, this fault tolerance capability is lost, but the original data remains intact.

 RAID 1 has only 50 percent capacity: Only half of the total drive space is available for usage. RAID 5, on the other hand, has $n-11$ capacity, where n equals the total number of drives in the system. A RAID 5 system with four 20GB drives has a 60GB capacity, whereas a RAID 1 system with four 20GB drives has only a 40GB capacity.

RAID 4—Striping with a Parity Drive (Block Level)

RAID 4 is identical to RAID 3 except that instead of laying data down a byte at a time, data is written an entire block at a time. The same advantages of fault tolerance apply; however, write speeds are slower for RAID 4 because small changes require rewriting an entire block, whereas with RAID 3, the same change can be made with a few bytes. Neither RAID 3 nor RAID 4 is seen or used frequently in the PC server industry, because both standards rely heavily on type-specific usage—for example, frequently reading large contiguous data that was written at the same time for RAID 3 or smaller, more randomly written data for RAID 4. This process works well for large files or database-type applications. But because it is difficult to dedicate any given PC server exclusively to either of these functions, RAID 3 and 4 are unrealistic in the marketplace.

 You will need to be familiar with RAID levels 0, 1, and 5 for the exam. RAID 0 is not truly fault tolerant, and RAID 5 only allows for recovery of a single drive failure. Multiple drive failures can only be recovered for stacked RAID configurations.

RAID 5—Striping with Parity

RAID 5 is by far the most popular implementation of RAID. Although RAID 5 is commonly known as striping with parity, the feature that sets it apart is that the parity data is striped across all drives along with the data itself. This eliminates the single point of failure of a parity drive found in RAIDs 3 and 4, while still implementing the same degree of fault tolerance. RAID 5 writes slightly faster than a single disk drive, but not as quickly as RAID 0 because the additional parity information must be written as well.

 Remember that one of the focal points in the Server+ exam is to ensure that you understand how servers differ from desktop systems. Fault tolerance and high availability are critical considerations.

Stacked RAID

Stacked RAID is exactly what it sounds like: multiple RAID levels that have been combined within a single system in order to take advantage of the features of both RAID levels and eliminate or reduce the drawbacks of each. RAID 10 is a popular stacked RAID configuration in which RAID 0 and 1 are combined as striped sets are mirrored to provide the highest performance while still enabling fault tolerance. RAID 50 (AKA RAID 0/5) is also known as RAID 0 striped sets, which are in turn striped with parity (RAID 5) in order to provide and allow for multiple drive failures.

Note: Although Other RAID Levels are available, they are neither standardized nor do they strictly apply to data storage. RAID 6 has been known to be representative of redundant components such as power supplies or cooling fans.

RAID Types

Choosing an appropriate RAID solution also involves choosing between hardware- and software-based RAID types. The most important factors in choosing software-based over hardware-based RAID are price and cost of implementation. The most important factors in choosing hardware-based over software-based RAID are speed and true fault tolerance.

Hardware-Based RAID

Considering that most hardware RAID is implemented using SCSI drives, we will consider implementation and installation of SCSI RAID configurations. Limited hardware-based RAID is possible with ATA drives and controllers, but this is frowned upon in the server world for the same reasons (speed and feature limitations) that cause software-based RAID to be poorly regarded. Remember that a single SCSI bus can support up to 15 drives, and multiple buses can exist within a single computer, thus making the array potential virtually limitless. This does not mean that all RAID is SCSI. On the contrary, IDE RAID controllers are now available that handle limited RAID functionality such as striping and mirroring.

Hardware-based RAID features are varied, but some research is necessary prior to choosing any given RAID system. The particular hardware employed can dictate how recoverable—and expensive—a given RAID system is. Almost all hardware-based RAID solutions require that all drives be identical in some form or fashion. Inquire with the manufacturer as to whether the same drive type and model is necessary or whether identical drive size will do. In addition, find out whether there are differences in drive requirements between RAID levels. Mirroring usually requires identical drive sizes, but it is not always required for striping.

Internal RAID usually is shipped from the manufacturer; however, any given server can be upgraded to internal RAID with the appropriate SCSI controller, cables, drives, and sufficient drive bays to support two or more drives. Internal RAID is appropriate only for small to midsize companies because it is easier to deal with than an external array device. One drawback is that the system is tied to the internal array for the duration of its existence. A situation could conceivably arise where you need to upgrade the current drives to higher capacities, but the BIOS might not support those higher capacities. As a result, you might need to simply purchase additional drives—which you might not have room for on the internal system. When considering the purchase of an internal array server, make sure that external SCSI support is available so that you have the option of upgrading to an external RAID configuration.

External RAID has the capability of being more flexible and functional than an internal hardware RAID implementation. With internal RAID, the drive array fails if the server fails. External RAID has the admirable feature of being somewhat portable. It can be plugged into any appropriately connected server quickly and, with a few administrative changes (depending upon the network operating system), the data can be accessible to the network public in a matter of minutes. As mentioned earlier in the SCSI section, it is also possible to place an external drive array onto the SCSI bus of two different computers, thus adding additional fault tolerance and opening the gate for clustering functionality.

 Remember that SCSI drives are numbered and that numbering occurs on the drive itself. RAID Array configuration goes a step further to "anchor" the SCSI ID numbers appropriate to the bay in which the drive resides. Remember that a RAID array is simply a SCSI bus with a chassis built around it. The only difference is that the array's controller firmware must keep track of who lives where in order to track what data lives on what disk appropriately. This information is vital for recovering from a failure should the need arise.

External RAID is a mature solution. New technologies have allowed the evolution of what can be termed a "standalone RAID box" that serves data over the network as though it were its own server, without server-specific software and administration. This is called Network Attached Storage (NAS). NAS devices can be accessed by multiple operating systems. These network servers seamlessly see NAS devices as their own internal drives. This results on all but the most basic foundations in both Unix and Windows servers being able to access—and share—data on the same NAS device. The advantages of NAS are many: it is portable, it can be plugged into any appropriate network, it can be accessed by multiple operating systems, it requires less administrative overhead because network operating system overhead has been eliminated, and storage can be increased without downing either server or network.

Hardware-based RAID also runs faster than software RAID. This is because RAID controllers often have their own processor that handles the I/O load normally handled by the server CPU in software RAID applications. Additional physical-related RAID functions not found in software-based RAID are available with hardware-based RAID, namely hot plug and hot spare functionality. Hot plug is the ability to remove a failed hard drive and replace it with a known good drive. A hot spare is another drive in an array that is not being used, but which has power applied to it and whose drives spin. The advantage of a hot spare is that if a drive in the array fails, the hot spare is immediately utilized and data is rebuilt on the fly without human intervention.

Hardware-based RAID quite often also supports advanced management tools such as remote failure notification and predictive failure analysis. Remote notification, similar to the same functionality for tape backup and UPS applications, sends notification of a drive failure via SMTP email or pager (and an analog phone line). Predictive failure analysis is an advanced technology that looks at the current performance and read/write failures and compares them with known baseline data, extrapolating the health and welfare of a given drive. Predictive failure analysis literally can predict how long a failing drive will last, and it will preemptively notify you before the failure occurs. Array management and automatic features, such as manually "failing" a drive for replacement and manually kicking off a regeneration process, can be performed with these management tools.

Software-Based RAID

Software-based RAID can be called a poor man's answer to fault tolerance, because although software-based fault tolerance can be achieved with it, it is not without several significant gotchas:

➤ Software-based RAID places an additional load on the server CPU.

➤ You cannot stripe the boot disk with software-based RAID. The RAID does not physically exist until the server operating system is fully booted. Any software-striped boot disk will be completely unreadable when the system boots.

➤ Software-based RAID requires administrative intervention in order to recover fully from a drive failure.

➤ Hot plug and hot spare features are not available with software-based RAID.

➤ Software-based RAID requires that a server be brought down in order to recover fully from a drive failure.

➤ Software-based RAID does not require that the disks be of the same make and model (this can be an advantage in terms of flexibility).

➤ Software-based RAID does not always require that the disks be of the same capacity. The operating system usually addresses drives as drive letters, which can be assigned based upon partitions or volumes. If software RAID is performed based upon drive letter addresses as it is in the Microsoft world, then the drives themselves do not need to be the same size.

➤ Software-based RAID does not mix well with other network operating systems' disk management features, such as volume spanning.

If, after you implement RAID, CPU utilization increases greatly and users begin to complain about access times, you can almost be certain that a server is running software-based RAID. Three solutions can solve this problem: upgrade the CPU, add a second CPU, or switch to hardware-based RAID. Be aware that upgrading or adding a CPU can somewhat reduce the problem, but it might not eliminate it completely.

NetWare, Windows NT, and Windows 2000 all support software-based RAID in some form or another. NetWare's SFT can handle RAID 1 mirroring and duplexing, while the Microsoft products support RAID 0, 1, and 5. The NetWare mirroring product automatically continues to service data requests when a drive in a mirrored set fails; however, Microsoft NT requires that the mirror be broken and that the secondary drive be designated as the primary drive before functionality can resume. Microsoft Windows 2000 simply requires that the system be rebooted and set to boot from the mirrored drive.

Practice Questions

Question 1

> You are a server administrator, and your boss arrives one afternoon and
> explains that he has some data on an external hard disk that he would like
> to hook up so that you can copy all the files to your server. Your server has
> an ultra ATA/66 controller and the external enclosure is an Ultra2 device.
> How do you get to the data on your server?
>
> O a. Install a cable adapter and a 132 ohm terminator on the server
>   and move the files.
>
> O b. Remove the drive from the external enclosure and install it in your
>   server. Move the files to the server's hard disk.
>
> O c. Install a SCSI controller in a spare PC and move the files.
>
> O d. Tell your boss you cannot retrieve the information.

Answer c is correct. The Ultra2 device is SCSI and you must find a system capable of SCSI communications with your server. Answers a and b are incorrect
because SCSI devices are not capable of being installed in a system that has only
an ATA (IDE) controller. Answer d is incorrect because unless the drive itself is
damaged beyond repair, there is always a way to retrieve the data, albeit annoying
or expensive.

Question 2

> What is the maximum number of devices that can be installed on an ATA
> (IDE) controller?
>
> O a. 1
>
> O b. 2
>
> O c. 4
>
> O d. 8

Answer b is correct. The ATA bus is capable of supporting two devices: a master
and a slave. Each controller supports one bus. Answer a is incorrect because the
assumption is that a maximum number of devices would be higher than one.
Answer c is incorrect because most servers have two ATA controllers installed,
allowing four devices in a machine. Answer d is incorrect because SCSI can support eight devices on a bus, but ATA/IDE cannot.

Question 3

You have an Ultra3 SCSI controller installed in your computer and have been given an Ultra2 SCSI external hard drive to install. What do you do?

- ○ a. You purchase a 50-pin to 68-pin adapter and install a 132 ohm terminator.
- ○ b. You install a 110 ohm terminator.
- ○ c. You purchase a 50-pin to 68-pin adapter and install a 110 ohm terminator.
- ○ d. You tell the person who gave you this task that these devices are not compatible and you cannot install the hard drive.

Answer c is correct. The Ultra3 SCSI controller has a 68-pin connector and the Ultra2 hard drive has a 50-pin connector. To make the connection you will need an adapter. The correct termination is 110 ohm for active termination, allowing both of the devices to operate in LVD mode. Answer b is incorrect because a 110 ohm terminator alone will not solve the problem. Answer a is incorrect because if you use the 132 ohm terminator, you will be using passive termination, and the bus will revert to SE mode and limit the bus speed. Answer d is incorrect because it is possible to attach an Ultra2 SCSI drive to an Ultra3 SCSI controller.

Question 4

You are replacing a failed HVD Fast SCSI CD-ROM with an LVD Ultra3 SCSI CD-ROM. What do you do?

- ○ a. Purchase a 50-pin to 68-pin adapter and install a 110 ohm terminator for active termination.
- ○ b. Install a 132-ohm terminator.
- ○ c. Purchase a 50-pin to 80-pin adapter and install a 132 ohm terminator for passive termination.
- ○ d. It will not work.

Answer d is correct. HVD and LVD are not compatible. The old HVD CD-ROM had to be installed on an HVD controller. The LVD CD-ROM is not going to work with the controller. Answer a would be correct if both devices were HVD or LVD, but they are not. Answers b and c are incorrect because a 132-ohm terminator is only required for SCSI-1.

Question 5

> You are installing a 20GB ATA hard drive. You want to have a 4GB boot partition. Which way should the BIOS be configured?
>
> ○ a. Enable LBA support and disable INT13h.
>
> ○ b. Disable LBA support and disable INT13h support.
>
> ○ c. Disable LBA support and enable INT13h support.
>
> ○ d. Enable LBA support and enable INT13h.

Answer d is correct. You should enable support for both of these features. Most operating systems access the hard drive using LBA, but they do not do this until after they have booted. During bootup, they access the hard drive using CHS translations, which requires INT13h extension to access partitions greater than 528MB. Answer a is incorrect because INT13h support is necessary. Answer b is incorrect because both LBA support and INT13h support are necessary. Answer c is incorrect because LBA support is necessary.

Question 6

> You have just installed RAID on your server, and as soon as the server is booted, you notice that the memory pages per second increases dramatically and CPU utilization decreases. What is wrong?
>
> ○ a. You need to install more memory.
>
> ○ b. You need to add more hard drive space.
>
> ○ c. You need to upgrade to hardware-based RAID.
>
> ○ d. You need to upgrade the CPU.

Answer b is correct. All RAID configurations except for RAID 0 involve a reduction in available drive space. It is safe to say that there has been a reduction in drive space as soon as RAID is implemented. Answer a is incorrect because nothing has changed to truly alter the amount of RAM required by the system, yet the paging activity has increased. Answer c is incorrect because the decrease in CPU utilization shows that hardware-based RAID is already being implemented. Answer d is incorrect because CPU utilization is not overburdened.

Question 7

You have just installed RAID on your server, and as soon as the server is booted, you notice that the memory pages per second decrease dramatically and CPU utilization increases. What is wrong?

    I.   You need to install more memory.

    II. You need to add more hard drive space.

    III. You need to upgrade to hardware-based RAID.

    IV. You need to upgrade the CPU.

  ○ a. I and II

  ○ b. III and IV

  ○ c. I or II

  ○ d. III or IV

Answer d is correct. We can see that this is software-based RAID because the CPU utilization has increased so much. Possible solutions for this are to upgrade to hardware-based RAID or upgrade the CPU. Answers a and c are incorrect because installing memory or adding hard drive space has little or no effect on CPU usage. Answer b is incorrect because after upgrading to hardware-based RAID, the CPU should not need upgrading at all.

Question 8

You are considering installing an external hard drive drive on your server. Which interface is best?

  ○ a. RS232

  ○ b. USB

  ○ c. SCSI

  ○ d. IEEE 1394

Answer c is correct. SCSI interfaces are faster than the others listed. Answer a is incorrect because serial connections are the slowest and are being replaced by USB. Answer b is incorrect because USB is slower than IEEE 1394. Answer d is incorrect because IEEE 1394 is slower than external SCSI.

Question 9

You are the server administrator for a group of servers that reference a 12-drive RAID array configured with RAID 5. Predictive failure analysis indicates that drive 10 is failing. What should you do?

- ○ a. Let it fail, hot swap it, and let it regenerate.
- ○ b. Perform a tape backup on drive 10 and hot swap it.
- ○ c. Use the management software to fail the drive, hot swap it, and let it regenerate.
- ○ d. Use the management software to fail the drive, hot swap it, force regeneration, and restore the data from tape.

Answer c is correct. Management software can be used to manually fail the drive as if it had failed on its own, allow it to be hot swapped, and permit regeneration to occur automatically. Answer a is incorrect because letting the drive fail on its own runs the risk that the failed drive will negatively impact system performance during mission-critical hours and usage. It is better to schedule a safe time to administer the array. Answers b and d are incorrect because it is impossible to perform a tape backup or restore to a specific drive.

Question 10

You have been researching RAID solutions for your midsize company. You've chosen to implement hardware RAID, but the remaining budget is slim as a result and fault tolerance is still very important. Which RAID level should you choose?

- ○ a. RAID 0
- ○ b. RAID 1—mirroring
- ○ c. RAID 1—duplexing
- ○ d. RAID 5

Answer d is correct. RAID 5 provides a better utilization of disk space than RAID 1. Answer a is incorrect because RAID 0 has no fault tolerance. Answers b and c are incorrect because they do not utilize disk space as efficiently as RAID 5.

Need to Know More?

 Boswell, William. *Inside Windows 2000 Server.* Indianapolis, IN: New Riders, 2000. ISBN 1-56205-929-7. Contains intermediate to advanced information on everything about Windows 2000, including RAID implementation.

 Craft, Melissa, Mark A. Poplar, David V. Watts, and Will Willis. *Network+ Exam Prep.* Scottsdale, AZ: The Coriolis Group, 1999. ISBN 1-57610-412-5. Contains in-depth information on RAID.

 Minasi, Mark, Christa Anderson, and Elizabeth Creegan. *Mastering Windows NT Server 4 Fourth Ed.* Alameda, CA: Sybex Network Press, 1997. ISBN 0-78212067-9. An ideal administrator's companion for Windows NT 4, covering mostly basic to intermediate content with several advanced topics covered. Microsoft RAID support and installation topics are included.

 Reeves, Scott, Kalinda Reeves, Stephen Weese, and Christopher S. Geyer. *A+ Exam Prep, Third Edition.* Scottsdale, AZ: The Coriolis Group, 2001. ISBN 1-57610-699-3. Great for specifics on RAID and SCSI topics.

 Zacker, Craig and Paul Doyle. *Upgrading and Repairing Networks.* Indianapolis, IN: Que Corporation, 1996. ISBN 0-78970181-2. An excellent reference for specifics and how-tos on RAID and SCSI technologies.

 www.adaptec.com. *Let's talk about RAID.* This article provides in-depth information about RAID.

 www.ata-atapi.com. A thorough and definitive Web site by Hale Landis on ATA/ATAPI.

 www.novell.com. *SFTIII for Netware.* This article provides information about the NetWare equivalent to clustering and load balancing. SFT is a complete system mirroring solution and does not currently span more than two systems.

 www.paralan.com/glos.html. This Web site, developed in San Diego, CA, offers a great glossary on SCSI terminology.

www.pcguide.com. This site, developed by Charles M. Kozierok and similar to TechRepublic, contains a wealth of information on many IT topics.

 www.scita.org. The SCSI Trade Association Web site contains historical and technical information and member info.

 www.storage-area-networks.com. *Reducing Enterprise Backup Windows*. A good article by Kevin Trotman about the ins and outs of SAN purchase and configuration.

 www.storecase.com. This site contains extensive information (and plenty of white papers) about SCSI technologies and compatibility.

 www.t13.org. The T-13 organization, based in Washington, DC, is ultimately responsible for standardizing ATA and ATAPI technologies. Meeting notes and new and proposed technologies are available on this Web site.

 www.techrepublic.com. A wealth of information on any and every IT topic imaginable—everything from hardware and component-level data all the way to management decisions and political trends. An excellent source for up-to-date definitions and information ranging from the novice to the expert.

CPU and Memory

Terms you'll need to understand:

✓ Data bus

✓ ROM

✓ RAM

✓ Byte

✓ Bit

✓ Overclocking

✓ Cache

✓ Math coprocessor

✓ SIMD

✓ L2 Cache

✓ ECC

✓ SEC

✓ DIB

✓ BIOS

✓ ZIF/LIF

✓ Bus controller

✓ Memory controller

✓ DRAM

✓ EDO RAM

✓ SDRAM

✓ Parity

✓ SIPP

✓ SIMM

✓ DIMM

Techniques you'll need to master:

✓ Determining the proper CPU for your server functionality

✓ Installing and upgrading a CPU

✓ Determining the proper RAM for your server

✓ Installing and upgrading RAM

CPU

The brain of the computer is the Central Processing Unit (CPU). It is embedded in a special container that protects the delicate components from the environment, from technicians, and more importantly from pirates who want to copy the complex design. A look at Figure 4.1 shows the major components of a server motherboard.

The CPU is where the most important computer operations take place. With a nonworking CPU, the rest of the hardware simply cannot function. The CPU is involved in nearly every aspect of your computing experience. It dictates how fast or how slow the computer is able to run. The holy grail of computer science is to make the CPU faster and stronger.

In this section, we examine the genesis of the CPU, look at the different types, and explain their advantages and limitations. We will focus on the microprocessors found in the PC, particularly server systems that are covered on the exam, and discuss a bit of additional background information to assist you with the skills and concepts that are expected from a Server+ certification holder. The

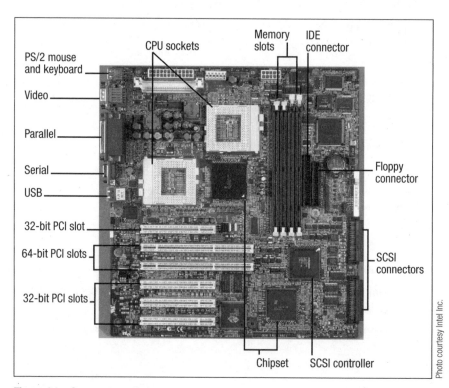

Figure 4.1 Server components.

good news is that the CPUs in mainframes and minicomputers work according to similar concepts. In consequence, microcomputers have been able to borrow many methodologies and engineering concepts from the mainframe world.

The Data Bus

The microprocessor does not exist in a vacuum. The processor needs something to process so it loads instructions from memory, either read-only memory (ROM) or the larger random access memory (RAM). Once the instructions are executed, a place to store the results is needed. This means a communications channel is needed to feed the CPU and retrieve the results. The CPU is so critical to the operations of the computer that many different devices need to be connected to it at the same time. To facilitate this level of access, the CPU and the various communications partners are placed on a data bus.

The data bus is a series of connections that carry the same signal to all components. It is similar to running a long wire and applying 20 volts of electricity. If we install taps along the wire and measure the voltage with a volt meter, we will see 20 volts at each tap. If we lower or raise the voltage, the change occurs down the entire length of the wire. This common bus lets the CPU communicate with the various components without requiring a separate connection to each device. This bus arrangement makes it easy for the manufacturer to add additional devices that need to communicate with the CPU without having to redesign and rewire the microprocessor.

There are two separate data buses. The internal data bus lets the CPU communicate with the various circuits and internal caches of memory that are incorporated as part of the chip's design. Typically, this bus is extremely fast and is independent of the rest of the computer. The external data bus communicates with the rest of the computer. The fastest CPU can be constrained by the slowest external bus to produce a totally worthless computer.

The speed of the bus is like the speed on the highway—very fast. Because each line can only carry a single signal, either a logical 1 or 0, a single line bus is like the oldest of country roads. Each line has to line up, and there is no passing. Manufacturers of the earliest microprocessors realized that a single data bus was digital suicide, so they started with a bus equal to the most common unit of computer measurement, the byte.

The byte is comprised of eight bits. The bits represent the single ones and zeros. Thus, a megabit is equal to approximately one million bits, and the megabyte is approximately eight million bits, or one million bytes. Even the latest muscle bus from the state of the art labs of Intel does not use a megabyte bus; the current champ uses just 64 communication wires. The earliest personal computer's CPU had only eight wires, or an eight-bit bus.

Just like a highway, the more lanes you provide, the more traffic, or data, you can move between components. Just how crowded are the main traffic lanes of the computer? All hardware that uses data is connected in some way to the data bus or is connected to some device that is connected to the data bus. Contrast Los Angeles rush hour traffic to a small two-lane road through midwest Wyoming. If you do not have a lot of traffic, two lanes will suffice, but if you are moving billions of bytes of information at top speed, a 64-bit bus is the only thing that can do the job. Buses are discussed in more detail in Chapter 5.

Clock Speed

All of the components in the computer are tied to the metronome of the computer's internal clock. Most computers have at least two clocks, one to keep track of the time and date and another to provide synchronization signals to the various components to ensure one part of the computer does not overwhelm the other parts.

Many CPUs also have internal clocks to help control internal functions related to processing and input/output communications. The clocks are developed to produce timed signals that are measured in hertz. Most modern CPUs operate in megahertz, or millions of cycles per second. Some of the newer chips are penetrating the lofty heights of gigahertz, or billions of cycles per second. Each cycle gives the microprocessor the opportunity to complete one, or several operations. Because timing is critical in processing, the faster the clock, the faster the processor.

It is possible to speed up the operation of a microprocessor by speeding up the clock. This is called *overclocking*. Overclocking makes the CPU work harder and faster by giving it faster timing pulses. In some cases, overclocking is a cheap method of upgrading. Some manufacturers test processors at different speeds. Those that consistently and reliably operate at higher speeds are sold with the higher speeds as the defined standard. Chips that are not as reliable at these high speeds may operate fine at some of the lower clocking options. These chips are sold and warranteed at the lower speed. Many motherboards support a variety of speeds. Keep in mind that overclocking a processor is not supported by the manufacturer. Overclocking taxes the chip, causing additional heat and stress. Never overclock mission critical machines and be forewarned that you do risk damaging an otherwise operational CPU. If you need additional speed, either upgrade the CPU or upgrade the system and add a second processor.

Register Width

Microprocessors need to have a temporary storage space to load data into during processing. These are called registers. Registers are also used to shift data back and forth, performing multiplication and division. Registers are where the logical and arithmetic operations are performed.

Larger registers can manipulate larger chunks of data at one time. This means that two CPUs with the same data bus and the same clock frequency are not equal if one has a larger set of registers. You need to consider this when purchasing and installing multiple CPUs into the same server.

Upgrading to a multiprocessor system is not as simple as purchasing any CPU that fits into the slot on the server. Ideally, you need to purchase a CPU that is identical to the first CPU. Quite often this is impossible because CPUs change so quickly. There are two solutions to this problem. One solution is to follow the n+ rule, whereby a manufacturer assigns a "version" to each CPU and subsequently guarantees that if the version number is incrementally one above or below your existing processor version, it will be compatible. The second solution is to purchase two new CPU chips at the same time, ensuring that they are compatible with the motherboard on the server.

Address Bus and Cache

CPUs cannot store all of their data in registers. They need some form of permanent or at least semipermanent storage. This means memory. In the "Memory" section of this chapter we discuss the various types of memory, but let's briefly examine how the CPU talks to the various components of RAM and ROM via the address bus.

The address bus works in the same way as telling a taxi where to take you in the city. You can tell the driver, "I need to go to the 1523rd house on 32nd Street", and the driver knows where to go. But what if you can't count past house 1024? You will never be able to ask to go to any house with a higher number. A limitation on older computers was that the address bus was only 20 bits in length. It could only address memory locations to 2^{20} (1048576) or 1MB of RAM.

In addition, the addressing limitation was associated with the speed of memory access. If the CPU asked for something in memory, it frequently had to wait for data to be delivered. Frequently the CPU could not process any more data until the requested information could be located and retrieved from its memory location. When the computer has to wait for data, it is called a *wait state*. Wait states means a loss in productivity. To combat wasted time, chip engineers created *prefetch caching* where memory could not only get the requested information, but also other information surrounding it. This local memory is called a *level 1 cache*. The cache is normally stored on the CPU chip itself and runs using the internal clock and an internal data bus. The CPU no longer has to wait for data as it is stored in a fast and nearby internal cache. Some manufacturers offer near-chip cache called level 2. Level 2 cache is typically easier to upgrade because it isn't part of the main processor package, but it is slower than level 1.

Understanding the interrelationships between the data bus, the clock frequency, register sizes, address buses, and internal caches is one of the primary responsibilities of a chip designer. Familiarity with these components is a good starting point for examining each processor class.

Server vs. Workstation

When selecting a microprocessor, it is important to determine the primary purpose of the computer. If the computer is not intended to perform intense processing, such as running a database or email application, purchase a decent processor, but spend most of your money on the hard drive, memory, and network infrastructure.

Keep the various relationships of the components that support the CPU in mind. Consider the clock frequency and the width of the data bus. The fastest processor in the world will just have to wait around if the other components are not fast enough to keep up. Keep your system in balance by ensuring that all components run at the same speeds,especially when considering the systems within a server. When managing servers, you will be dealing with traffic, usage, and frequencies that are higher, bigger, and greater than a standard desktop. An unbalanced system can create bottlenecks in a variety of ways.

Specifications

In order to understand the relationships between the dizzying arrays of computer offerings, you need to be able to compare apples to apples. The 486-66 MHz machine of yesteryear does not run at even half the speed of a Pentium 133 MHz computer. To be able to competently discuss the differences of each microprocessor, keep the information discussed in the previous sections in mind.

The Birth of the Microprocessor

The first commercial shipment of the microprocessor happened on November 15, 1971. Intel was commissioned by Busicom, a Japanese calculator manufacturer, to create the 4004 computer chip. It ran at 108 kHz and had a 4-bit data bus. It could address a scorching 640 bytes of RAM. In 1971, Gary Kildall started programming in PL/1 for the 4004 processor, which prompted Intel to create a more powerful version, the 8008. Don Lancaster took this next generation of chip, the 8008, and described the design for the first personal computer. This masterpiece of engineering was featured in 1973 as a "TV Typewriter" in *Radio*

Electronics Magazine. That same year, the first home computer using the 8008 microprocessor, the Scelbi 8h, was sold in kit form. Shortly thereafter an upgraded kit known as the Mark-8 was finding its way into the eager hands of the amateur hobbyist. Several additional processors soon hit the market, the 6502, the Z80, the ZX-80, and the ZX-81, but the precursor to the home computer revolution, for better or worse, was the Intel 8080 processor.

Intel 8080

The 8080 was first commercially produced in 1974. It was the processor in the Altair 8800 home computers. The Altair name comes from a Star Trek planet, which lead the computer where it has never gone before. This computer was placed on the market by the MITS calculator company and was sold in kit form. Bill Gates and Paul Allen wrote the BASIC programming language for MITS, which was used on the Altair computer, and it started Bill's meteoric rise to his present level of success.

Intel 8086 and 8088

The Intel 8086 was released on June 6, 1978. It was Intel's first 16-bit microprocessor. It was designed to be fast and powerful. The 8086 boasted a 4.77 to 10 MHz clock speed, 16-bit registers, and an external 16-bit data bus. It also had a 20-bit address bus to address 1MB of RAM. When IBM entered the computer business, the 8086 was considered too expensive, and oddly enough, too powerful to fulfill "Big Blue's" vision of a computer. The result was that Intel essentially "dumbed down" the 8086 processor and called it the 8088.

At this point, some of the factors that affected the overall speed of a computer can really be identified. The 8086 and the 8088 could run the exact same program and be set to the exact same clock speed. The 16-bit data bus would let the 8086 import and export the data to the chip at twice the speed of the 8088.

Intel 80286

The Intel 80286, commonly called the 286, started as a 6 MHz speed demon. Soon Intel pushed the envelope by upping the clock speed to 10, 12.5, and eventually 20 MHz. To add to the power, the 286 came with a 24-bit address path that allowed for a whopping 16MB of addressable memory. This chip was the heart of the IBM AT computer.

The 286 also offered two modes of operations: *real mode* and *protected mode.* These two modes of operation made the package operate like two separate chips in one package. Real mode operations essentially acted like an 8086 microprocessor.

The computer could run the 8088 and 8086 programs without requiring any modification to the programs. Every system instruction was available and fully functional when the 286 was operating in real mode.

This level of compatibility came at a price. The 80286 microprocessor essentially lobotomized itself, cutting back the addressable memory to 1MB. This made the old programs, not to mention the owner of the aforementioned programs, happy, but limited the full flexibility and functionality of the machine.

Protected mode operations allowed specially programmed applications many advantages over the older real mode programs. Protected mode applications were "protected" in that they were limited to writing only to their assigned memory. This helped to prevent applications from stealing or overwriting areas of memory that was originally designated to a separate application. The protected mode helped add stability and reliability to a machine that was rapidly becoming indispensable in the business environment.

The protected mode of operations also heralded in the invention of *virtual memory*, which allowed applications access to far more than the 16MB of physical memory. This meant that with up to 1GB of memory, larger applications could be loaded simultaneously and would be protected from fighting each other for memory.

Bill Gates' MS-DOS had a very tough time addressing this huge amount of available storage, so the 286 saw the rise of additional operating systems like Microsoft Windows, SCO Unix, and IBM's OS/2. The more powerful, true multitasking operating systems were still in the development stage, and the 286 was obsolete by the time some of the "beefier" operating systems like Windows 95, Windows NT, and Windows 2000 were introduced.

One major disadvantage to the two modes in the 80286 microprocessor was that the computer needed to be rebooted to change the operational mode. This led to a gradual shift from real mode applications to those natively written to take advantage of the many features of the 286.

Intel 80386

Intel changed the world of computing when it introduced the 80386 microprocessor on June 16, 1985. The 80386 was the first true 32-bit processor. All of the support circuitry, the external bus, the address bus, and the registers were a full 32 bits in width. The chip originally shipped with a clock speed of 12 or 16 MHz and could address 4GB of physical RAM and 65TB of virtual memory. One of the biggest advantages of the 386 was that it could switch between real and protected modes of operations without requiring a reboot.

The 386 microprocessor introduced an additional operating mode known as *virtual real mode*. This made it possible for the 386 processor to host virtual machines that enabled more than one application to actually run at the same time.

Intel eventually produced 90386 processors that could run at 25 and 33 MHz. Clone manufacturers weren't far behind as chief Intel rival, AMD, produced an 80386-compatible that ran at an unprecedented 40 MHz.

Intel charged a pretty penny for the flagship of their processor fleet. The big 80386 was out of reach for many businesses, so Intel decided to offer a smaller version that was designed to increase sales without dropping the price of the newest kid on the block. In June of 1988, Intel released the 386SX.

386DX and 386SX

The 386DX (Dual word eXternal) was the full-blown 80386 in its entire 32-bit glory. The 386SX (Single word eXternal) was created by disabling half of the 32 bits of the data bus to a single word or two bytes. This dropped it to the 16-bit, 286 levels. Intel also dropped the memory addressing to a miserly 24-bits, which limited the SX machines to only 16MB of RAM.

The one advantage of the 386SX was that it could be used to upgrade existing 16-bit motherboards. This extended the life of users' machines and also temporarily ensured that motherboard manufacturers had a few more months to unload their inventory before it all became paperweights.

Note: It's not unusual to find companies running older versions of NetWare on 80386 processor servers.

It was in the 80386–80486 years that Microsoft first produced the Windows operating system, and IBM released OS/2. NetWare ruled the server market, and it was only toward the end of 1990 that Microsoft started beta testing their first NOS, which would be known as Windows NT. Meanwhile, Unix was being used in corporate environments since the 8088 became available.

Intel 80486

The 486 processor was roughly twice as fast as a 386 running at the same clock speed. The four factors that contributed to this fact were:

➤ The 486 only took two cycles to execute an instruction, whereas the 386 took 4.5 cycles. This meant that the 486 could perform 2.5 operations for every one that the 386 could crank out.

➤ Intel moved the cache on the chip creating the first Level 1 cache available for mass production. This built-in cache had an average hit ration of 90 to 95 percent. This meant that when the processor needed data from memory, it was right there most of the time. This convenience almost eliminated the need for any wait states on the main CPU.

➤ Built-in math coprocessors were included in most versions of the 486. The coprocessor that greatly enhanced the mathematical prowess of the older machines was brought onboard the main processing chip. This meant no more trips to the bus to request information.

➤ Memory could be accessed using burst-mode memory cycles. This meant that the normal two-cycle memory access would proposition the circuitry for the next data transfer. Once the initial 32 bits were transferred in two cycles, the next 12 bytes could be had with only one clock cycle for each 32 bits, or 4 bytes. That meant up to 16 bytes of additional data could be transferred in as little as five cycles instead of the normal 8+ cycles required by the 386.

The first 80486DX processor was introduced by Intel on April 10, 1998, and the first systems started to appear the following year. The initial chip ran at 25 MHz, but remember, this outperformed a compatible 80386 50 MHz system.

486SX

Intel once again put the brakes on its premier processor to provide consumers with a cheaper, but slower, version of its flagship processor. The company accomplished this by removing the math coprocessor. Intel initially just turned the coprocessor off. This thrilled many hardware hackers as they discovered they could turn it back on and get a more expensive chip at a bargain. Intel fought back by actually removing the circuitry. Intel did offer an upgrade from the 486SX to the 486DX by installing the OverDrive processor to restore the missing circuits, but at the cost of reduced proximity to the main CPU circuitry.

Clock Doubling

Intel answered the increasing demands of speed by introducing the DX2 and DX4 processors. These machines ran at clock speeds of up to 100 MHz by taking the CPU and configuring it to run internally at double the external clock speed. This would take a normal 486DX running at 33 MHz and produce a 66 MHz speed demon. The DX4 would triple the external clock, making the same 33 MHz clock run the chip at 100 MHz. Keep in mind that this only affected the internal processes. The internal register transfers and computing would run at 100 MHz, but external calls for memory would only run at the normal 33 MHz rate. The DX4 also offered increasing amounts of internal onboard cache.

The new clock speeds and increases in circuitry generate a lot more heat and require external heat sinks and mounted fans to keep the chips from burning out. If you have an older machine that whines, it is probably because the fan mounted on the CPU has worn bearings. If the whining suddenly goes away, you should immediately check to ensure the fan hasn't given out. A dead fan soon leads to a dead processor.

Pentium Processors

Because you cannot copyright numbers, Intel decided to move to Latin to name its processors. Pentium is derived from the Latin word for five as the Pentium is the new 89586 family of microprocessors. The first, or Pentium I, was introduced on October 19, 1992, with the first chip shipping on March 22 the following year.

By this time, many corporations were migrating to client/server solutions that lived outside of the mainframe environments with which most people were familiar. Windows NT Server was in full swing and competing vigorously with NetWare for an increasing market share. Unix had become more popular, however, not as mainstream as the other two network operating systems.

Fans and cooling methods are covered on the exam. You need to know that CPU fans are attached to the CPU chip itself. Computer fans cool the internal components of the server, and cabinet fans are designed to cool a rackmount cabinet full of computers.

The Pentium was the first chip to offer superscalar technology. This meant that the Pentium featured twin data paths, which allowed the processor to execute two instructions at the same time. These two buses were called U and V. The U pipeline was designed to process the entire instruction set of the Pentium. The V pipeline offered a subset of instructions. This allowed the processor to divide the instructional tasks into discrete operations that were then shared between the two pipelines. Software that is designed to take advantage of the multiple paths is known as multithreaded applications. Windows NT was one of the first operating systems that was specifically designed to take advantage of this technology.

The Pentium also boasted a 64-bit data bus with a built-in math coprocessor. These machines also come with twin internal 8KB caches. One cache is used for data and the other is designed to store programming instructions.

The first generation of Pentium processors did not double the external clock, whereas the second generation had a clock multiplier of 1.5 or 3 depending on the model. Thus, the Pentiums ran from 33 to 200 MHz.

Pentium Pro

In 1995, the Pentium Pro was introduced. This processor was aimed at the higher-end servers and workstations. The Pentium Pro added a second memory-caching chip. This was the first Pentium that supported the Reduced Instruction Set Computer (RISC) processor. All of the other Pentiums only ran the Complex Instruction Set Computer (CISC) processor. Because a Pentium Pro was really a Pentium at heart, it also incorporated a CISC to RISC translator. Additional features like three-way superscalar execution and dynamic execution made this chip a powerhouse.

Pentium MMX

More and more applications began to rely on high-speed graphics. This manipulation was taxing even the fastest Pentium processors. To address this "need for speed" Intel released the third generation Pentium in 1997, which included a pipelined Multi-Media extension (MMX) chip. This provided a dedicated processor designed for Single Instruction Multiple Data (SIMD), which lets a single command operate on different sets of data.

The SIMD feature of the MMX chip transformed the graphics industry, particularly in the games arena. In order to have the "latest and greatest," you had to have MMX. To upgrade to MMX, you needed to have a Pentium motherboard that matched the "socket 7" specification. The 233 MHz MMX essentially ended the original Pentium line in June of 1997.

Pentium II

In 1997, the first Pentium with MMX built-in to the chip was introduced. This was the Pentium II. The chip added several features that revolutionized the processor market. These features included:

➤ 512KB L2 cache in addition to the separate L1 caches that the Pentium already supported.

➤ Error Correction Coding (ECC) of the L2 Cache bus, which ensured that the data being transported was checked and correct.

➤ Single-Edge connector (SEC) packaging, which protected the internal circuitry and made installation much easier and less prone to error.

➤ Multiple branch prediction, which "looked-ahead" in the processing cycle and prefetched information along decision branches. This meant that when a decision was reached, the requested result was already loaded and ready.

➤ Dual Independent Bus (DIB) design, which isolated the system bus from the cache bus. It allowed complete synchronization between the CPU and the various caches without being interrupted by any system calls.

> Speculative execution, which executed operations based on "best-guess" results. This kept the pipes full and boosted system performance.

> Data-flow analysis where the processor actually reorders the order of execution to ensure speedy processing. This required the CPU to actually analyze the instructional relationships between the different commands and avoid breaking the order too radically.

Intel Celeron

The consumer market was finally introduced to the speed increase of the microprocessor with the SX designation. The Pentium II was oriented more towards the business market, as businesses were the only ones with the pockets deep enough to purchase Intel's powerhouse. To keep the revenue stream alive and provide the home consumer with more power, Intel introduced the Celeron.

The Celeron was a pretty decent processor in comparison to other cloned processors on the market. It sported the MMX technology that was such a huge success in the home entertainment market. It also provided some of the Pentium II's sexier features like multiple branch prediction, data-flow analysis, and speculative execution.

Xeon

The Xeon first became available in 1998 and soon became "the chip" for high-end servers. This chip supported a clock speed that ranged from 450 MHz to 1 GHz. The multiprocessing capabilities made this the prime choice for application servers where raw processing power is king. The Xeon designation was applied to the Pentium II and Pentium III chips to establish a CPU that was specifically designed for the server environment. Figure 4.2 shows a Pentium III Xeon processor.

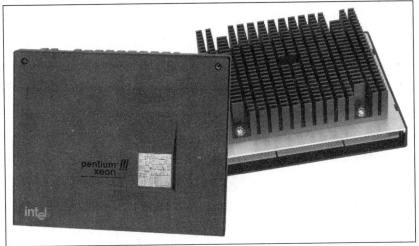

Photo courtesy Intel Inc.

Figure 4.2 The Pentium III Xeon processor.

Pentium III

The Pentium III added streaming SIMD enhancements for mathematical processing and graphics rendering. It also provided additional support for power control, which allowed the processor to conserve power and generate less heat when in an idle state. As shown in Figure 4.3, the Pentium III is no longer a single chip.

Pentium 4

The Intel Pentium 4 was designed for pure speed. The first Pentium boasted two pipelines, but the Pentium 4 has 20. It is part of the Intel Netburst microarchitecture. Additional features include:

➤ 400 MHz system bus that delivers 3.2GB per second to the memory controller.

➤ Internal Arithmetic Logic Units that run at twice the clock speed.

➤ Advanced dynamic execution that enhances the prediction of execution flow.

➤ 128-bit, 144 instruction, streaming SIMD design for crisp, and, more important, really fast graphics.

Intel-Compatible Processors

Several manufacturers have produced outright clones or variations of the Intel line of processors. After Intel figured out they could name the chip after something they could copyright, that is, the Pentium, it became difficult for consumers to know which CPU clone would offer the same or better performance with lower prices.

Weitek was one of the first competitors that manufactured and sold math coprocessors. These processors were well designed because they were actually

Figure 4.3 The Pentium III processor.

Photo courtesy Intel Inc.

created by several Intel engineers. Intel originally contracted Weitek to develop the coprocessor for the 386 computers, which resulted in the Weitek 1167. The funny thing is that the 1167 was not compatible with the 80387 and needed a different mounting socket than the standard Intel chip. This caused somewhat of a war between the two manufacturers. Weitek's current lack of predominance in the market speaks volumes about the wisdom of taking a closed architecture approach.

Other companies, such as Cyrix, IDT Winchip, and AMD, who made a faster 486 than Intel, soon followed. The array of competitors spurred Intel to continue to grow and gave consumers several options. Many end users chose to stick with Intel, as there were various reports of incompatibility with the clones. Many current motherboards are designed specifically for Intel or some of the competitor's CPUs and cannot be mixed and matched.

Installing a CPU

First ask yourself, "Is this worth the trouble?" Remember what we said earlier in the chapter about the importance of balancing the speeds of all the components in a system. If you have a slow, insufficient motherboard, all the processors in the world will not help to speed it up. You'll need to remember that all of the CPU power and speed will do a server no good if the motherboard is too old to handle it, or if other components are so slow that the CPU spends more time waiting for everything to catch up than it does actually doing work.

When you upgrade a Pentium I computer, you can usually keep the floppy drives, the mouse, and other minor components. Some people also keep the old 2MB graphics card and inexpensive sound card (which shouldn't be on a server system anyway). Upgrading additional components like the drive controller will depend on whether you want to ensure a balanced system and add fault tolerance or whether you are willing to deal with bottlenecks that will restrict the upgraded performance of the overall server. If your new system is not designed to be a high-performance server, the old IDE drives should be sufficient. (Refer to Chapter 3 for more about IDE drives.)

Pentium II upgrades usually involve just the CPU and maybe the motherboard as well. It really depends on whether or not you want a new case. There are two major case shapes or form factors you need to pay particular attention to: the AT and ATX. They do not fit the same box and some processors will not fit in the same socket.

Pentium III upgrades normally only require that you swap out the chip. You may be suboptimizing the system by relegating it to a slower clock or system bus, but results vary. Just make sure the motherboard's chip set supports the new processor.

Before and After the CPU Installation

Before the CPU is installed on a system, you need to check with the motherboard manufacturer to determine whether the proposed CPU is compatible and will fit in the socket. It may also be necessary to upgrade (also known as flashing) the BIOS to allow the system to recognize the upgraded CPU. It is almost always necessary to do this when installing a second CPU on the system.

After installing a second CPU, you need to obtain NOS specific drivers and components in order to allow the NOS (Windows NT, Windows 2000, NetWare, Unix/Linux) to recognize and utilize the processor. In Windows NT and Windows 2000, this is done by obtaining an updated Hardware Access List (HAL) for the system. NetWare requires an additional NetWare Loadable Module (NLM) to be loaded with the system.

Plugging in the CPU

To directly swap out an existing CPU, you normally need to remove the old one. This can be accomplished in a couple of ways. Chips on the older machines, which are the 8086 variety, need to be desoldered. However, we will primarily focus on the Low Insertion Force (LIF) and the Zero Insertion Force (ZIF) socketsets.

The LIF socket is really a misnomer. It takes between 60 and 100 pounds of force to leverage the chips out of the socket. For best results, use the special tool that usually comes with the chip. This tool should be inserted between the chip and the motherboard. You then alternate sides to ensure an even level of extraction and avoid bending pins. If you don't pry the chip out evenly, you could damage the chip, the socket, and your wallet.

Intel introduced the ZIF socket with the newest 486 and Pentium processors. To remove the chip, you simply lift a lever and the CPU is released. No muss, no fuss, and no more cracked sockets.

Once the chip is removed, install the replacement chip, ensuring compatibility by checking the specifications of the motherboard and the processor *prior* to the installation. Because some ZIF sockets are pretty generic, make sure you know where pin 1 goes and properly align the chip. Setting the chip in incorrectly can damage the chip and the main board.

SEC slot 1 upgrades are a little different. You may need to purchase an additional fan and heat sink to dissipate the astounding amounts of heat the higher-end Pentiums produce. SEC removal is simply a matter of moving two plastic pins and pulling out the old CPU. Reverse the process to replace the chip. Ensure that your new CPU has the two guides properly aligned, and press the CPU in place. Reposition the two pins, and the CPU is installed.

Remember to check the manufacturer's documentation to ensure that you know which slot to use as you may have a multiprocessor motherboard, or you may have a special expansion card that needs to be installed if the second slot is to remain unoccupied.

It is essential that any cooling fans on the processor be properly installed and operational. All processors later than the 486 generate enough heat to destroy themselves in a very short time. Test to ensure that the fans are working properly before you replace the outer case.

Chipsets

Motherboards provide a place for all expansion and internal components to reside. They govern communication between the various components and dictate expansion compatibilities. One of the overriding factors in dealing with the motherboard, or system board, is the chipset.

The chipset normally consists of four primary elements:

➤ *Bus controller*—This acts as a traffic cop that decides who can communicate, how fast communications can go, and what format the communications assume. Current maximum bus speeds include 66, 100, and 133 MHz frequencies. These frequencies are like speed limits on the freeway; no single device can travel faster than the speed limit. Most buses support device speeds that are less than the maximum bus speed, but devices that attempt to communicate faster than the speed limit simply will not work. Most devices also support speeds that are less than their own maximum operating speed; however, many proprietary or cheaper devices do not. Beware of this little gotcha when purchasing component equipment. Devices that run on the bus controller range from RAM to hard disk controllers and everything in between.

➤ *Memory controller*—This chip handles the requests for reading and writing to the various forms of memory on the computer. It is the memory controller and the functions it supports that determine the maximum memory capacity on the motherboard.

➤ *Data and address buffers*—These specialized chips are designed to provide data to the processor and other components in a timely manner, usually before the component specifically asks for it.

➤ *Peripheral controller*—This element lets the rest of the external world provide services to the main board. Communications to such devices as keyboards, disk drives, and sound cards must flow through the controller to move to and from the external devices and the CPU.

Some motherboards provide additional chips in the chipset to handle specific services like specialized high-speed buses or additional cache memory. Some manufacturers also include integrated peripherals, like video cards, network adapters, and sound cards. This may lower the overall cost of purchasing these devices separately, but may cost more in the long run as these integrated devices are usually impossible to upgrade without creating IRQ, DMA, or memory resource conflicts. Add-on cards usually offer additional features and better performance than the vanilla components found in many combination motherboards.

Remember that while installing any internal computer component, you need to be grounded in order to prevent an Electrostatic discharge (ESD) event from zapping your server. Static electricity can cause damage to a computer. Usually, you don't even know that you are carrying an electrostatic charge until you come in contact with something else. Both you and the computer can be carrying a charge. Ideally, the best way to eliminate the possibility of an ESD event is to ground yourself and the computer so that neither is carrying a charge. The best way to do this is in a lab using heel straps that automatically ground you to the floor or wrist straps that can be plugged into a bench. Because most of us do not live in an ESD sensitive environment, the best workaround is to make sure that the charge you carry is at the same charge level as the computer. If you and the computer carry the same charge, there is no reason for electrons to jump from you to the computer or vice versa. You do this by leaving the computer plugged in but powered off. You *neutralize* yourself to the computer by touching it. The best way to keep this electrostatically neutral status while you are working is to purchase a wrist strap that has an alligator clip on it, which can be attached to the computer's chassis.

Memory

Although the processor is the brain of the CPU, it needs some form of storage in order to function. There are different types of memory designed to perform different tasks. Memory is also the single most important factor when creating a high-performance system. If your server is memory constrained, you will not get the overall functionality, reliability, and performance for which system it was designed.

Memory primarily consists of ROM or RAM. The combination of these two forms of storage provide initial boot services and give the ever-faster processor somewhere to store its results.

ROM

ROM is used to store data even when the main computer is powered off. It is typically used to provide the root instructions that tell the computer what to do prior to loading and running the regular operating system.

ROM is also used to configure system settings and control how the overall machine deals with the installed peripheral devices, like disk drives and even RAM.

The most important ROM is the system Basic Input/Output System (BIOS). The BIOS controls how the various components communicate at the equipment layer. You normally cannot do anything to the system BIOS, but the BIOSs on some machines are able to load new commands or perform flash upgrades. Never interrupt a flash upgrade as it can quickly render the chips unusable, requiring a physical replacement. BIOS functionality is discussed in more detail in Chapter 5.

RAM

RAM is a more popular option to replace or upgrade than the CPU. This is particularly true as the prices of RAM continue to plummet. Memory configurations that were unheard of in the early mainframe days are now commonplace on both entry-level computers and servers. RAM is usually measured in megabytes, but some servers and very high-end workstations now sport multiple gigabytes of physical, not virtual, memory.

One of the challenges of memory upgrades is determining the appropriate types of memory to purchase. This can cause several trips to the computer store as different types of memory chips cannot be combined. Improper memory upgrades can cause erratic behavior when installed in the wrong place or in the wrong motherboard.

Dynamic RAM (DRAM)

DRAM refers to memory that is normally stored by charging and discharging very small capacitors. These capacitors only hold a charge for a fraction of a second, which necessitates frequent refreshes. Needless to say, DRAM "forgets" everything when the power is terminated.

Fast Page Mode DRAM (FPM DRAM)

FPM DRAM provides faster access by taking advantage of the physical layout of computer memory. Because memory is comprised of rows and columns, FPM speeds up the process of paging, or loading and unloading data, by retaining the row address of the data and modifying only the column. This does require dividing memory into pages ranging from 512 bytes to a few kilobytes long, which speeds up access by providing much fewer wait states for the cache and CPU when retrieving contiguous memory locations.

FPM DRAM lead to further improvement, such as *burst mode addressing*, which was first introduced on the 486 microprocessor.

Extended Data Out (EDO) RAM

EDO RAM made its debut in 1995. EDO is a modified form of FPM that is also known as Hyper Page Mode RAM. The main differnce between EDO and FPM is that the data output drivers on the chip are not turned off when the memory controller removes the column address to begin the next cycle. This allows for a small time overlap that saves approximately 10 ns per cycle.

Memory access time is improved because the memory controller is able to begin a new column address instruction while it is reading data in the current address. This is nearly identical to what older systems used to perform by interleaving banks of memory. The huge advantage over interleaving is that you do not need to install redundant banks of RAM.

Burst EDO (BEDO) RAM

BEDO RAM is the same as normal EDO with an added burst feature to speed access of contiguous blocks of data. The main disadvantage is that only one chipset, the Inter 440FX Natoma, supports it. Synchronous DRAM (SDRAM) was introduced soon after, and the increase in speed ensured a short life cycle for BEDO.

SDRAM

SDRAM runs in synchronization with the memory bus, which removes latency as the control signals are already in time with the motherboard's clock. SDRAM is dramatically faster than FPM or even EDO RAM. Initial latency is the same, but burst access is very fast, consisting of only 8 system bus cycles as opposed to 11 for EDO and 14 for FPM.

Double Data Rate (DDR) SDRAM

DDR SDRAM is a clock doubler. It transfers information twice on a single clock cycle. This is the same technique that enabled the Advanced Graphic Port (AGP) to exceed Peripheral Component Interconnect (PCI) for graphics speed.

Rambus DRAM (RDRAM)

RDRAM, an Intel standard, works by doubling the internal data bus from 16 to 32 bits. Intel also tweaked the internal clock to 800 MHz, which produced a maximum bandwidth of 1.6 GHz per second. Rambus (the sole manufacturer of this unique type of RAM) provides an independent control and address buses. It also supplies internal 64 bit interleave, which supplies a 128-bit 100 MHz data path to the rest of the system. The biggest problem with DRDRAM is that you have to license the design. This is rather expensive and pretty much eliminated its adoption.

Synchronous Link DRAM (SLDRAM)

SLDRAM has a 64-bit bus and a 200 MHz clock speed. Because it is a doubler, it can transfer data at 400 MHz. It has many of the same features of DRDRAM with one notable exception: SLDRAM is an open source, which means no licensing fees are required.

Parity

One of the primary axioms of the computer industry is Garbage In, Garbage Out (GIGO). If your data becomes corrupted in memory before it is delivered to the CPU for processing, the results will be worthless. Parity chips, usually odd or even, act like a quality control agent. If the 8 bits add up to an even number and the even parity bit is clear, you should have good data. If the 8 bits add up to an odd number, the parity bit should be set. If the parity bit is clear, producing an odd sum, the data is corrupted and should be discarded. This simplistic example shows how bad data can quickly be identified and, if available, restored from source media.

ECC

What happens if the data *and* the parity block are corrupted or if more than one bit is corrupted? If you are using simple parity checks, the error could go undetected and the result is garbage. ECC adds additional information about the bits, which is examined to determine whether there are problems. ECC is more accurate than standard parity checks, but can be slower.

Many manufacturers believe that modern production controls mostly eliminate data errors. Operating systems and sophisticated CPU algorithms can also identify and correct errors. The current trend is to ignore parity and errors in memory. This produces a fairly significant burst in speed, but could compromise data integrity.

Memory Packaging

Early versions of RAM were installed as single chips, usually a bit at a time in a Dual Inline Pin (DIP) chip. Some were hard soldered to the motherboard, but most were simply seated in a socket. To upgrade memory, you needed to remove and replace the chips, usually eight or nine at a time—nine only if you were using parity.

As memory capabilities increased and prices decreased, manufacturers offered several different installation forms:

➤ Single Inline Pinned Packages (SIPPs) were circuit boards that had DRAM chips mounted on it. The reason that SIPPs were shortlived was that the board had an array of small and relatively fragile pins protruding from the bottom. These pins were easily broken and impossible to repair.

➤ The Single Inline Memory Module (SIMM) was functionally identical to the SIPPs except they did not have those nasty pins. The lower edge of the board had 30 contacts that simply slipped into the connector. Initially, SIMMs came in only 30 contact versions, but some custom configurations numbered over 200.

Contact versions of 30 and 72 are the most widely used. SIMMs are usually installed in banks that depend on the depth (256KB–32+MB) and the width (1 bit–16+ bits). Normally, you must fill individual banks in even divisions of 8 or 16 bits. If you are using parity, you must fill individual banks in even divisions of 9 or 18. The 72-contact SIMM allows wider chips, in terms of bits, which allow the motherboard to hold more memory without crowding the other components.

➤ The Dual Inline Memory Module (DIMM) comes with 168 contacts and has an entire bank of memory on a single board. It is easier to install as it is normally dropped straight in as opposed to the SIMM "swing" installation.

When installing server RAM, check with the manufacturer regarding the following issues, to ensure that they do not become a problem:

➤ The maximum amount of RAM that the server can handle. Also check for the maximum allowed SIMM size.

➤ SIMMs of differing sizes and/or speeds might not work together, even though they are individually compatible with the server.

➤ SIMMs of different sizes and/or speeds might work together only if they are installed on separate memory banks on the server.

Cache Memory

The faster caches that appeared on the later processors needed to have high-speed chips. Normal DRAMs were not quick enough to deal with the never-ending demands of the mighty 486. Special chips called Static RAM (SRAM) were used. SRAM does not use capacitors to store information. Instead SRAM uses a special circuit called a flip-flop. DRAM needs to be refreshed frequently as the capacitors lose their charge rapidly. The SRAM, once set, retains its setting without a refresh. Because it is more complex to build and is much faster than DRAM memory, SRAM is much more expensive.

Write-Back and Write-Through Cache

The primary job of the cache is to speed up processing and limit the number of wait states the CPU has to execute. Some slower caches will immediately send all data that is given to it directly to memory. Although it is operating, the CPU may need to execute a wait state, which is called the *write-through cache*. Because the CPU needs to wait, it cannot perform, which slows the entire process.

The *write-back cache* takes a more powerful approach. This cache has special circuitry and logic that ensures that the CPU never has to wait while the cache is writing to memory. This cache is much harder to manufacture and is therefore more expensive.

Practice Questions

Question 1

A technician replaces an existing 128MB RAM DIMM on your server with a 256MB RAM DIMM. When the server starts, it only recognizes 128MB RAM. Why?

   I. The RAM's speed is higher than the bus speed.

   II. The motherboard's chipset will not support that much RAM.

   III. The RAM's speed is lower than the bus speed.

   IV. The RAM is the wrong voltage.

  ○ a. I or II

  ○ b. II or III

  ○ c. III or IV

  ○ d. I or IV

Answer a is correct. Either the RAM's frequency is more than what the bus will allow or the chipset will not support that much RAM. Answers b and c are incorrect because most buses are compatible with lower speed components. Answer d is incorrect because voltage does not come into play when choosing RAM.

Question 2

Which of the following CPU components provides a path for data to travel between CPU components?

  ○ a. Clock

  ○ b. Register

  ○ c. Cache

  ○ d. Data bus

Answer d is correct. Any bus can be described as a road that exists between two or more components. Answer a is incorrect because the clock maintains the timing sequences for components within the CPU. Answer b and c are incorrect because both the register and the cache are different types of memory storage facilities.

Question 3

Which CPU chip is specifically designed for high-end server applications?

○ a. Pentium II

○ b. Xeon

○ c. Celeron

○ d. Pentium 4

Answer b is correct. The Xeon processor's multiprocessing features were specifically designed for high-end applications servers. Answers a, c, and d are all potential server implementations; however, you are very likely to also find them in desktop systems.

Question 4

You have installed a second CPU on your server system. What else must be done in order to complete the installation?

   I. Flash the BIOS

  II. Upgrade the memory

 III. Terminate the data bus

 IV. Upgrade the NOS drivers

○ a. I and II

○ b. II and III

○ c. III and IV

○ d. I and IV

Answer d is correct. You need to flash the BIOS and upgrade the NOS drivers in order to provide both base system support and NOS recognition of the second CPU. Answers a, b, and c are incorrect because upgrading the memory is not required for a CPU upgrade and terminating the data bus is impossible because it lives within the CPU chip.

Question 5

> BIOS information is stored in what location?
>
> ○ a. ROM
>
> ○ b. RAM
>
> ○ c. Hard disk drive
>
> ○ d. Cache

Answer a is correct. BIOS information is located in ROM. Answer b is incorrect because RAM requires a steady power stream: BIOS information would be lost every time the system is powered off or unplugged. Answer c is incorrect because the system requires hard drive specification information to read from the hard disk, and that information is provided by the BIOS. Answer d is incorrect because cache is a temporary "anticipatory" memory store.

Question 6

> Which of the following describes DIMMs?
>
> ○ a. Contain DRAM chips
>
> ○ b. Contain 30/72 pins
>
> ○ c. Contain 168 pins
>
> ○ d. Require swing installation slot

Answer c is correct. DIMMs are 168-pin memory cards. Answer a is incorrect because SIPPs contain DRAM. Answers b and d are incorrect because SIMMs are either 30 or 72 pins and have a swing installation slot.

Question 7

When installing memory and RAM components on a server, what must you do?

   I. Ground yourself and the server

  II. Back up the server data

 III. Unplug the server power

 IV. Wear rubber-soled shoes

  ○ a. I and II

  ○ b. II and III

  ○ c. III and IV

  ○ d. I and IV

Answer a is correct. Grounding yourself prevents ESD events from occurring and data backup is essential to ensure recoverability in any situation. Answers b and c are incorrect because you need the ground circuit in order to ensure that the server is well grounded. Answer d is incorrect because rubber-soled shoes at best are a method of ensuring that static electricity does not flow from you to the computer through your feet.

Need to Know More?

 Reeves, Scott, Kalinda Reeves, Stephen Weese, and Christopher S. Geyer. *A+ Exam Prep, Third Edition.* Scottsdale, AZ: The Coriolis Group, 2001. ISBN 1-57610-699-3. This book contains basic information on bus and BIOS.

 www.pcguide.com. This site, developed by Charles M. Kozierok and similar to the TechRepublic site, contains a wealth of information on many IT topics. In particular, it has great articles on BIOS.

 www.intel.com. A great source of information about the latest BIOS trends.

 www.phoenix.com. This site is run by the manufacturer of one of the most complex and feature-laden server BIOS chips.

Bus and BIOS

Terms you'll need to understand:

✓ Bus mastering
✓ Throughput
✓ Processor bus
✓ Cache bus
✓ Backside bus
✓ Memory bus
✓ Frontside bus
✓ Local I/O bus
✓ Standard I/O bus
✓ ISA

✓ MCI
✓ EISA
✓ VESA
✓ PCI
✓ AGP
✓ BIOS
✓ POST
✓ IPMI
✓ WFM
✓ SNMP

Techniques you'll need to master:

✓ Calculating bus throughput
✓ Explaining the difference between bits and bytes
✓ Explaining which buses are plug and play compatible

✓ Upgrading/flashing the BIOS
✓ Explaining the various BIOS features that can be found on a server

How Data Moves

Before you can begin to understand Basic Input/Output Systems (BIOSs) or even buses, you need to figure out how data gets from one place to another. The best way to do this is to examine the individual components of a computer in order to get a better idea of what data is and how these individual components talk to each other.

Bits and Bytes

In the same way that an atom is the smallest component of matter, the smallest component of data is called a bit. Computers only talk in ones and zeros. In the programming world, this is known as a logical data type. In reality, all information received by a computer is translated into ones and zeros in order for the computer to understand it. A bit is simply a container that can hold a one or a zero. A single bit containing a one or a zero really does not convey much information at all. Consider the game show "Name That Tune." Naming a tune that consists of only one note is nearly impossible, but combining several notes gives us a chance to figure out what the song is. Similarly, when 8 bits are combined, the computer can begin to make sense of the information presented. Eight bits is also known as a byte.

One thousand bytes is the same as one kilobyte (KB), and subsequently 1000KB is the same as 1 megabyte (MB). This is where some confusion arises. Traditionally, when discussing data, 1MB is really 1024KB. But when I/O (input/output) is discussed, the standard metrics of 1000KB is the same as 1MB. Because data storage is not discussed in this chapter, the method of referring to bytes, kilobytes, and megabytes is used.

Because the same methods and labels are used to describe quantities for data storage and data transfer, it is easy to forget that a megabyte is not necessarily a group of data. For example, a megabyte really is a parking lot that can contain eight million cars, or bits of data. The computer gets information not based on the types of cars that are in the parking lot, but whether each space actually has a car in it. Each parking spot is the same as one bit, and a full parking space holds one bit.

Now let's talk about how data gets from one parking lot to another. The parking lots are analogous to the components in your computer, such as the CPU, hard disk drives, and peripheral components. In order to get the data from one parking lot to another, you basically need to build a road . As you build this road, you need to make sure that it is at least as wide as one car in order to ensure that a vehicle can get from one parking lot to another. This works as long as you do not have very much data going from place to place; however, you are prone to traffic jams when you try to put more than one car on a single-lane road at the same time. The solution, then, is to build an extra lane. Two lanes might work well in a rural environment, but not in a metropolitan area, which is what a computer or server is.

In order to handle the amounts of traffic in a computer, you need to build a multilane highway. Each lane must be the width of a single car, which is one bit. Highways in the computer world are called buses. A bus is a multilane highway that acts as a passage between different components (parking lots) in a computer.

Bus Mastering

Once a highway is built, you still need to be able to provide some amount of assurance that traffic accidents will not occur. The ultimate authority is the CPU. However, realistically a lot of these tasks are delegated to a traffic cop known as a bridge. When the CPU is the authority, it is known as the bus master. It is also possible to have other components take on the task of being the bus master. Situations where this might be beneficial include tasks that contain large chunks of data that need to go across the highway, and neither the source nor the destination involves the CPU. Of course, this does take a certain level of responsibility in order to avoid mayhem occurring on the highway. For this reason, only certain components are allowed to have bus mastering authority. By-and-large, when you hear about bus mastering, the reference is to hard drives. Bus mastering does require an operating system that at least emulates 32-bit multitasking. Currently, bus mastering is supported only for Windows 9x, NT, and 2000, and Linux.

Throughput

Once the highway is built, the bus master is placed in authority, and a bridge is established, you need to calculate how much data to move across that bus in any given point in time. Let's say you have a 16 bit wide bus, which is similar to a 16-lane highway. In order to calculate how many bits can travel on this bus every second, you need to determine the speed limit on the highway. In the computer world, this speed limit is given in electrical frequency measures called megahertz (MHz). As shown in Figure 5.1, 1 MHz essentially means that one million bits can travel on a single highway per second. Remember that each lane is really labeled as a "bit." So, the 16-bit wide bus running at 10 MHz can handle 16 million bits of information per second. There are 8 bits in a byte, so this equates to 2 million bytes per second, which is the same as 2000KB, or simply 2 megabytes per second (MBps). You need to be able to understand the difference between bits per second and bytes per second. Many marketing materials will indicate that the products runs at 40 million bits per second, which sounds a lot more impressive than 5 million bytes per second, or just 5MB.

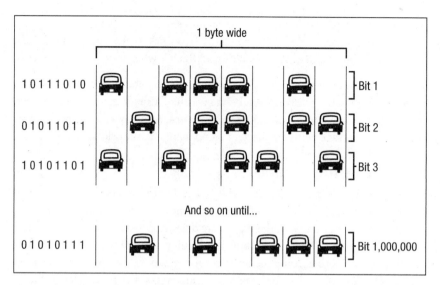

Figure 5.1 An 8-bit wide bus. If bits 1 through 1,000,000 were to occur in one second, the bus speed would be 1 MHz.

One other point for you to remember: When talking about the maximum capacity of a bus, you are literally talking about the highest amount of data that this bus is capable of handling. As you can see in Figure 5.1, not all bits are "occupied" with data, so you will almost never see a parking lot full of data unless there is trouble on the highway. In reality, it takes extra time to exit the parking lot, get on the freeway, get off the freeway, and park again. And don't forget about the traffic cop/bridge who makes sure that each bit gets safely on and off the freeway to begin with. Translated into computer terms, the time spent waiting at the bridge for the traffic cop to give the OK to go is called overhead and latency. Despite the delays of overhead and latency, it is very real and very possible to overload the bus and create a traffic jam on the bus. The need then arises to upgrade the highway into a wider and faster means of getting from point A to point B. We will discuss this evolution as it pertains to I/O buses in the section entitled "I/O Bus Types."

Bus Types

Five different types of buses reside in every PC or server. Keep in mind that each of these buses can be built to only go between point A and point B, or they might have multiple connections to different locations along the way. The five bus types include:

➤ *Processor bus*—The processor bus actually resides within the CPU chip. It is the fastest running bus on the computer and connects to the high priority L1 Cache in the processor portion of the CPU.

➤ *Cache bus*—The cache bus is also known as the backside bus. It also is internal to the CPU chip. It connects the lesser priority L2 Cache and the processor portion of the CPU. The cache bus is not as fast as the processor bus, but is faster than all of the other buses on the computer or server.

➤ *Memory bus*—The memory bus is also known as the frontside bus. It is both internal to the CPU chip and external to the actual RAM boards on the system. It is with this bus that you start to see serious degradation in speed. The degradation in speed is very much understandable if you consider that the internal processor and cache buses are all parts of the same CPU body chip. It doesn't take as much time for your brain to talk to your hand as it does for you to talk to someone else. RAM access speed via this bus is much faster than the speeds used to access other devices in the system. This is primarily because the bus is not as wide, and some buses are more efficient than others. (Hard drives are slower than memory because drives have mechanical parts and RAM does not.)

➤ *Local I/O bus*—The local I/O bus is also known as the expansion bus. This bus connects to plug-in cards for video, network, modem, and any number of other types of peripherals. There are two types of local buses that are used: Video Electronics Standards Association (VESA) local bus, and Peripheral Components Interconnect (PCI). Each of these local buses is discussed further in the "I/O Bus Types" section of this chapter.

➤ *Standard I/O bus*—The standard I/O bus is basically a catch-all phrase for all other expansion buses that are not local. This can include Industry Standard Architecture (ISA), Extended Industry Standard Architecture (EISA), and Micro-Channel Interconnect (MCI) buses.

Other buses exist on or between most systems, such as Universal Serial Bus (USB), Ethernet, parallel, and serial. In this chapter, only I/O buses are discussed as well as how the BIOS is associated with them. Other buses, such as USB, Ethernet, and so on, are discussed throughout this book when referring to peripherals and storage devices. The same methods of calculating speed, throughput, and width apply to all bus types, so remember what you have learned in this chapter when considering how fast components run.

Bus Fault Tolerance

Although not utilized in the standard fault-tolerant components such as hard disk drives and power, there is such a thing as bus fault tolerance. Certain systems and servers have built-in redundant local I/O buses. These fault-tolerant buses are designed to isolate systems that are prone to overloading a single bus rather than for swapping in the event that one single bus should fail; however, moving fault-tolerant bus-attached devices is possible. Physical layout of a bus is nothing more than wires laid out on a circuit board called runs. Component failure, as seen with a hard drive or power supply, does not exist on a bus. This is simply because if the bus fails, the wire runs on the circuit board would be damaged, and in general, you would worry about the entire motherboard in that situation.

In my experience, fault-tolerant local expansion buses are usually seen on servers that handle or expect to handle hardware RAID (discussed in Chapter 3). Keep in mind that everything on the computer is plugged into a bus. This also includes hard disk controllers and other essential peripheral equipment. Just like any huge factory, the system that runs multiple hard disk drives, and even multiple controllers, is very likely to cause a traffic jam on the bus when communicating with other system components. The solution is to create an exclusive highway just for the RAID array. This not only speeds up drive communications, but also improves other system communications that would otherwise come to a grinding halt if everything were on the same bus.

I/O Bus Types

A thorough understanding of the different types of I/O buses requires something of a history lesson. This is primarily because the original PCs were designed as "green screen" devices that looked like a mainframe terminal, yet behaved similar to a Unix machine.

Note: Historically, IBM created the first 16-bit PC and needed assistance in building an operating system for it. After attempting alliances with the creators of Control Program for Microcomputers (CP/M) and Digital Research, IBM ended up working with an embryonic company known as Microsoft.

Industry Standard Architecture (ISA)

IBM originally created the ISA bus as an expansion bus for the first PC. The ISA bus was originally 8 bits wide and completely linked to the CPU. This intimate link to the CPU was eventually found to be dangerous in other bus types; however, the main problem with the 8-bit ISA bus was simply speed. Between the hard disk, the CPU, and memory, it was very easy to flood the bus with data and cause a traffic jam. When the 80286 CPU chip became available in 1984, a 16-bit ISA bus was created for it. The computers associated with the 8-bit ISA bus (8088, 8086 processors) were also restricted in the number of peripherals they could handle because only interrupt request (IRQ) numbers one through eight were available. (PC and server peripherals require IRQ numbers to interface with the CPU and bus appropriately.) With the 80286 processor, the 16-bit bus allowed access to the additional IRQs of 9 through 15.

At about the same time that the 80286 machines became available, Microsoft began working and releasing a product that would be known as Windows. "Windows 1.0" was simply a file management tool with a graphical interface that lived on top of the operating system (OS), which at the time was disk operating system (DOS). DOS was an OS that was created in the days of the 8086 and 8088 processors to handle user interface with the hardware. Its behavior and mannerisms were based on Unix, and although many commands were similar, functionally it fell short of the mark.

Note: Incidentally, the attempts to emulate Unix are still prevalent in the PC and server market. Not only was DOS a spin-off of Unix, but Windows NT (and subsequent versions of it) was also a licensed and drastically modified version of Unix.

Both 8-bit and 16-bit versions of the ISA bus were restricted to an 8.3 MHz clock rate, which only provided enough throughput to handle approximately 16 MBps. The CPU at the time was certainly able to handle the kinds of processing needed for the graphics available in the early versions of Windows. However, this same additional graphics load presented problems for the 16-bit ISA bus.

Micro Channel Interconnect (MCI)

Anyone who has worked with an MCI card is able to recognize its uniqueness simply by the fact that every MCI card had a blue plate instead of a metal plate on its side. The MCI bus was created as a proprietary "upgrade" to the ISA bus. It was a 32-bit bus that ran at 10.33MHz and allowed 40MBps throughput. This was a great improvement over ISA; however, the biggest problem was that it really wasn't an upgrade.

IBM had been the market leader of mainframes for a very long time. When the company created the IBM PC, it never even considered that someone might come along and try to clone it. IBM made the bus architecture open ended in order to allow other vendors to create peripheral cards to go into its computers; however, when manufacturers began to clone PCs with a much lower price tag, IBM suddenly began to lose the market that it had created. In addition, strategic infighting began to occur with Microsoft over the purpose of OS/2; the alliance eventually fell apart, and Microsoft aggressively began development of what would become known as Windows 3.1. The response to this market betrayal appeared to be a two-pronged attack by IBM: OS/2 and MCI. OS/2 was the first true 32-bit, multitasking operating system that seemed tailor-made to go with the 32-bit MCI bus. Strategically this would not have been a bad thing; however, IBM made a huge mistake: MCI was neither backward compatible with ISA peripherals, nor did it contain or utilize open standards. The result was that manufacturers could not develop peripherals for the MCI bus without first obtaining name approval and licensing from IBM. MCI did see some action in the server market due to its high speeds and throughput. It never quite made it to the desktop market primarily due to pricing. The proprietary MCI equipment and peripherals were more expensive than ISA peripherals, which usually did not have any speed problems for standard desktop applications. Most users did not need more than what was provided with a modem, a network card, and a video monitor. Disk I/O was also not an issue for a single user. As time went on, the desktop market data changed due to advances with the dominant operating system, which was Windows. Windows began using more and more graphics that required additional communications with the CPU in order to provide the interface. This resource requirement eventually grew into a demand for a better bus to handle the additional load. In the meantime, IBM's competitors began to work on a new bus type to surpass IBM's MCI.

Extended Industry Standard Architecture (EISA)

In response to the MCI proprietary issues of backward compatibility, AST, Compaq, Epson, Hewlett-Packard, NEC, Olivetti, Tandy, Wyse, and Zenith (all, PC-compatible manufacturers) all worked together to create the EISA bus. EISA was almost identical to MCI in that it had a 32-bit wide bus, but ran slightly slower. At an 8.3 MHz speed, the throughput was nearly 32MBps, which was a remarkable speed at the time. The biggest difference was its backward compatibility; ISA components could be plugged into the EISA bus.

Again there was not much demand for EISA in the desktop market because the operating system simply did not demand enough throughput to offset the additional costs associated with creating 32-bit peripherals. EISA did however see quite a bit of usage in the server market. Today you still see quite a few servers running EISA buses despite the fact that subsequent buses run much faster. The reason for this is price: 32-bit EISA devices are not compatible with any of the other faster bus types, and because EISA equipment was something of a financial investment at the time, many companies are reluctant to upgrade or eliminate it completely.

Both EISA and MCI introduced a couple of new features that are widely in use today: bus mastering and very limited plug and play. The particular flavor of plug and play that was used by both MCI and EISA relied on a single disk or CD-ROM.

Installation and configuration of ISA components required that the user install the card, manually configure the jumpers for IRQ and direct memory allocation (DMA) on the card, install drivers into the OS, and configure the drivers for those IRQ and DMA addresses. Installation and configuration of EISA components required that the user install the card and boot to a floppy or CD drive; the boot program would subsequently query the new hardware and install the appropriate drivers. Disaster recovery for EISA and MCI systems could become quite hairy, as it became necessary to shuffle between these "automatic driver" disks and operating system disks.

 Component installations that deal with buses follow this pattern: turn off the server, install the hardware, power up the server, and install drivers in the OS.

Video Electronics Standards Association (VESA) Local Bus

A VESA local bus is similar to a patch, an upgrade, or an add-on to an original ISA bus. It utilizes the same ISA bus that every other component utilizes; however, an add-on bus is aligned with one or two ISA slots to provide a full supplementary 32-bit bus. The VESA local bus was introduced about the time that the 80486 processor became available. This was also about the time that users and desktop demand for graphical resources began to increase. The idea was to provide a supplement to the ISA bus that could handle the increasing graphical resources and still allow full backward compatibility with ISA technology with little or no disruption to the overall system. Basically, the VESA bus was an add-on that provided additional functionality for graphics.

There were two major problems with the VESA local bus: It was intimately tied to the CPU, which required that VESA components be designed to run at the CPU clock speed. If you decided to upgrade the CPU, you had no guarantee that your VESA components would function at the increased speeds. In addition, it was possible to bog down the CPU with graphics information that it did not need to deal with because there was essentially a fulltime open line between the CPU and the bus.

Although the VESA local bus was essentially backward compatible, it was definitely not backward compatible when it came to equipment upgrades and improvements. Even though the VESA bus did not seem to have very many problems in the desktop market, there were some problems with the CPU/video connection in the high-end desktops and occasionally in the servers as well.

Peripheral Component Interconnect (PCI)

PCI is the default bus that is currently shipped with nearly every server and desktop currently on the market. Many desktops still provide one or two slots for ISA components, but ISA component sales are rapidly declining. Many servers and desktops still utilize ISA firmware technology; however, PCI is still the dominant bus.

A PCI bus is a 32-bit or 64-bit bus that runs at 33 or 66 MHz. The throughput can reach 132 MBps for a 33 MHz machine and 500MBps (the uppercase "B" signifies mega*bytes* per second, not megabits per second) for a 66 MHz machine (without overhead). This is an incredible improvement over the ISA, MCI, EISA, and VESA buses. PCI supports up to five slots, and of those five, only one can be 64 bits per bridge. Remember that a bridge is like a traffic cop for the PCI highway.

PCI also has several features that were either not fully utilized or not seen at all in previous bus architectures. PCI is the first BIOS that is fully compatible with plug-and-play technology. When the system boots, the BIOS automatically queries the PCI bus to determine if there are any plug-and-play compliant devices plugged into the bus. These plug-and-play compliant devices have the capability of dynamically configuring DMA, memory, and IRQ addresses, requiring no user intervention. If there are plug-and-play–compliant devices, the BIOS determines the configuration data and stores it in a table that is subsequently passed to a plug and play operating system such as Windows 9x or Windows 2000. PCI technology also allows for IRQ sharing, which effectively removes any limits on the number of peripherals that can be plugged into any given server. The PCI bus is also unique in that it fully supports bus mastering in the sense that it not only allows a single device to be a bus master but also allows multiple devices to be bus masters.

Another feature that is available with the PCI bus, when supported by the BIOS, is PCI *hot-plugging*. This is essentially a fault-tolerant feature that allows PCI expansion cards to be plugged into the bus without powering down the system.

 Some of you veteran technicians might be thinking that it's already possible to install a PCI card without powering down the system, but you definitely need to know that unless the system supports and is enabled for PCI hot-plugging, you run the risk of frying the motherboard, hard disk drive, RAM, CPU, and basically any component on the server. This includes an additional risk to yourself should you inadvertently discharge a capacitor.

Other Expansion Buses

PCIX buses are similar to VESA in that they appear to be a fully backward compatible add-ons to the standard PCI bus. Only one PCIX slot can exist on a bus that is 64 bits wide. It runs at 133 MHz, which allows for a 1GB per second capacity. This is an awesome capacity; however, for the technology and cost involved, it is best suited for servers and in particular for RAID cards.

AGP is also similar to VESA in that it was designed specifically for video usage. In reality, AGP is not a bus but rather a port. It runs at 66 MHz and is 32 bits wide, but it allows for only one device that is specifically a video card. Redundancy is always stressed on the Server+ exam. Although it is unlikely that a server itself will have enough graphics activity to truly justify an AGP port, it is still a good idea to implement and use AGP on your servers to clear bandwidth from the PCI bus for usage by more critical systems such as a hard disk.

BIOS Overview

BIOS activity occurs when the system boots. Until the operating system begins to load, the BIOS is in absolute control of everything in the system. The BIOS performs the following operations at startup:

1. *Power On Self Test (POST)*—When the server power is turned on, and after the power supply is fully initialized, the CPU wakens and immediately waits for instructions from the BIOS. The BIOS really doesn't *do* anything. It just tells the CPU what to do. In response to the first set of instructions, the CPU basically flips the power switch for the other components on the system. The BIOS has its own power source (a battery) that essentially keeps it alert and awake, waiting for the power supply to give the go-ahead for launch, so it can feed instructions to the CPU, which then starts the other components.

2. *Turn on video and hard disk drive*—The video is turned on almost immediately because users tend to think that the computer is not working if the screen remains blank until the OS begins to load. Additional events also occur at this time that troubleshoot some other system components, but for the most part, the video is turned on at this stage simply to get it ready for when the OS loads. The hard disk drive is also turned on because the OS cannot load without it. (Technically you can load the OS from a floppy, CD, or other media, but ideally the OS is loaded from the hard disk drive.) The hard disk drive is a major mechanical component in what is largely an electronic system, and sufficient time is required to allow it to "spin up" and basically initialize itself so that it is available when the OS needs to load.

3. *Startup screen*—The startup screen is then displayed. For most servers, the startup screen is simply a splash screen that contains the BIOS manufacturer's logo. Many BIOSs allow you to turn this screen off provided the manufacturer has not disabled the switch.

4. *System test*—Memory is tested along with other components, such as the keyboard, the DOS mouse, the SCSI array, and so on.

5. *Inventory and system configuration*—The BIOS actually takes something of an inventory of the available system components and adds this information to a database type table that is made available to the OS for interface usage.

This configuration includes both communications (COM) ports and line printer terminal (LPT, or printer) ports, initialization and plug-and-play detection and configuration. This plug-and-play feature is exclusive to a PCI bus, and is a proactive process where the BIOS (actually the CPU acting on its behalf) checks all components attached to the PCI bus to see if they are plug-and-play compatible. If they are, the BIOS essentially assigns IRQ and memory configurations to the cards, and then places this information in the configuration table mentioned earlier.

6. *Boot to OS*—Once all of the tests are complete and the hard disk drive is initialized, the BIOS essentially tells the CPU to look at the hard disk's master boot record (MBR) for the next set of instructions. BIOS activity then gradually decreases to a bare minimum as the OS initializes itself with appropriate component information referenced in the BIOS data table.

Advanced BIOS Features

It is not necessary for you to know the basic BIOS features found in every PC on the market. You do, however, need to know how and when you access the BIOS information, and how to change BIOS settings. Although this information varies from manufacturer to manufacturer, there are some similarities you can rely upon. When the system boots, a prompt appears that basically tells you to press certain keys to enter a setup program, which is the BIOS setup. Many server manufacturers have additional configuration utilities that are accessed similarly. Be very careful that you do not change anything that you do not intend to. Most BIOS setup programs include the following options:

➤ *Multi-boot*—Most systems have the capability of booting to either a floppy disk or a hard disk drive. Many of the more advanced systems and servers also have the capability of booting to an LS120 (a 3.25 inch floppy that holds 100MB of data), a Zip drive, a DVD, a CD-ROM, and even a USB (with the proper BIOS switches turned on).

➤ *Hot-plug PCI*—This feature that can be enabled within a BIOS to permit the PCI bus to accept additional expansion cards without powering down the system. This feature was originally implemented as a fault-tolerant mechanism; however, it is most widely used to add components, such as hard drives, without requiring server downtime. This is an essential feature for high-availability servers.

➤ *Remote console redirection*—This feature is a security measure for servers. Remote console redirection allows a server's keyboard, mouse, and video signals to be redirected to another system via a serial connection or another direct connection. Keep in mind that, as with all BIOS settings, this is just a switch that allows the feature to be possible. Many features, such as this one, either require on-board OS support or additional software be installed in order to truly perform this function. This feature is ideal in a situation where security is a concern. It is also ideal for highly stable systems that require little or no configuration changes where it simply is not necessary to have a monitor or keyboard attached.

➤ *Host floppy redirection*—Similar to remote console redirection, the floppy drive can be redirected as well. This can be used as another security feature to help prevent tampering with a server. It would certainly be difficult to actually harm the data on a server if you could not see the interface, enter information, or even use a boot disk to reboot the system. This feature also provides additional convenience for an administrator to apply updates on a "headless" system without having to visit a system and hook up a monitor.

➤ *Memory mapping*—During the system startup, the BIOS performs several tests on system components. Most notably, the BIOS has the ability to physically check RAM bit by bit. (You also have the capability of turning this checking feature off, but we recommend against it for servers, due to the criticality of the machine.) If an error is found in RAM, normally the system will issue a beep code and either prompt for instructions or completely stop. Memory mapping is similar to a "flag-and-redirect" feature, which has been in use for a very long time in the hard disk drive world. Basically, when the system encounters a bad spot on the hard drive, the spot is marked with a flag, and the data is redirected to an alternate location. Memory mapping is the RAM equivalent of this feature.

➤ *Advanced configuration and power (ACPI)*—Different server BIOSs support different levels of ACPI. ACPI is basically a power-saving standard that allows different server components to be shut down when they are not in use. Although it is not in huge demand in the United States, it has become a legal requirement in some parts of Europe and Asia. Advanced power management (APM) is a similar power management tool. It was never recommended for server systems because quite often it turned off more than necessary and thus accidentally disconnected mission critical services and functions even after the system was fully "awakened." (In the wake of the California power crisis, power management is seeing some renewed interest in the United States, so it is not a bad idea to become educated on the subject.) Unlike APM, which was fully managed by the BIOS, ACPI is managed by the operating system. The OS determines which components should be shut down or put to sleep and when this should occur. However, the BIOS still performs the task. ACPI has many additional features that are not necessary for you to know, but suffice it to say that you should not turn on ACPI until and unless you either need it, or you test it fully to ensure that it awakens appropriately.

➤ *USB boot*—This is a new feature that you need to be very aware and wary of. In general, it is recommended that USB be completely disabled on server systems simply because of the inherent security risks. There is always a possibility that someone could access your system and plug in new equipment that could cause critical damage ranging from system instability to full-blown hacking.

➤ *Crisis recovery*—This feature is a safety net in the event that the system loses power while flashing the BIOS (see the "BIOS Upgrades" section of this chapter). Bare-bones BIOS information is stored in a special memory chip that is only updated after x number of successful system boots occur after a flash. In the event that power is lost, crisis recovery kicks in and allows the BIOS to essentially rebuild itself to the point that it can figure out the rest of the information.

➤ *Multiprocessor failover*—In the event that you are running a multiple CPU server, it is possible to recover from a CPU failure in the same manner that hard disks can recover from a drive failure. Unlike RAID 5, recovery from a CPU failure does involve rebooting the system twice—once to confirm that the CPU has failed and a second time to redirect the boot process to the secondary CPU.

➤ *Intelligent Platform Management Interface (IPMI)*—IPMI is a remarkable technological breakthrough that allows physical sensors to be enabled within the chassis or cabinet of the server. IPMI can be enabled within the BIOS and subsequently configured in the server manufacturer's setup/configuration program to allow a server to constantly check items, such as temperature, voltage, power supply, and so on, for any noteworthy configured event. IPMI can literally notify you via the network or other means of a situation where the temperature is too high or someone has opened the chassis door.

➤ *Intelligent I/O subsystem (I2O)*—This is an industry standard feature that essentially allows PCI bridging. This feature allows two different PCI buses to be bridged together to enable data to travel faster between the two with little or no CPU involvement.

➤ *Wired for Management (WFM)*—This is a suite of features built specifically for server systems where remote management is made available using features such as wake on lan, wake on ring, and Simple Network Management Protocol (SNMP) traps. Wake on lan and wake on ring both complement ACPI features to enable a sleeping server to wake up when the server is the target of LAN communications or a modem ring. SNMP is a protocol, which is used by many network and server management applications, that utilizes a series of "traps." These traps constantly check for configured warning signs—such as CPU thresholds and network utilization—and notify designated administrators via email, network broadcasts, or any number of other methods. WFM allows SNMP to incorporate more hardware oriented information that, along with advanced diagnostics, can diagnose a failing component such as a hard drive, extrapolate when it will fail, and proactively notify an administrator so that the part can be replaced in an orderly fashion. WFM is truly a technology advance that should be taken advantage of whenever possible—simply to reduce and eliminate unscheduled downtime in the form of drive failures.

BIOS Upgrades

BIOS data is stored on a ROM chip. Another term that you may hear for this ROM chip is nonvolatile RAM. Unlike its name implies, you can write the BIOS ROM providing you follow the appropriate steps. The process of writing a BIOS is called upgrading, or flashing the BIOS. The process of performing the upgrade usually varies slightly from manufacturer to manufacturer, so you will always need to check with the system documentation or the manufacturer's Web site in order to determine the appropriate process. In general, flashing a server's BIOS is actually quite easy if you follow these steps:

1. Download and create an upgrade boot floppy per the manufacturer's instructions.

2. Back up all system data and as much configuration information as you can.

 If you upgrade the BIOS and something subsequently fails, you have a problem because either the upgrade was not applied correctly, or the update was faulty to begin with. If you are lucky, you can recover by reflashing the BIOS. If you are unlucky, you will probably need to find another server and restore the backup data from tape.

3. Power down the server, and reboot with the boot disk installed. Make sure that the server's boot order includes the floppy disk drive before the hard disk drive.

4. Quite often all you need to do at this point is reboot the system and remove the floppy disk. Updating the BIOS in advanced servers is a bit more complex and involves confirmations, and sometimes even multiple disks and reboots.

Practice Questions

Question 1

How many bits are in a byte?

○ a. 4

○ b. 12

○ c. 8

○ d. 64

Answer c is correct. There are 8 bits in a byte.

Question 2

Data can travel on a bus in speeds measured in:

○ a. Frequency

○ b. Bits

○ c. Bytes

○ d. Megahertz

Answer d is correct. Bus speeds are measured in megahertz, which is a *unit* of frequency. Both bits and bytes are measurements of data. Therefore, answers a, b, and c are incorrect.

Question 3

> Which of the following describes bus mastering?
>
> ○ a. Non-HDD devices traveling at the same speed to accomplish bulk data transfers
>
> ○ b. Non-HDD devices controlling the bus to accomplish bulk data transfers
>
> ○ c. Non-CPU devices controlling the bus to accomplish bulk data transfers
>
> ○ d. Non-CPU devices traveling at the same speed to accomplish bulk data transfers

Answer c is correct. It is possible to have non-CPU devices control the bus in order to accomplish bulk data transfers. Answer b is incorrect because an HDD controller can be the bus master. Answers a and d are incorrect because bus mastering has nothing to do with speed.

Question 4

> A 32-bit bus running at a 33 MHz frequency has what throughput?
>
> ○ a. 132MBps
>
> ○ b. 8.25MBps
>
> ○ c. 500MBps
>
> ○ d. 40MBps

Answer a is correct. 132MBps is what a 32-bit bus running at 33 MHz is capable of running. Throughput calculation is accomplished by taking the bit width of the bus, dividing it by 8 to get the number of bytes, and then multiplying that number by the frequency. The result is megabytes per second.

Question 5

Standard I/O type buses do not include which of the following?

○ a. ISA

○ b. EISA

○ c. MCA

○ d. Processor

Answer d is correct. Processor buses are their own type. Answers a, b, and c are incorrect because they are all types of standard I/O buses.

Question 6

Plug-and-play is fully supported with which bus types?

○ a. ISA

○ b. MCI

○ c. PCI

○ d. AGP

Answer c is correct. Plug-and-play is fully supported with PCI buses. Answer a is incorrect because ISA does not support plug-and-play whatsoever. Answer b is incorrect because MCI only partially supports plug-and-play. Answer d is incorrect because AGP is not really a bus type and does not apply.

Question 7

Which of the following is not a supported boot device?

○ a. Floppy disk drive

○ b. RAM memory

○ c. Zip drive

○ d. USB HDD

Answer b is correct. RAM can hold data but cannot be configured to hold data long enough to boot the OS. Floppy disks, Zip drives, and USB hard disk drives are all capable of being configured as boot devices within the BIOS. Therefore, answers a, c, and d are incorrect.

Question 8

Which bus type runs between the processor and the L2 Cache?

○ a. Frontside bus

○ b. Backside bus

○ c. Processor

○ d. Local I/O

Answer b is correct. The backside bus travels between the processor and the L2 Cache. The frontside bus travels between the processor and the memory. The processor bus is internal to the CPU, and the Local I/O bus is an expansion bus. Therefore, answers a, c, and d are incorrect.

Question 9

What is the process for upgrading a server BIOS?

○ a. Back up the server, download the data to a boot floppy, boot the system using the floppy, reboot.

○ b. Download the data to a boot floppy, back up the server, boot the system using the floppy, reboot.

○ c. Reboot, download the data to a boot floppy, back up the server, boot the system using the floppy.

○ d. Download the data to a boot floppy, boot the system using the floppy, back up the server, reboot.

Answer b is correct. The first thing you do is download the flash information and put it on a bootable floppy disk. Most manufacturers will provide you with a data file that will automatically create a bootable disk when the file is executed. When you are ready to flash the BIOS, you need to back up the server, boot the system using the bootable floppy, and reboot.

Need to Know More?

Reeves, Scott, Kalinda Reeves, Stephen Weese, and Christopher S. Geyer. *A+ Exam Prep, 3rd Edition.* Scottsdale, AZ: The Coriolis Group, 2001. ISBN 1-57610-699-3. This book provides basic information on buses and BIOS.

www.intel.com is a great source of information about the latest BIOS trends.

www.pcguide.com, developed by Charles M. Kozierok, is similar to TechRepublic and contains a wealth of information on many IT topics. In particular, it has great articles on BIOS.

www.phoenix.com is home to the maker of the most complex and feature-laden server BIOS chips.

Peripherals and Network Interfaces

Terms you'll need to understand:

- ✓ UPS
- ✓ USB
- ✓ NOS
- ✓ SNMP
- ✓ KVM
- ✓ VPN
- ✓ SAN
- ✓ Parallel port
- ✓ NLM
- ✓ Serial port
- ✓ IEEE 1394
- ✓ Ethernet
- ✓ Token Ring
- ✓ Fast Ethernet
- ✓ Gigabit Ethernet
- ✓ 10Base-T
- ✓ 100Base-T
- ✓ Cat3
- ✓ Cat5
- ✓ NIC
- ✓ Firewall
- ✓ Repeater
- ✓ Hub
- ✓ MAU
- ✓ Switch

Techniques you'll need to master:

- ✓ Installing peripherals
- ✓ Identifying network cables
- ✓ Installing network cables
- ✓ Installing network cards

Server Peripherals

Most dictionaries define "peripheral" with words like "auxiliary, supplementary, or on the side." Computer peripherals are generally items or pieces of equipment that are not necessary for the proper functioning of the base equipment itself. In this section of the chapter, we will discuss the varieties of peripherals that will be covered in the exam, their functionalities, and the ways in which they interact with other components as part of a complete server system.

Peripherals for computers vary widely in range and caliber. Due to the mission-critical nature of server computers, however, the Server+ exam discusses only a few peripherals that could (and quite often should) be found on a server. The Server+ exam mentions peripherals that are part of standard operating procedures—such as monitors, keyboards, and mice—but does not require specialized knowledge about them. Just keep in mind that they are default peripherals for server computers that are covered in this exam.

UPS

UPSs, or uninterruptible power supply units, are external battery-run units that are connected to the power input of one or more servers. The function of a UPS is to provide power to a server so that the server will not ungracefully shut down during a power outage. An "ungraceful" shutdown is a nice way of describing what happens when a computer unexpectedly loses power—an event that often causes data loss and corruption. Imagine, for example, that the power goes out on an unprotected server just when it is updating a file. Every file on a hard drive is listed in a table of contents on the hard disk. That table also shows the file size and the date and time when it was last modified. If a power failure occurs while the file is being edited, and if the file is a different size from the listing in the table of contents, the file has become corrupted. This particular type of file corruption can be repaired using disk repair tools included with network operating systems (NOSs) such as NetWare, Windows NT/2000, and OS/2. Corruption can occur in other ways that are even more difficult to track and repair.

When microcomputer servers first reached the commercial market, they were simply file and print servers. Essentially, all they did was handle the base functions associated with sharing files and print devices. A UPS was necessary to help prevent corruption in the event that a power failure might occur when a user or NOS file was open. Early UPS systems of this type provided surge suppression and line filtering, and they charged the battery that kept the computer running until either the power came back or someone was able to manually shut down the server. As time went by, microcomputer servers evolved into client-server applications that eventually became the application servers we know today. Unlike file and print servers, application servers don't simply wait around for a user to request data; instead, they proactively perform tasks associated with, leading up to, and cleaning up after user requests. This level of activity increases the likelihood that a power outage will corrupt an open file in ways that are more difficult to fix than the example just given.

The increased risk of data loss led to increased demand for UPS functionality. UPSs in turn offer features that are available only with a data connection between the UPS and the server system. The connection is traditionally made to a serial port on the server system; however, recent software upgrades have enabled USB support as well. The following is a list of features that can be found on UPS units with these types of data connections:

➤ SNMP (Simple Network Management Protocol) support that enables customized emails to be sent to administrators or users in certain circumstances

➤ Remote UPS and systems management via modem connections on the UPS unit

➤ Pager notification via modem connections on the UPS unit

➤ Network broadcast message that notifies users that the server will go down

Generally, when companies choose a UPS unit for a single- or multiple-server environment, UPS management applications and features such as those listed above come in handy. Many companies, however, will reject such a UPS configuration due to price. Keep in mind that in lieu of an automated shutdown, a manual shutdown will be necessary to ensure data integrity during a power outage. And with manual shutdown, quite often a greater battery capacity (and more time) will be required in order to support the system until personnel can safely shutdown the server(s).

Certain measures can be taken to increase the amount of time a battery-powered UPS unit will sustain a server(s) and equipment attached to it. Removing noncritical peripherals and attachments is a good start but can lead to confusion. For example, a KVM (keyboard, video, mouse) switch unit whose power is not drawn from a UPS can be a problem during a power outage. The loss of keyboard and mouse would force a server to be manually—and ungracefully—shut down because many systems do not react well to a plug-and-play philosophy. Realistically, the best thing you can do to increase the battery life of a UPS is to get in the habit of shutting off the monitor when it's not in use.

Many server-caliber UPS units have LED displays on the front of the unit that indicate status items such as current battery state, estimated power load, and the battery time remaining under such a load. Using these indicators, you can experiment with adding several servers to a UPS unit. Keep in mind, however, that a monitor is the single biggest energy-eater in any system. Improve your battery time, save energy, and reduce the likelihood of overloading your UPS by purchasing a KVM unit.

Modems

Modems are communications devices that function by dialing analog phone lines and communicating with other modems that answer the call. Modems that are attached to and utilized by servers can be divided into two separate categories: those used for purposes of the server, and those used for purposes of the network.

Server-based modems are usually used for administrative and server remote control through applications such as Symantec's PCAnywhere. Although remote control applications are rare on NetWare servers, they are common among Windows and OS/2 servers, which require remote administration and maintenance capabilities. With the increasing technical and physical capabilities of the Internet, these types of server/modem applications are becoming less common due to virtual private networking (VPN), which can handle most, if not all, of the functions required by server-based modems. VPN is the capability of accessing a business network securely through an Internet connection.

Network-related modems are usually used for dial-up services that enable remote users to dial into and access local network resources. Shared fax, paging, and other forms of remote communications usually require that both server-based and network-related modems be available.

Modems are usually connected to a serial port on the back of the computer. In certain specialized situations, however, multiple modems are configured in a modem bank with a proprietary connection and hardware. Such configurations will not be covered in the Server+ exam.

Printers

Printers are output devices that can be either directly connected to a server system or virtually connected through a network or other print server hardware. In the past, printer mechanics were slow and cumbersome, rendering high connection speeds unnecessary. Technology improvements have made printers faster but more complex in terms of color and resolution, causing most printers to continue having issues keeping up with the amount of data being processed. Data bottlenecks result in lost print jobs and garbled output; one solution is for printers to have on-board memory as a temporary storage place for queued print data while the server sorts through other print items.

In the early years of computing, printers were connected directly to a parallel port on the server system. This type of connection is still common for single-user systems, but parallel port connections place limitations on the physical distance between a printer and a server and are therefore impracticable in many corporate situations. Most NOSs have added functionality that allows printers to be virtually connected to a server through Transport Control Protocol/Internet Protocol (TCP/IP) or NetBIOS addressing on the network. Virtual connection options increase security and flexibility and allow printers to be moved from place to place. This particular flavor of network connectivity is specific to both printer and NOS and will therefore not be discussed in the "Connectivity and Installation" section of this chapter.

Tape Drives

Tape drives are quite often the backup method of choice for a server. Other methods, such as backing up to removable drives or a SAN (storage area network) are also available, but tape is often the preferred method due to its portability and archive capabilities.

Tape drives come in several shapes and sizes, depending upon connection method, capacity, and whether the drive is internal or external. Internal drives are usually connected via a small computer systems interface (SCSI) or IDE (ATA) interface (discussed in Chapter 3). External tape drives are usually connected via SCSI, parallel, and more recently, USB connections. In the past, tape drive installation was unique for each server system because the software drivers required to run the tape drive were almost always proprietary to the backup application rather than being provided by the OS or NOS. What this meant was that you could not access the tape device or data without having the backup application on the system, and the OS/NOS did not automatically recognize that the tape device even existed. More recently, however, tape manufacturers have begun producing separate drivers to run under Windows 2000, Windows NT, and NetWare, thus making the tape backup process less dependent upon hardware support within the application and more dependent upon the OS itself. This is an overall improvement because the shift in control allows the NOS to handle access control and security for the tape drive device, something that most backup applications were ill equipped to deal with in the past.

External Drives

External drives can include fixed media such as hard drives, but in most cases they encompass Zip, ORB, floppy, CD, or CD-R (CD-recordable) drives. These types of drives attach to a server via parallel, SCSI, or USB connections and are usually used for backup or data portability. Although Zip, ORB, floppy, and CD-R drives are ideal for backup purposes, the storage capacities of these types of devices are significantly less than those of a tape drive. Because of capacity limitations, you are more likely to encounter these drives on workstation PCs than on servers.

Connectivity and Installation

Installing and connecting peripherals can be tricky. Thankfully, the scope of the exam is limited to those items most often used by servers. In this section, we will talk about parallel, serial, and USB connections. SCSI and ATA connectivity is limited to drives and is covered in Chapter 3.

 | Connection speeds by type of connection run in the following order from fastest to slowest: SCSI, ATA, IEEE 1394 (FireWire), USB, and parallel.

Parallel Connections

The parallel port on the server is a 25-pin female connector. IRQ settings are set to 7 by default for LPT1 and to IRQ9 for LPT2. Parallel ports are used primarily by printers and external drives. The data input/output rate for parallel connections is very slow by comparison to any other connection method other than serial connections, and there does not appear to be any major breakthrough on the horizon that will enable parallel connection speeds to match those of USB and IEEE 1394 (FireWire).

Four types of parallel connections exist, all of which are backward-compatible with older connection types. Unidirectional parallel ports (UPP), the oldest type of parallel connection, are one-way connections that send data from the server to the print device but do not allow information to be sent back to the server. Bidirectional parallel ports (BPP), the next oldest type, are a step up, enabling communications to occur both from the server to the device and from the device back to the server. The advantage of bidirectional connections is that it allows printer functionality to be reported to the computer. In order for a user to receive an Out Of Paper notice, a BPP or higher port type is required. Both UPP and BPP ports communicate between 50 and 150 kilobytes per second.

Just when printer technology began to advance out of the dot-matrix and daisy-wheel stage, the available data rate increased with EPP (enhanced parallel port) technology, which allows throughput ranging from 500 KB per second to 2MBbs. But it was only when the ECP (extended capability port) data compression technology became available that external drives and parallel devices became known in the retail marketplace as legitimate—and affordable—devices. ECP technology also supports multiple logical devices, meaning that more than one device at a time can be hooked up to the same port.

Parallel devices are installed by plugging the device into the parallel port on the server, applying power, and then installing an appropriate driver for the operating system—Windows NT/2000 and OS/2, or NLM (Netware Loadable Module) for NetWare. Windows 2000 plug-and-play features may detect the new device, depending on whether the port is already configured for a different device. Up-to-date drivers and NLMs are usually available from the manufacturer, but many devices can be installed from the NOS manufacturer's installation disks.

Serial

Serial ports, also known as RS-232 ports, are usually male 9-pin connectors on the computer. Some older servers have a 25-pin male connector, but this is rarely seen in newer systems. Serial connection speeds run up to 921,600 bits per second (bps), which translates to 115,200 bytes per second. Sound familiar? It should, because this is the maximum data rate by which your computer can connect with a modem.

Serial devices on a server are usually modems; however, other devices, such as a Personal Digital Assistant (PDA) and a mouse, can connect through the serial port as well. If a server does not have a modern PS/2 connection for the mouse, then the mouse must be connected via the serial port. If a modem is also necessary for the server, an additional serial card can be purchased and installed on the server in order to allow installation of additional hardware. A microcomputer server can have a maximum of 4 serial ports, assigned the names COM1, COM2, COM3, and COM4. COM1 has a default IRQ of 4 that is shared with COM3. COM2 has a default IRQ of 3 that is shared with COM4.

Pay attention to default IRQ settings for common peripherals on a system.

IEEE 1394

Commonly known as FireWire, the IEEE 1394 standard originally was used almost exclusively by Apple Macintosh systems. Servers are usually not equipped with FireWire ports, and in order to obtain this functionality, you would need to purchase a 1394 controller card and install it on the bus. 1394 connections are supported under Windows 2000 and will soon be supported by NetWare; however, it is currently not natively supported on OS/2 or Windows NT. Driver installation under all operating systems is almost completely dependent upon the device manufacturer. All of this effort can be worthwhile, however, because 1394 connections support data rates of up to 400 million bps, which translates to 50 megabytes per second (MBps).

 When compared to other external connection methods, IEEE 1394 is faster than everything else available, except SCSI and ATA.

Universal Serial Bus (USB)

USB is a close cousin to FireWire. It's easy to confuse the two, as the connectors look similar. The data rate is 12 million bps, which translates to 1.5 megabytes per second—still quite impressive in comparison with serial and parallel connections.

Native USB support is available only under Windows 2000, and installation usually involves plugging the device in and waiting for the plug-and-play feature of the OS to recognize the device. Additional USB driver updates are usually available from the manufacturer and may add additional features to those provided by the Windows 2000 drivers.

Network Interface Types

Network cards and interfaces are, by definition, peripherals, just as external drives and UPS systems are. Each of the peripherals described previously are designed to communicate between the device and the server. Network interface cards also communicate with the server but are different in scope from other peripheral devices and components. After all, communications are at the heart of networking, whereas communications for other peripherals are simply a means to an end.

The Server+ exam does not specifically cover protocols and topologies; much of that information is covered in the Network+ exam instead. To be properly prepared for the exam, you will need to be familiar with network interface types, cabling, network interface hardware, and other networking devices.

If you glance briefly at the headings that follow, you will notice that the network interfaces (sometimes called LANs, for local area networks), cabling, and interface cards belonging to a particular network interface type all have common features. That's because once an interface type has been chosen, all components are built around that definition.

Ethernet

Ethernet can be termed as a connection methodology based upon the IEEE 802.3 standard, according to which devices configured in a bus or star topology communicate using a set of rules known as carrier sense multiple access/collision detection (CSMA/CD). CSMA/CD is basically a set of traffic laws that are followed by all devices on the network in order to reduce the number of accidents, or *collisions*. CSMA/CD also defines what to do when collisions do occur. Standard Ethernet runs at up to 10Mbps and continues to be the most popular connection method to date.

Token Ring

All but extinct now, Token Ring was once the preferred networking method because it provided the best performance for large numbers of connections at the highest speed. Token Ring is based upon the IEEE 802.5 standard that was originally defined by IBM. Instead of the CSMA/CD traffic rules of Ethernet that are designed to handle multiple vehicles on the road, Token Ring is just the opposite: Only one vehicle is allowed on the highway. The vehicle is called the token, and it constantly travels in a circular route from computer to computer. Any communications that need to cross the network hop onto the token as it passes by, in the same way that a person hops on a commuter bus or train. When the train stops at the appropriate destination, the data hops off and other data hops on. The only difference between a train route and our token is that the token carries only one passenger. Token Ring runs at either 4 or 16Mbps. Token Ring was the preferred network interface method for some years: Not only did it run faster, it also had a faster practical run rate because there were no collisions—only one "vehicle" could be on the road at a time. Token Ring began to decline in popularity when Fast Ethernet became available at greater speeds and at a lower cost.

Token Ring has found some favor in the fiber media world in FDDI (Fiber Distributed Data Interface) applications, in which dual Token Rings are configured with servers residing in one or the other ring. FDDI is a fault-tolerant enterprise networking solution because each ring has a link to the other ring at two separate points. This linking configuration enables at least partial network recovery in the event that one of the sustaining members of a ring fails.

Fast Ethernet

Fast Ethernet has all of the same qualities and features of standard Ethernet, except that Fast Ethernet runs at speeds up to 100 Mbps. This is why Fast Ethernet is also called 100 Ethernet. Fast Ethernet is based on an addendum to the IEEE 802.3 standard called 802.3u. Most Fast Ethernet devices are backward compatible with Ethernet devices, but it's important to know that a mixed Fast and Standard Ethernet is only as fast as its slowest common link. We will discuss this speed limitation in the section entitled "Cabling and Connections."

Gigabit Ethernet

Gigabit Ethernet has all of the same qualities and features of Standard and Fast Ethernet, with the exception that Gigabit Ethernet runs at speeds up to 1000 Mbps. Gigabit Ethernet is based upon an addendum to the IEEE 802.3 standard called 802.3z. Because of cabling and interface costs (Gigabit Ethernet requires fiberoptic media), Gigabit Ethernet is not seen widely in the real world. It is used more often for server farms and SAN (storage area networks—see Chapter 3) than for standard desktop connectivity applications.

Cabling and Connections

Network cabling is arguably the single most important element of any network. Cable length, quality, and type can make or break the data rate and efficiency of a network. Cables mentioned and covered in the exam are usually twisted pair copper 10Base-T cable in varying pairs and configurations. Fiberoptic media are also mentioned in conjunction with Gigabit Ethernet, but considering that fiber applications of this type are highly specialized, it is not necessary for you to know more information than what we have already discussed.

Ethernet cabling and connectivity come in two different base types: telephone-type cable and coaxial cable. All networking cables are limited to a certain length. Before communications satellites came along, all intercontinental phone calls from the US traveled to Europe or Africa or Asia via a huge telephone-type cable that was laid beneath the ocean. The further away the connection, the longer the delay between when you said something and when the other person heard it. Static, echoes, electrical interference, and other conversations might bleed into the line, causing problems understanding what the other person on the line is saying. These same concepts apply with network cables. A human conversation is recoverable because people can usually fill in any missing information interactively and reach an understanding of the topic. Computers cannot take these intuitive leaps; so specific limitations are placed on the length of cable that can be handled over a network. The range of a network can be increased slightly when pairs of wires are twisted in such a manner as to be able to resist intrusion by several frequencies of interference. Even with added shielding, excessive cable lengths can result in lost data and terrible network performance due to jitter (when interference occurs) and attenuation (when the signal fades due to excessive distance).

10Base-T

Telephone-type cable is usually called 10Base-T cable—easy to remember because the T can stand for telephone. 10Base-T requires a specific type of cable known as Category 3 (CAT 3 for short) and is basically two pairs of twisted copper wires. Although material differences exist between CAT 3 and the regular phone cord you use in your home, more than one Ethernet network has been built successfully on telephone cable with no one the wiser. Both 10Base-T and 100Base-T cables are connected using RJ-45 connectors, which look similar to the RJ-11 connectors that are used for standard telephone connections except that they are slightly larger. Unlike RJ-11 connectors, RJ-45 connectors have eight terminals to accommodate eight wires instead of the four that you would find in RJ-11. 10Base-T (or CAT 3) cable has a maximum length of 100 meters before attenuation sets in.

100Base-T

100Base-T, also called Category 5 (CAT 5) cable, is a higher quality of cable that consists of 4-pair twisted cable. Speeds of 100Mbps can also be achieved using 2-pair high quality cable; however, pricing and availability are a factor, and most implementations use 4-pair twisted cable with the same RJ-45 connectors used for 10Base-T. 100Base-T is backward compatible with 10Base-T, but there are a few hitches. First, CAT 5 cable is more expensive than CAT 3 and is not always required for a smaller network. These days, it is more difficult to build a 10Base-T network due to cabling availability. On the other hand, 100Base-T (also known as 10/100 Ethernet) network interface cards are more expensive than plain 10Base-T Ethernet cards. To maintain 100Mbps speeds reliably, the same 100-meter maximum length applies to both 100Base-T networks and 10Base-T networks.

You will be expected to know the cable pinouts for 100Base-T cables. As shown in Figure 6.1, there are two types of cable configurations, known as standard and crossover cables. Standard cables utilize pins 1, 2, 3, and 6 and are used to connect interface cards with hubs. When two computers are connected, the wires literally need to be crossed so that the talking wires on one side are going to the listening wires on the other side and vice versa. This is called a *crossover cable.* Crossover cable uses the same pins and makes direct connections between two servers or between two hubs that do not handle that crossover within a designated crossover port on a hub or switch.

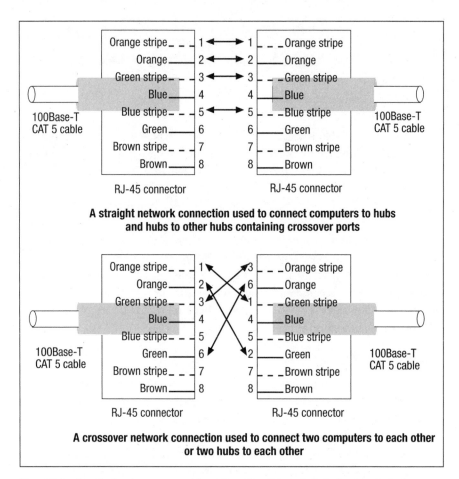

Figure 6.1 Standard and crossover cable configuration. Arrows in both diagrams indicate data-carrying wires.

For the purposes of the exam, hub-to-hub connections will not occur with crossover ports.

Coaxial

Coaxial cables are primarily used for audiovisual applications today, but formerly they were used for local area networks because the cable was cheaper, better shielded to help eliminate jitter, and could be longer than the telephone cable for 10/100Base-T. Coaxial cable is physically laid out in a line with computers that are linked via BNC connectors and terminating resistors on each end of the line to prevent data from literally falling off the end of the network. Coaxial, or coax, cable (also called 10Base-2, RG-52, or thinnet) is less flexible than phone cable and can carry more data. However, its maximum length is 185 meters, and the maximum data rate is 10Mbps, a fact that essentially slated it for mainstream extinction as soon as 100Base-T technology became available.

Another older coaxial type of cable exists called thicknet. Thicknet was a more expensive coaxial cable solution by which a main coax trunk or backbone existed to which all computers were attached. Attaching a computer was not a matter of plugging in a cable as it is with standard coax or RJ-45 connections. Connecting a new computer to a thicknet network consisted of literally cutting into the thick cable shielding and tapping into the main copper trunk. Once a connection was moved or removed, the connector remained in place; however, several random connectors could lead to jitter all by themselves, a fact that caused the connectors to be nicknamed "vampire taps."

Interface Cards

There are two types of network interface cards: Ethernet and Token Ring. Ethernet cards can be subdivided into 10/100Base-T and coaxial cable types. Network interface cards originally were circuit boards that were plugged into the motherboard bus.

These days, network interface card (NIC) boards are also being replaced by USB and wireless network cards. These latter technologies are less likely to be seen on server systems than on desktops, but they do bear mention as potential trouble-shooting tools and as useful technologies in temporary circumstances. Newer, exciting technologies for internal interface cards are becoming more common as systems gain the capability of booting to the network with the appropriate network card and BIOS support. Again, this USB networking technology is less common in server systems than PCI-based NICs but remains flexible enough for systems deployment and thin-client options.

Installing a network interface card is usually fairly easy. After the board itself has been installed and a network cable connected, a driver needs to be installed on the NOS in order to awaken the NOS to the card's presence and allow it to be used. For Windows NT and OS/2, this means specific drivers for the respective NOS. NetWare requires that NLMs be downloaded and installed for the hardware to function. Windows 2000 attempts to detect and install the network card during its boot process using plug-and-play technology. If the detection process or the driver fails, an updated Windows 2000-specific driver must be obtained from the manufacturer to complete the configuration process.

Windows NT, Windows 2000, and NetWare all support NIC-based routing, which is also called multihoming. When two separate networks require connectivity between one another without losing autonomy, a router is normally required to transfer the data from one network to the other. The multihoming features of these NOSs, on the other hand, literally connect the same computer to both networks using two separate network cards. This is also known as a "poor-man's router" because most true hardware routers add filtering, firewalling, and other security-related functionalities.

Other Networking Equipment

As we learned in the above section, all network cables have maximum lengths beyond which quality communication cannot occur. In order to extend a network's functional distance, a device called a repeater must be added to the network. A repeater simply takes the signals received form the network, amplifies them, and then rebroadcasts them. Today's advanced technologies have allowed the repeater's functionality to be added with other multiple-connection hardware devices to provide ever faster and more reliable networks.

For LAN connectivity, coax is the only cable type that does not require an intermediate connection device for the network to function. This is because computers are connected in-line with the coax cable itself and communications proceed apace. 10Base-T connections, as shown in Figure 6.1, require different pinouts depending upon the devices being connected. Repeaters do exist for Coax networks, but they are not common and are expensive. The price break between coax and 10/100Base-T usually occurs at the point where repeaters become necessary.

Hubs

Hubs are Ethernet devices that both repeat and amplify signals and act as central access connections for multiple networking devices. A hub literally connects devices in the star topology common for Ethernet. Hubs come in 10Base-T, 100Base-T, and 10/100Base-T speeds, with ports ranging in number from 4 to 64. It is possible to connect two computer devices using a crossover cable, and it is also possible to connect three computers using multiple network cards, but the best method of putting together a true Ethernet network is to purchase a hub and connect all systems to the hub. Because hubs are also repeaters, they can be used to extend the physical length of the network several times. Keep in mind, though that there is a logical limit of three hops from top to bottom before signal degradation begins to occur despite amplification. What this means is that a main hub can have a child hub, a grandchild hub, and a great-grandchild hub, but no more. Multiple children can exist in each generation, but the total number of generations should not exceed three. Connections between hubs can occur using either crossover cables or a straight cable connected to special crossover ports on each hub. Hubs can also be used to connect two separate networks in a similar manner to routers. The difference is that routers and multihomed systems are usually used to bridge wide-area or diverse networks.

MAUs

A Multistation Access Unit (MAU) is the Token Ring equivalent of a hub. Similar to a hub, the MAU contains the Token Ring that the network is based on. Computers are connected to MAUs either via RJ-45 connections or via IBM proprietary connectors.

Switches

Switching hubs, commonly called switches, are fast, intelligent hubs. To be more specific than this, it becomes necessary to describe different hub types in more detail. Most hubs simply rebroadcast traffic to all ports on the hub. These are called dumb hubs (for lack of a better term). Intelligent hubs continue to broadcast to all ports on the hub, but they also enable an administrator to manage the ports in such a manner that data and traffic can be monitored and optimized. Switching hubs take this feature one step further by identifying destination information in network packets (packets are bits of network data) and delivering the packet to the appropriate destination port rather than broadcasting the information to all ports. Instead of routing between networks like a router does, a switching hub routes between ports.

Routers and routing are not really covered in the Server+ exam because these technologies are internetworking-related rather than server-related. Don't be fooled: Any mention of routers or CSU/DSU units is meant to throw you off the scent.

Practice Questions

Question 1

What types of devices should be connected with the RJ-45 cable shown in Figure 6.2?

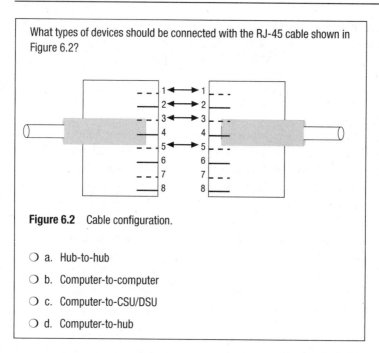

Figure 6.2 Cable configuration.

○ a. Hub-to-hub

○ b. Computer-to-computer

○ c. Computer-to-CSU/DSU

○ d. Computer-to-hub

Answer d is correct. Straight cables run from computer to hub. Answer a is incorrect because the exam assumes that hub-to-hub connections are made with a crossover cable. Answer b is incorrect because a direct computer-to-computer connection requires a crossover cable. Answer c is incorrect because CSU/DSU units are not covered in the exam.

Question 2

What types of devices should be connected with the RJ-45 cable shown in Figure 6.3?

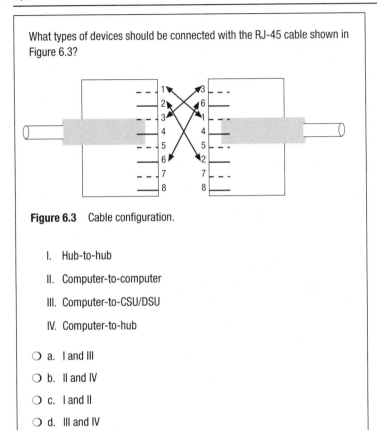

Figure 6.3 Cable configuration.

    I. Hub-to-hub

    II. Computer-to-computer

    III. Computer-to-CSU/DSU

    IV. Computer-to-hub

  ○ a. I and III

  ○ b. II and IV

  ○ c. I and II

  ○ d. III and IV

The correct answer is c. Crossover cables are required for both hub-to-hub connections and computer-to-computer connections. Answers a and d are incorrect because the exam does not cover CSU/DSU units. Answer b is incorrect because a computer-to-hub connection is a straight-through connection, which is not what is shown in the illustration.

Question 3

> Which interface method is the fastest?
>
> ○ a. SCSI
>
> ○ b. USB
>
> ○ c. IEEE 1394
>
> ○ d. RS232

Answer a is correct. SCSI devices run faster than all others on this list. Answers b, c, and d are all incorrect because they are not as fast as SCSI.

Question 4

> You recently hooked a UPS to your server and when you power the system on, the UPS shows an alarm indicating that the battery is overloaded. What caused the overload?
>
> ○ a. Monitor
>
> ○ b. Modem
>
> ○ c. CPU
>
> ○ d. KVM

Answer a is correct. The monitor adds the greatest power load to the entire system. Answer b is incorrect because a modem consumes little power and in many cases is not mission-critical, so it is probably not attached to a UPS to begin with. Answer c is incorrect because you should assume that the UPS was rated for this server prior to purchase. Answer d is incorrect because a KVM does not consume as much electricity as a monitor.

Question 5

You have connected a modem to your server and rebooted the system. What else must you do to complete the installation?

○ a. Load the proper NLM

○ b. Run setup from the NOS installation disk

○ c. Exit and down the server again

○ d. Nothing

Answer a is correct. The driver must be loaded for the modem to work. Answer b is incorrect because running setup from the NOS disk will install the NOS. Answer c is incorrect because there is no reason to reboot the server again. Answer d is incorrect because device drivers must be loaded in all situations.

Question 6

You have connected a USB printer to your server and it does not work. You connect it to a different server and it does work. What's the problem?

○ a. The printer is broken.

○ b. The USB port on the first server is malfunctioning.

○ c. The USB port on the second server is malfunctioning.

○ d. USB devices are not supported on the first server.

Answer d is correct. Of all of the NOSs covered in the exam, Windows 2000 is the only one that supports USB connections, which means that not only is the USB port on the second server working (answer c) but also that the printer is not broken (answer a). Answers a and c are therefore incorrect because the printer works on the second server. Answer b is incorrect because hardware failure is far less likely than lack of NOS support.

Question 7

You are in the process of documenting emergency procedures during a power outage. You determine that in order to increase UPS battery time, several devices can be powered down without compromising server availability. What are these devices?

   I. Monitor

   II. UPS

   III. Hub

   IV. Tape Drive

  ○ a. I and II

  ○ b. III and IV

  ○ c. I and IV

  ○ d. II and III

Answer c is correct. Both the monitor and the tape drive can be powered off without reducing server availability. Answer a is incorrect because powering off the UPS will cause the server to lose power also. Answer b is incorrect because a hub is what provides network availability to the server. Answer d is incorrect for both reasons: powering off the UPS will cause the server to lose power, and powering off the hub makes the network no longer available to the server.

Note: Keep in mind that although a given piece of equipment might be without power, other parts of the network might still be receiving power. You need to maintain that network availability to the server.

Question 8

On which multi-connection networking device would you find a crossover port?

I.   Hub

II. MAU

III. Switch

IV. NIC

○ a. I and III

○ b. II and IV

○ c. II and III

○ d. I and IV

Answer a is correct. Hubs and switches can have crossover ports. Answers b and c are incorrect because MAUs are used for token ring networks and do not require crossovers to communicate directly between devices. Answer d is incorrect because NICs don't utilize multiple connections.

Question 9

Which of the following is not a peripheral?

○ a. UPS

○ b. Printer

○ c. SCSI array

○ d. Modem

The correct answer is c. The SCSI array—even when it's external—is essential to the functionality of a server; therefore it is not a peripheral. Answers a, b, and d are all incorrect because any given server can perform basic standard functions without these devices.

Need to Know More?

 Craft, Melissa, Mark A. Poplar, David V. Watts, and Will Willis. *Network+ Exam Prep*. Scottsdale, AZ: The Coriolis Group, 1999. ISBN 1-57610-412-5. Information on networking and cable connectivity.

 Zacker, Craig and Paul Doyle. *Upgrading and Repairing Networks*. Indianapolis, IN: Que Corporation, 1996. ISBN 0-78970181-2. An outstanding reference for specifics and how-tos on everything networking. If there were a single non-exam-related source of information that is covered in the exam, this book would be it.

 www.novell.com. This Web site is a general source for documentation on supported technologies such as USB and IEEE 1394.

 www.pcwebopedia.com. This Web site is a great launch pad for any IT research project. Enter the name of any IT topic that interests you, and not only will the definition appear, but hyperlinks to other technical definitions for words used in the definition are also shown, as are hyperlinks to sites on the World Wide Web that have more in-depth information on that topic.

 www.mouse.demon.nl. *Connector Reference Chart* contains drawings of every type of known PC connector. It is a great reference for the proper names for these connectors.

 www.hardwarebook.net. This is a comprehensive adapter, cable, connector, and circuit Web site containing pinouts and diagrams for every conceivable type of cable and connector.

Diagnostic and Management Tools

Terms you'll need to understand:

✓ Diagnostic
✓ Baseline
✓ BIOS
✓ NOS
✓ MSD
✓ MEM
✓ IPCONFIG/IFCONFIG
✓ NETSTAT
✓ HWCONFIG
✓ DFSPACE
✓ ESD
✓ POST
✓ Paging
✓ SNMP
✓ MIB
✓ RMON

Techniques you'll need to master:

✓ Gathering active and passive baseline information
✓ Taking system inventory
✓ Avoiding electrostatic discharge on a system

With the Server+ exam, there are several terms and concepts that you will not find on any other CompTIA exam. For the most part, these are specific to a server platform and are pretty much tied into the concept that a server must be up and running more reliably than an average desktop. Certain standard utilities, such as PING, IPCONFIG, IFCONFIG, and TRACERT, are more tuned toward configuration and troubleshooting and will be covered in Chapter 10. Server-specific applications, concepts, and utilities are covered in this chapter.

Diagnostic and Baselining Tools

Diagnostic tools are utilities and programs that are used to determine the health and welfare of a server. Just like human babies or pets, servers do not necessarily talk in a manner that you can understand. When we suspect that something is wrong with a baby or pet, we take them to a doctor or veterinarian who is trained in the art of healing and knows what to look for and expect with the patient. Unfortunately, we cannot do this with servers because we are the ones who are supposed to be the doctors in this particular situation. Despite the differences in our "patients," we can learn techniques from doctors and other scientists by looking at their methodologies and adapting them to suit our needs.

One of the main things that doctors know about a patient is what the "norm" should be for several different critical indicators. For instance, there are well-known factors that can indicate a state of healthiness such as heartbeat, temperature, and blood pressure along with a host of others. In the computer world, these factors are called *baselines*. In the same way that a doctor can measure your temperature and compare it with a healthy baseline, you can check certain functions within a server and compare those functions with known baselines in order to determine the relative healthiness of the server. Without a baseline to reference, a doctor would not know if a human temperature of 105 degrees Fahrenheit is bad or not; the same concept applies to computers as well. Unfortunately, servers come in all shapes, functions, and sizes, and it is difficult for administrators to simply look up one of these baselines in a book and memorize it. Instead, you need to carefully monitor the health and welfare of your server in order to gather "known good" data.

Methods of Gathering Baseline Information

There are two different ways of gathering baseline type information: *active* and *passive*. Let's consider the previous human doctor analogy. A doctor uses a stethoscope to listen to your heartbeat and determine how many times a minute it is beating. Before the doctor can use the stethoscope to measure your heartbeat, he must know that you have a heart to begin with. Doctors spend quite a while learning the parts of the human body, and you need to spend some time learning about the parts of a server. Because servers are different from one another, it is important to recognize that just knowing there is a CPU, memory, and a hard disk in a server is not sufficient to do the job. It is also important to know the speeds and capacities of these components. This type of information is called passive because it generally does not change.

The actual process of measuring a patient's heartbeat, however, is an active means of gathering information because the doctor is actually doing something to gather information, which itself is dynamic. Transitioning this scenario to the computer world should be pretty easy: You all know that computers must have RAM in order to function. The amount of RAM that is on board a server is a passive piece of information. Monitoring memory usage, however, is an active means of getting some information because you actually look at how well something is doing its job.

Personal experience will tell you that if memory usage is zero, something is very wrong with your server, and you need to begin to troubleshoot the problem. If, on the other hand, information shows that 256MB of memory are being used when you only have 128MB, this might also be cause for concern. As with any human illness, you need to know the server components that contribute toward wellness as well as their levels of activity when they are healthy.

Passive Baseline Information

As we hinted previously, passive baseline information consists of a mid-to-high level inventory of the critical components in a server system. For the most part, these components include CPU, memory, and hard disk drives. Often you need to include external information such as network connections as well. Basically, anything that is mission-critical to the hardware functionality of the server should be properly catalogued.

BIOS

As discussed in Chapter 5, the BIOS is basically the system coordinator when the server is first turned on. Quite often, the BIOS contains information on the major components of a server such as memory, the CPU, and hard disk drives. Network information is usually not shown at this stage because it is not necessary at boot. The information that the BIOS actively uses is often displayed on the screen during the boot process.

SCSI information usually does not appear as part of the BIOS because many SCSI controllers have their own processors that handle this information. The BIOS queries the SCSI devices, which then display specific information on the screen after the initial BIOS display is complete.

Operating System (OS)/Network Operating System (NOS) Tools

Many operating system and network operating system tools exist for the purpose of gathering passive and active information about the server. DOS-based versions of NetWare can use MSD, MEM, IPCONFIG, and NETSTAT to gather information about the entire system, memory, and networking components. Windows NT and 2000 can use MEM, system information, Control Panel|System, IPCONFIG, NETSTAT, and listings shown in system properties to get information about memory, the entire system, and networking. Unix and Linux both utilize HWCONFIG, DFSPACE, NETSTAT, and IFCONFIG to show system information, disk drive information, and networking properties. All OS/NOS versions covered on the exam will run FDISK, which is a utility that tells you about the hard disk drive partitions and configuration.

➤ MSD.EXE is an application that was originally included with Windows 3.1, but has been shipped with MS-DOS and Windows 9x. If your NetWare system runs DOS, or a clipped version of Windows 95 or 98, you might use MSD.EXE to give you a thorough rundown on system hardware, memory, IRQs, direct memory access (DMA) calls, and memory addresses.

➤ MEM.EXE is an application that is available with all Microsoft platforms and operating systems. Earlier versions of MEM were used to help shuffle loaded memory apps into upper and extended memory in order to allow enough lower memory to run active applications. This particular "shuffling" practice effectively became obsolete when Windows 95 was introduced because Windows 95 handled extended memory management outside of the DOS shell. The **MEM** command has three valuable switches for use in baselining: **/P**, **/D**, and **/C**. The **/P** represents program. Entering **MEM /P** results in an output of all loaded applications. The **/D** (debug) switch is similar to **/P**, but provides additional entries for device drivers and environmental variables.

➤ IPCONFIG and IFCONFIG are utilities for the DOS/Windows and Unix platforms, respectively. Both utilities display the current IP addresses assigned to network cards on the system. They also re-lease and renew leased IP configuration information obtained from a DHCP server. There are several switches available with IPCONFIG and IFCONFIG; however, all you really need to be aware of right now is the **/ALL** switch, which is shown at the top of Figure 7.1. Notice that the system shown in the figure is a DHCP client that has received its TCP/IP configuration information from a DHCP server.

➤ NETSTAT.EXE (shown in the lower portion of Figure 7.1) shows current connections to or from the system. **NETSTAT -R** shows the routing table for the current system. **NETSTAT -A** shows all connections and ports that are being used on the system. **NETSTAT -E** shows Ethernet statistics for the

```
C:\>ipconfig /all

Windows 2000 IP Configuration

        Host Name . . . . . . . . . . . . : bullet
        Primary DNS Suffix . . . . . . . :
        Node Type . . . . . . . . . . . . : Mixed
        IP Routing Enabled. . . . . . . . : No
        WINS Proxy Enabled. . . . . . . . : No

Ethernet adapter USB:

        Connection-specific DNS Suffix  . :
        Description . . . . . . . . . . . : EZ Connect USB/Ethernet Converter
        Physical Address. . . . . . . . . : 00-E0-29-94-39-99
        DHCP Enabled. . . . . . . . . . . : Yes
        Autoconfiguration Enabled . . . . : Yes
        IP Address. . . . . . . . . . . . : 192.168.0.212
        Subnet Mask . . . . . . . . . . . : 255.255.255.0
        Default Gateway . . . . . . . . . : 192.168.0.1
        DHCP Server . . . . . . . . . . . : 206.80.192.1
        DNS Servers . . . . . . . . . . . : 206.80.192.1
                                            204.147.80.5

        Lease Obtained. . . . . . . . . . : Saturday, June 16, 2001 12:38:18 PM
        Lease Expires . . . . . . . . . . : Saturday, June 23, 2001 12:38:18 PM

C:\>netstat

Active Connections

  Proto  Local Address          Foreign Address             State
  TCP    bullet:1600            msgr-ns46.msgr.hotmail.com:1863  ESTABLISHED
  TCP    bullet:1959            PROFESSIONAL:netbios-ssn    ESTABLISHED
  TCP    bullet:1966            pop.phnx.uswest.net:pop3    TIME_WAIT

C:\>_
```

Figure 7.1   IPCONFIG and NETSTAT.

system. From the -E switch in particular, you get a good idea of what the average percent error rate is.

➤ HWCONFIG can be used on a Unix or Linux system for both passive and active baselining. When used with the -C switch, HWCONFIG checks for device conflicts, which is something you may need to do when troubleshooting; however, you must first determine the normal status. Sometimes conflicts are okay as long as the proper functionality is working. Windows NT and 2000 are similar to Unix in that much of the system functions are logged-in-user specific. The HWCONFIG utility displays the configuration for the current user. Other users can be queried by using the -F switch and defining a separate input file.

➤ DFSPACE is similar to the Microsoft utility CHKDSK. DFSPACE displays disk space used, percentage occupied, and total disk space available. Incidentally, DFSCK will repair problems. CHKDSK essentially performs the job of both DFSPACE and DFSCK combined.

For the exam, you need to be aware that both IPCONFIG and IFCONFIG are used to show TCP/IP information on the server. Most servers are not DHCP clients, but you also need to know that these tools can release and renew DHCP information.

Third-Party Tools

Many companies offer third-party tools that essentially inventory the hardware and software on your system. Because an inventory process is easy to carry out, most of these tools also include active diagnostic, troubleshooting, and remediation tools. When purchasing third-party tools of this type, ensure that they are designed to work with the NOS and version that you are running on your server.

 I once had a utility that tracked and reported directory service information on the fly. It was a very good tool to have handy; however, it had a memory leak and caused the server to dump once a week. It took hours of downtime and troubleshooting to find the culprit because it was so difficult to determine exactly what change was causing the problem. My personal advice to you is that you should not put any application on your server that is not essential to its functionality.

In the interest of maintaining stability within your server environment, it is a good idea to thoroughly investigate the utility before using it. If it maintains a system process or daemon (a piece of the app that is awake all the time, waiting for or performing tasks), you might want to disable that function or uninstall the app when you do not need it.

Server Management Tools

Server management tools, although similar in nature to the BIOS in that they perform essential system functions, can also contain passive types of information about the server. Server management tools are the de-facto standard for any true server on the market. These management tools—called by any number of different marketing type names—are usually glorified BIOS applications that are accessible via a boot disk, partition, or CD. They basically take all of the more complex parts of a server configuration process and make them simpler by wrapping a graphical user interface around them.

Server management application utility features include BIOS configuration, disk management and configuration, Simple Network Management Protocol (SNMP) settings, component installation and configuration, and basic diagnostics. Most of these management programs also include a feature that will eliminate and then reload the operating system for you. With the possible exception of SNMP settings, each of these features can be used to glean information about your server. The reasoning behind such a hefty group of features is primarily for ease of use and configuration. Keep in mind that a fully loaded server may have multiple CPUs, RAID, fault-tolerant PCI buses and memory banks, redundant fans, and power supplies.

Physical Inspection and a Word of Warning

There should always be a way for you to determine a basic hardware inventory. If for some reason you cannot, or if your company requires detailed inventory information for a capital asset program, you may need to open the system and take a look at the internal components. If you do, do not expect to garner much information. Unless you are running a very old server, CPUs are covered by heat sinks nowadays. Therefore, you will only be able to tell whether you are running multiple CPUs, a Pentium II processor, or a Xeon processor. With memory, you will only be able to tell how many single inline memory modules (SIMMs) are installed on which bays. Most SIMMs are not labeled with their capacity. Hard disk drives, on the other hand, are quite often labeled with manufacturer, model, and capacity information.

My personal rule of thumb is to avoid "cracking the case" to look inside a server unless something is broken and needs replacing. Even then, you should never do so without proper precautions. The reasons for this are simple: electricity and electrostatic discharge (ESD). Electricity and people do not usually go together and avoiding this particular health hazard usually involves shutting down the server—something that is often frowned upon because the goal is to keep your servers up and running as much as possible. ESD events are the static discharges that happen when you touch something that conducts electricity. When you accidentally discharge by touching a doorknob or car door, the effect is usually a small spark, a snap of pain, and some annoyance. The delicate components in a server (or any computer for that matter) are a different matter entirely. Computers contain circuits that are attached to various and sundry working electrical components. When an ESD event occurs on a computer, the wire you touched transmits the electrical charge along the circuit until one of four activities occurs:

➤ The circuit reaches ground and the charge is dispersed.

➤ The electricity follows the circuit to a component that safely absorbs and disperses the electrical charge.

➤ The electricity follows the circuit to a component that cannot absorb the electrical charge, and the component is damaged.

➤ The wire in the circuit is too small to carry the electrical current, and the current essentially burns a hole in the wire.

What makes ESD events so heinous is that they can be smaller than you might feel or detect, and you do not always need to physically touch something for the electrostatic charge to jump from you to the computer in the same way a lightning rod attracts lightning. You may have seen pictures of people dressed in big overall suits with gloves and masks and booties working at computer manufacturer plants such as Intel. These are just a few of the precautions taken to avoid ESD events, particularly because the circuits within a CPU chip are so very tiny that any electrostatic discharge will destroy the chip.

Even when the system is turned off, ESD events can occur when a person or object has an electrical charge that is different from that of the server. You can avoid damage in most environments by touching the server chassis while it is still plugged in. You can do this without additional equipment; however, it is better to purchase a wrist strap for a minimal cost at most computer stores or on the Web that clips onto the chassis. If you have a wrist strap, clip it on, and wear it any time you work on a server. If you do not, be sure to touch the server chassis often to compensate for movements you make (shuffling your feet on carpet, for example) that might incur a charge. Be aware that many servers' Wake-on-LAN may activate the server if any electrical current reaches the LAN port. Unplugging LAN connections can help avoid this occurrence, and ultimately disabling Wake-on-LAN eliminates this possibility altogether. If you feel more comfortable with the server unplugged, touch the server chassis anyway. The server itself may be holding an electrical charge, but as long as the two of you are holding the same levels, you should be okay.

If you are lucky enough to work in a more structured environment, you may be able to electrically neutralize yourself to ground by different methods involving wrist straps and heel straps. Wrist straps traditionally plug into tech benches that are grounded and should be worn and plugged in any time you work on a system. Many companies will add an extra dose of precaution by installing special flooring that is electrically grounded. Environments such as these require that you wear a heel strap made from conductive rubber that not only discharges static electricity, but also keeps you electrically neutral any time your feet touch the floor. Many companies use a combination of both wrist and heel straps along with grounded benches and floors in order to ensure complete and thorough protection for the equipment being serviced, maintained, or manufactured. The "bunny suits," or additional clothing and equipment you see worn by some people are used in environments where additional precautions are taken to avoid gathering an electrostatic charge by isolating the person from conductivity in the environment.

Active Baseline Information

Unlike passive baselining, active baseline information is gathered by taking measurable observations of different components working at normal efficiency. An advantage of gathering active baseline information is that the process is the same as the troubleshooting process. You may wonder why baselining is not part of troubleshooting. The reason is that troubleshooting involves trained problem-solving skills, which are difficult and require time to learn. The topic deserves its own chapter (and book, for that matter). Baselining uses many of the same tools you use in troubleshooting, but is necessary on its own because you need to know what the norm is in order to help with those problem-solving processes involved in troubleshooting.

Power On Self Test (POST)

As discussed in Chapter 5, POST is a very specific process performed by the BIOS during the boot process. The POST process basically queries the server's major components and determines whether they are functioning properly. If any of these components are not functioning, the server will beep a number of times to indicate the malfunctioning component. POST occurs before the monitor even receives data signals, so the POST has no choice but to respond to base-level hardware errors with beeps. In fact, the error could have something to do with the monitor itself. POST issues are primarily related to troubleshooting; however, there are times when POST beeps are the "norm" (such as headless systems), and you should record these normalities as baselines.

Note: BIOS is still a valuable tool for active baselining. Make a note of what comes up on the screen during a normal boot. That way you will know what to look for if a problem arises at the BIOS hardware level.

Network Monitor/Performance Monitor

Both Network Monitor and Performance Monitor are utilities exclusive to Windows. Although CompTIA focuses on vendor neutrality, there is no way to describe the functionality that comes with these two tools and their equivalent components within the NetWare, OS/2, or Unix world.

When performing active baselines, it is important to gather information on anything that could possibly slow down the server. In the process of doing so, you need to look at how hard disk, CPU, and memory usage work independently of each other, and also gather information on how they interrelate. In the troubleshooting world, it is a very good idea to understand how full or partial failures in one of these three areas affects the other two. The reason for this is because any given server or computer is a balanced environment consisting of several components working together. If one of those components fails, you might not see the negative impact immediately. Instead, the failure is likely to start a domino effect where other components become increasingly overloaded. Recognizing that an overloaded hard disk drive is not necessarily a hard disk problem is part of the "art" of troubleshooting. Again, before you can even begin to troubleshoot, you need baseline information on the individual components as well as baselines specific to interrelations between components.

➤ *Hard disk drive*—Gather baseline data on how often the hard disk drive is being used. Additionally, counters for faults and queue lengths can help determine whether a hard disk upgrade, replacement, or other action is necessary.

➤ *Memory*—Determine used and available amounts of memory. This information is an appropriate counter that is ultimately used in conjunction with paging baselines in order to determine if more RAM is required on a server.

➤ *CPU*—Determine how often the processor is being used as a norm. Percent utilization is an ideal counter that should tell you the kinds of loads the CPU is under.

➤ *Paging*—Determine the page file utilization. Most NOSs have a method of virtual memory that utilizes a page file located on the hard drive. The page file is usually a set size. This information provides a valid means of determining how well the hard disk and RAM are working together. When there is not enough RAM to perform a given task, the system will literally rip a "page" of active memory and shuffle it temporarily out to the hard drive. When it needs it again, it will shuffle it back. Windows client and server operating systems rely on paging even when RAM is available, so it is no longer safe to say that any paging activity indicates a RAM shortage. Again, this is why you need this active baseline: to determine the norm.

➤ *Application specific counters*—Determine application-specific counters. Network Monitor and Performance Monitor counters are sometimes available for specific installed applications such as Web services or database servers. In Microsoft NOSs, these counters will most likely be additional counters within Network Monitor or Performance Monitor. NetWare is more likely to have a separate console per application that displays efficiency results. Whichever NOS you use, you will need to gather data appropriately for baseline information.

 Gathering active baseline information is no small task. After all, if you gather information in the middle of the night, it won't do you any good because no one is using the system. You need to gather baseline information over the course of at least a few days, if not a week.

➤ *Network efficiency*—Determine percent usage on the wire, collisions, and bad packets of your network. If you are fortunate enough to have a Network Monitor, it might have features to measure percent usage baselines for these factors. All three are features you would use with a network analyzer tool; however, you may be able to find similar tools within a Network Monitor application. If you do not have a network analyzer (such as Fluke's LANalyzer) or a network monitor that will give you these baselines, Remote Monitor (RMON) may be the solution for you.

SNMP/RMON

Using the SNMP and RMON, you can set counters for specific network and computer information. These counters can be integrated into a reporting application that will give you your active baseline information. wewill focus more on SNMP and RMON in the "Management Tools" section of this chapter.

System Logs

Nearly all NOSs have a system log. System logs usually contain a variety of startup, shutdown, and major application events. Take a look at your system logs. Note all events other than startup and shutdown that should be considered "normal."

Management Tools

In addition to the server management tools discussed in the previous section, there are other utilities that are more focused toward reporting the current status of the server and specific server processes.

SNMP

Both SNMP and RMON are similar to Unix daemons, Windows NT services, or NetWare loadable modules (NLMs) . They are essentially little applets that stay awake all the time gathering information and waiting for a specific trigger to occur before performing a task. Unlike its name, SNMP is not really a protocol because it does not encapsulate and transport data across the wire. SNMP is a label for a standardized suite of services that live on a server and installed client machines.

SNMP consists of two parts: a manager and an agent. As shown in Figure 7.2, the manager application is usually installed on a server, and it is responsible for managing and coordinating the frequency and types of data that the agents gather. Agents, on the other hand, are installed on other servers or workstations and are responsible for gathering data per the manager's instructions. Each type of data that an agent reports on is known as a *trap* because the agent literally traps the dates and times that specific events occur. The manager coordinates these traps into miniature databases known as management information bases (MIBs) that can then be read and analyzed by a user interface application, such as Netview or Openview.

Both SNMP and RMON by themselves really do not do much. Commands basically include get, get next, set, and trap. With only these simple commands available, you can imagine that there are many functional limitations of SNMP and RMON. Realistically, if you want to view, analyze, and report on the data gathered by the agents and presented by the manager, SNMP and RMON must be adopted by

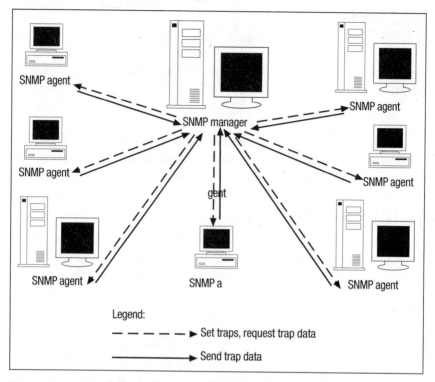

Figure 7.2 A typical SNMP configuration where the SNMP manager sets traps and requests trap data from each of the systems where an agent is installed. The agents, in turn, trap the requested data and send it.

an interface program such as Netview, Openview, or any number of other network management tools. Both SNMP and RMON do, however, use the UDP and IP protocols and require either Ethernet or Token Ring to function.

Many of these interface programs present system information graphically, where computer icons appear on the screen with corresponding colors to indicate whether the system in question is working or not. In past versions of the programs, it was possible to double-click on a computer's icon and view configuration information such as IP address and system name, but there were no hooks to remotely control the server from within the program, and there really was no way to interface with a server. One additional valuable feature that most of these interface programs did make available was the ability to page or email someone when a system became unavailable. This provided a huge advantage for administrators of mission-critical systems, especially because the technology supported this functionality coming from a system other than the affected—and downed—server.

When SNMP was first available, it could only report on whether or not a particular server was functioning based on trap responses. Because of this limited functionality, many user interface (UI) applications manufacturers added functionality to the core SNMP that was specific to their market segment needs. Eventually many of these manufacturers got together in an attempt to create a new version of SNMP. Unfortunately, opposing viewpoints and political infighting delayed the project indefinitely.

RMON

RMON came into existence by way of a group of people who were basically tired of waiting for SNMP version 2. Instead, they got together and agreed upon several add-on features for gathering data in nine additional categories. The result was a total of 10 different categories and functionality that acted much the same as SNMP. Quite often when you hear SNMP, people are really talking RMON, especially if the data has anything to do with network traffic.

Where strict SNMP monitors computer functionality, RMON can check noncomputer device functionality, such as hubs, switches, and routers as well as more in-depth information about the computers. Of course, in order to be able to do this, the devices in question must support RMON. RMON has the ability to do nearly everything that an advanced network analyzer can do without having to move about and plug into separate network segments.

The interface application, coupled with SNMP and RMON, still provides a graphical representation of computers with colors to indicate up or down status, but the additional RMON functionality tells you much more about the system as well as information about the network. With an RMON supported interface, an operator can double-click on the icon for a server and determine which protocols it supports, which ones are being used, and even how much network traffic it is producing. The same operator can double-click on a line on the screen representing a local area network (LAN) link and determine the network activity that is crossing that link down to the protocol and packet level. Similar to a network analyzer, RMON functionality can be tied into the interface application to filter, block, or allow network packets based upon their source or destination. Additional diagnostics can be performed based on filtered packets.

Figure 7.3 shows an ideal situation where RMON shines over SNMP. Notice that the Token Ring network is traveling clockwise.

Token Ring is different from Ethernet in that no two systems can communicate at the same time. Ethernet uses a method where many systems talk at once, and if they run into each other, they just say the words over again. Token Ring maintains

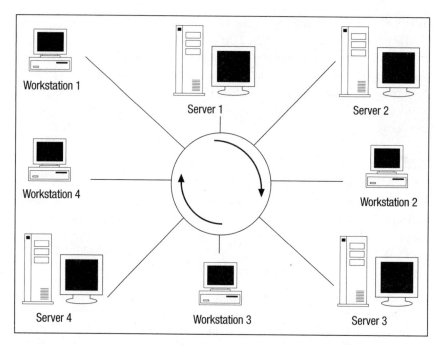

Figure 7.3 A Token Ring network where the token is traveling clockwise.

the "one at a time" rule by passing a baton, called a token, from one system to another. The token literally travels around the ring, being passed from system to system as in a relay race. For the sake of truly showing RMON functionality, let's discuss troubleshooting just a bit. Let's assume that all of the systems clockwise after Server 3 in Figure 7.3 are receiving numerous network errors. In the past, you needed to walk to the locations of each system, plug in a network analyzer on the network between each system, track the kinds of packets going back and forth, and determine which ones might be bad. Eventually, by plugging into cable after cable, you would find that a problem existed with Workstation 3's network card or ring speed. With RMON, you can analyze the same information between systems all at the same time (instead of gathering information one at a time manually) and without walking from system to system. The result is that you can target network problems exponentially faster by using RMON than if you used a network analyzer (which is very expensive) or if you were troubleshooting the problem in a more primitive manner by shutting down systems and isolating the problem in that way.

Practice Questions

Question 1

Which of the following is not a valid switch for the MEM.EXE command?

○ a. **/C**

○ b. **/D**

○ c. **/F**

○ d. **/P**

Answer c is correct. The switch /F is not a valid switch for the MEM.EXE command. The switches /C, /D, and /P are commands to classify, debug, and list programs in memory. Therefore, answers a, b, and d are incorrect.

Question 2

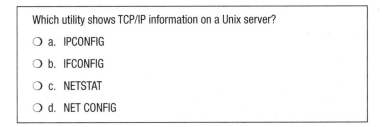

Which utility shows TCP/IP information on a Unix server?

○ a. IPCONFIG

○ b. IFCONFIG

○ c. NETSTAT

○ d. NET CONFIG

Answer b is correct. IFCONFIG is used to display and renew IP information on a Unix or Linux server. Answer a is incorrect because IPCONFIG is used on DOS/Windows platforms. NETSTAT shows the current network status; therefore, answer c is incorrect. Answer d is incorrect because NET CONFIG is a Microsoft networking command.

Question 3

> Which utility shows IP information on a Windows 2000 server?
>
> ○ a. IPCONFIG
> ○ b. IFCONFIG
> ○ c. NETSTAT
> ○ d. NET CONFIG

Answer a is correct. IPCONFIG is used to display IP information on a Windows 2000 server. IFCONFIG is used for Unix and Linux systems; therefore, answer b is incorrect. Answer c is incorrect because NETSTAT shows current network status, and answer d is incorrect because NET CONFIG is a Microsoft networking command.

Question 4

> Which application displays the status of a remote server?
>
> ○ a. SNMP
> ○ b. RMON
> ○ c. Performance Monitor
> ○ d. Network Monitor

Answer a is correct. SNMP will tell you whether a remote server is up or down. Answer b is incorrect because RMON displays additional server and network information. Answers c and d are incorrect because Performance Monitor and Network Monitor are both tuned toward local system statistics.

Question 5

> Which application displays the status of a remote hub?
>
> ○ a. SNMP
> ○ b. RMON
> ○ c. Performance Monitor
> ○ d. Network Monitor

Answer b is correct. RMON tells you information about network devices, whereas SNMP only shows you server up or down status; therefore, answer a is incorrect. Answers c and d are incorrect because Performance Monitor and Network Monitor are both tuned toward local system statistics.

Question 6

> You receive a page indicating that network utilization has reached 10 percent. What do you do?
>
> ○ a. Upgrade the network
>
> ○ b. Reboot
>
> ○ c. Nothing
>
> ○ d. Reset RMON to trap network utilization at 60 percent

Answer d is correct. A 10 percent network utilization is actually very low in a normal working environment. If anything, you should celebrate. Answer a is incorrect because there is no justification for upgrading the network. Answer b is incorrect because rebooting a single system or server is unlikely to change network utilization. Answer c is incorrect because you will still receive inappropriate notifications regarding network utilization.

Question 7

> Which of the following is not a Linux utility?
>
> ○ a. CHKDSK
>
> ○ b. IFCONFIG
>
> ○ c. DFSPACE
>
> ○ d. HWCONFIG

Answer a is correct. CHKDSK is exclusive to the Microsoft OS/NOS platforms. Answers b, c, and d are incorrect because they are all Unix/Linux exclusive commands.

Question 8

What is the name of the location where SNMP trap information is stored?

- ○ a. RAM
- ○ b. Hard disk
- ○ c. MIB
- ○ d. Local database

Answer c is correct. SNMP data is stored in MIB. Answers a, b, and c are all incorrect because, although they can be temporary storage locations for the MIB, they are not the storage location of the data.

Question 9

What's the difference between SNMP and RMON?

- ○ a. SNMP monitors network devices, whereas RMON monitors servers and workstations
- ○ b. SNMP monitors servers and workstations, whereas RMON monitors network devices
- ○ c. SNMP monitors servers and workstations, whereas RMON monitors servers, workstations, and network devices
- ○ d. SNMP monitors network devices, whereas RMON monitors servers, workstations, and network devices.

Answer c is correct. SNMP can monitor the state of a server or workstation. RMON does this as well and has the additional capability of monitoring network devices such as routers and hubs. Answers a and d are incorrect because SNMP cannot monitor network devices. Answer b is incorrect because RMON monitors more than just network devices.

Need to Know More?

 http://content.techweb.com/se/directlink.cgi?cwk1997082550061 contains the article "RMON Rocks On" by Oliver Rist, August 26, 1997, Issue 678. This exceptional article explains RMON functionality and the differences between RMON and SNMP.

 http://support.baynetworks.com provides great support and background information on SNMP.

 www.pcguide.com is a site, developed by Charles M. Kozierok and similar to TechRepublic, that contains a wealth of information on many IT topics.

Server Types

Terms you'll need to understand:

✓ Server-based networking
✓ Peer-to-peer networking
✓ Protocol
✓ Gateway
✓ Bridge
✓ Router
✓ Firewall
✓ Proxy
✓ Remote Access
✓ Mail server
✓ Database server
✓ Client/server
✓ Fax server
✓ SNA
✓ Web server
✓ FTP
✓ DNS
✓ WINS
✓ DHCP

Techniques you'll need to master:

✓ Describing server-based network structures
✓ Describing peer-to-peer network structures
✓ Distinguishing among different types of network servers
✓ Recognizing application server types
✓ Differentiating between name resolution and protocol servers

Network Types

When we first began working in the IT industry, the only PC-based servers were file and print servers loaded on a large piece of equipment located in a chilly, fireproof server room. At the time, Windows and OS/2 did not exist as networking platforms, Unix was not an option, and NetWare was the only NOS available for small and midsize companies. PCs were just becoming popular. I distinctly remember that most "computer" people were fascinated that computing now required a big box under their desks instead of a dumb terminal.

A few years later, two major technological innovations occurred in the PC industry. First, desktop systems became available with the same hardware qualifications as the best servers. Second, different types of PC-based servers became available, essentially changing the definition of a server from "box-based" to "function-based." If you were presented with a 386DX computer with 16MB of RAM, you could not be sure whether it was a server or a desktop computer. Confusion was rampant: A server could be defined as an ordinary PC on someone's desk, or worse yet, multiple server functions could be run on a single optimized computer. In order to prevent confusion in this chapter as well as on the exam, consider a server as a function or service that runs on a computer rather than the computer itself.

 Remember that when the word "server" is being used, it can refer to either a server computer or a server *process* running on a computer.

Server-Based Networks

Server-based networks are simply a group of networked computers where any number of different services are provided by a centralized authority server. As shown in Figure 8.1, network workstations request information from this centralized authority server. These different services are described as being network, application, or resolution and protocol servers. The centralized authority usually includes security and authentication that controls access to certain files, functions, and applications. Having a centralized authority does not necessarily require having only one server. Quite the opposite, as both NetWare and Windows NT/2000 support multiple servers not only to handle more services and better access, but also to provide redundancy and fault tolerance.

Keep in mind that for the most part, networking is not really a new idea. Most of the concepts, ideas, implementations, and engineering came from the mainframe or Unix world. DOS was based on the Unix command set, and Windows NT is also Unix-based. Even before DOS and Unix, the original computer network was a mainframe that allowed client "network" connections through a dumb terminal. Soon after the PC was invented, the industry saw the need to connect the

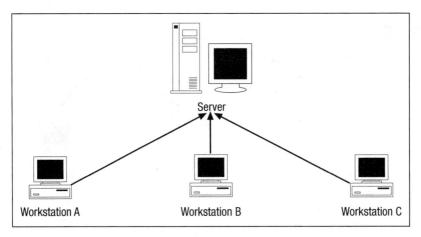

Figure 8.1   Server-based network workstations make requests to a centralized server.

PC to the mainframe in order to take advantage of the mainframe's power and the local processing available on the PC. Once connected to the mainframe, the need arose to be able to share some of the local files on the PC in the same way that files could be shared on the mainframe. Thus, a server was essentially born to handle file and print sharing in a similar, albeit drastically simplified, manner.

Peer-to-Peer Networks

Soon after server-based networks were introduced, the PC industry seemed to be in a state of confusion trying to deal with few or no standards pertaining to applications and hardware. Remember that not too long ago PCs were very expensive and purchasing a PC was a definite commitment and investment in technology and computing. Keep in mind that a server is not really a server unless it can serve something to other computers; so having a centralized powerful server was an additional investment that some small-to-midsize companies did not want to make.

During this state of standards chaos, a new type of network evolved that contributed to the uncertainty of what a server really was. Instead of utilizing a centralized server to hold files that needed to be shared and manage printers for everyone to use, this new type of network allowed individual computers to be responsible for sharing its own files and printers with the rest of the network. This type of networking was called *peer-to-peer networking*. As you can see in Figure 8.2, each computer was responsible for its own network resources, making it both a server and a client. All systems were essentially the same, or peers.

Until Microsoft introduced Windows for Workgroups (and incidentally coined the term "workgroup" as a peer-to-peer network), Lantastic was the peer-to-peer networking solution of choice. Unfortunately, Lantastic required proprietary hardware to function. Also during this time, Microsoft began to grow powerful,

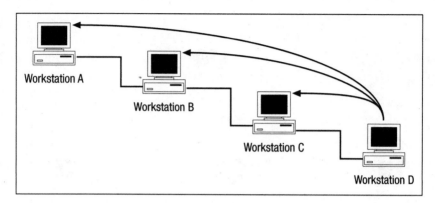

Figure 8.2 A workstation in a peer-to-peer network requests information and data from several workstations on the network.

networking standards were established, and the industry settled on the 802.*x* standards for networking. This new standard left Lantastic behind. Both Ethernet and Token Ring was supported by Novell NetWare and DOS/Microsoft, whereas the Lantastic investment would only work with Lantastic.

Peer-to-peer networking, however, did not die. Microsoft continued to provide peer-to-peer networking as a solution until and beyond the release of its server-based networking solution, Windows NT. It turned out that this particular move was rather savvy, enabling Microsoft to provide both peer-to-peer and server-based networking solutions for different types of companies on broader budgets.

 For the purposes of the exam, Windows NT/2000, OS/2, and Unix can be installed for both server-based and peer-to-peer networks. NetWare is the only platform that can handle only server-based networking. In the real world, OS/2 only appears to be used in large company legacy situations, and Unix is so flexible that it can do just about anything when used by a skilled administrator.

Keep in mind that a server is defined by the service it provides, not by its hardware. Most of the server types listed in this chapter are considered for server-based networks only; however, some of the server services can be supported and implemented in a peer-to-peer network, depending on the NOS.

Because of the caliber of applications and services provided, server-based network servers usually demand more powerful architectures and overall hardware in order to supply the performance required. Network servers also offer another important feature: redundancy. If a user's desktop dies, the user is unable to work, which costs the company money. The actual number associated with this loss is called the cost of downtime (CODT). The CODT associated with a single desktop computer is relatively small because it only deals with one user. When a server dies, however, the CODT is significantly larger because more users are not able to access network data. Additional connections to that server may be down as well. For example, if a Web server that is being used for e-commerce is drawing data from a file and print server that is down, not only are the other file and print users not functional, but that Web server is not functional. Downtime prevention technologies now exist to assist in reducing and eliminating CODT. A true hardware server will have just as many fault-tolerant and redundant components as it has mission-critical components. Mission-critical, showstopper components can include hard drives, power supplies, buses, network interface cards, failure recovery bootable multiple CPU chips, and error correction RAM.

Note: Calculating the CODT is probably the single most potent weapon you can use to convince management to support the purchase of additional technologies.

Network Servers

Standard servers are loosely defined as servers that provide access to and from resources on a network. You can find most of these server types in a peer-to-peer network and in server-based networks. For exam purposes, however, you're unlikely to see a gateway, router, bridge, firewall, or proxy server in anything but a server-based network.

File and Print

File and print servers (FNPS) were the original PC-based servers. These types of servers provide file and printer services (FPS) to network clients. In order for a file and print server to operate properly, it must have direct and usually exclusive access to the files and printers that it serves. File and print servers usually require a lot of hard disk space, but because they do not interact with the user, they usually do not require an inordinate amount of RAM. Certain NOSs, such as NetWare, have specific HDD-to-RAM formulas that are used to determine how much RAM is necessary, depending upon how much HDD is installed.

Files are usually located on the server machine itself, but they can exist on a RAID array attached to the server, on a Storage Area Network (SAN), or on a Network Accessible Storage (NAS) box. A NAS allows multiple servers to access the same files and is the only current situation where a server does not require exclusive control over the data.

Printers can be attached either directly through the server parallel port or on the network with a network interface card installed on the printer. The network interface requires that both the printer and server support the same protocol so that they can talk to each other. When configuring a network printer using a network interface, keep in mind that the protocol the printer and server use to talk to each other does not need to be installed on all of the network client machines. The clients communicate with the server, which in turn passes instructions to the printer.

A protocol is basically an agreed-upon language that computers use to talk to each other. Just like different human languages, some protocols have greater flexibility and inflection, allowing for a greater understanding, whereas other protocols are shorter and more to the point, allowing for faster communications.

Server-based file and print servers provide additional security by not allowing a user to access files and printers until they are authenticated against a centralized database. This kind of authentication is commonly known as a logon process. An administrator creates a user account and requires the user to log on to the server or network with a username and password. Additionally, the administrator is responsible for assigning appropriate security permissions that allow the user to access only those files that he or she needs.

Peer-to-peer file and print servers can also provide authentication security. By default, these servers allow full access to files and printers. They can be configured for additional user-based security; however, this can turn into an administrative nightmare fairly quickly. Think of it like this: each peer on the network serves files to other computers on the network. If security is implemented, not only do you need to create user accounts on each peer computer, but you need to maintain passwords on each computer as well. The bottom line is this: if you really want security, use a server-based network operating system that can handle a centralized user database along with user and password management and synchronization.

Gateway

For those of you with networking experience, you may first think of a default gateway for TCP/IP configuration when you hear the word gateway. After all, a valid IP address is required to surf the Web, but without a default gateway, communications won't proceed beyond the boundaries of the local area network. A gateway in this particular context is usually a router or a multihomed system that routes traffic from a local area network out to the Internet. Although this particular application *is* a gateway, keep in mind that the true definition of a gateway is a bit broader. Strictly speaking, a gateway is a piece of hardware or software that connects two different types of network architectures or network applications together. The key definition of a gateway is that gateways have logic. Logic cannot happen without some level of software; therefore, gateways all have software either in the form of literal software or firmware that has been burned into a hardware device.

As you can see in the list that follows, gateways can serve any number of purposes. Token ring to Ethernet, PhoneNet to Ethernet, and Ethernet to wireless are all distinct gateways used to link different local area networks together. Ethernet to Frame Relay, broadband, and digital subscriber line (DSL) to Cable, are all examples of gateways involved with wide area networking or Internet access. Oracle to SQL Server, Sybase to DB2, Exchange to Notes, and Lightweight Directory Access Protocol (LDAP) to X.500 are all examples of database gateways. Oracle, SQL Server, Sybase, and DB2 are all database applications. Exchange and Notes are email specific applications, and LDAP and X.500 are directory services. Basically, all software related gateways are designed to translate information from one database to another database.

➤ Token Ring to Ethernet

➤ PhoneNet to Ethernet

➤ Ethernet to Wireless

➤ Ethernet to Frame Relay

➤ Ethernet to Broadband

➤ DSL to Cable

➤ Oracle to SQL Server

➤ Sybase to DB2

➤ MS Exchange to Lotus Notes

➤ LDAP to X.500

 Although Lotus Notes is not just an email application, the Exchange to Notes gateway specifically handles email only. Windows 2000 Active Directory, NetWare Novell Directory Services (NDS), and Lotus Notes all share LDAP directory services in common. Gateways are currently being created to allow directory service information to be transferred between these three NOS powerhouses.

Hardware and network-based gateways usually live as dumb devices that reside on a network and pass all data back and forth between networks. Installation involves little more than plugging in the device and hooking up both types of networks. Smart gateways do exist where the device determines what data goes back and forth between networks. A router is an example of a smart gateway.

Software-based gateways usually require more RAM than what you would see in a traditional server because of the overhead involved in the translation between these types of applications. Another reason for the extra RAM rests heavily on the fact that a software gateway usually resides on the same computer as an application server.

Bridge

A bridge is almost synonymous to a gateway in that it can connect two different types of networks. But the difference is that a gateway can also translate between network applications. A router can connect two different types of networks, but just like a network-type gateway, a router incorporates embedded software that allows for some logic. Routers send data between two different networks based on the protocols used to transport the data packets. Bridges simply send the information between two networks without any potential filters, subnets, logic, rhyme, or reason. When thinking about a bridge, try to remember this: you can build a box that takes signals from a round wire and places them on a square wire, but the signal will still be round. This is what a bridge does. In order to have the square signal at the end of the square wire understand the round signal, some sort of logic needs to be applied to the signal in order to literally translate it from round to square. This is what a gateway does.

You may be asking yourself why you would ever purchase a bridge. The reason is simple: Hardware works faster than software. If you have a bridge handling the signal movements from one network media to another, you can have a piece of software handle the translation functions. In the end, this split solution might cost less money than purchasing a full gateway to handle both functions, plus it may be more efficient. You do not see many stand-alone hardware bridges in the workplace anymore because more and more companies have chosen to connect to the Internet, which quite often requires a router of some kind. It is cheaper to add on bridging features to a router than it is to have a router simply translate protocols and have a separate bridging device.

Router

A router is a specialized gateway that transfers information to and from a data line, ultimately connecting either to a different building or office, or to the Internet. Routers usually come in two different varieties: a multihomed PC or a dedicated router device.

A multihomed PC is simply a box that has two different network cards, which are connected to two different networks. In addition to card and cable installation, appropriate drivers need to be installed within the NOS. After the hardware and drivers have been installed, the NOS automatically routes data between the two networks. Novell NetWare, Windows NT, and Windows 2000 all support multihomed routing.

 Router devices, such as Cisco or Bay routers, are not specifically covered on the exam. It is safe to assume that routers are multihomed.

In many ways, routers are responsible for extending the definition of a gateway. Routers do not connect different applications, such as e-mail or databases, and they do not connect different network media types such as Ethernet and Token Ring. Routers connect networks that run different protocols. An ideal router configuration translates network basic input-output system (NetBIOS) protocol data packets, which do not travel well, into TCP/IP packets, which do. This is a rather advanced router function that can only be found with a multihomed computer and specialized routing software, or with a router device. Other advanced router functions can also include firewall and security features. Both multihomed and device routers are most often implemented as gateways between TCP/IP networks. Without going into too much networking detail, you need to be aware that TCP/IP is a touchy protocol because it requires that every computer on the network have a different, completely unique number within that network. Routers were originally used to connect local area networks to wide area networks. This is still the primary implementation of a router, but because Internet usage requires that clients run TCP/IP, routers are also being used to minimize network traffic on a local area network by essentially creating two separate networks with a router between the two.

NOS-based routers tend not to consume very much memory because the data throughput between network cards is exclusively based on the capacity of the wire, the network card, and the PCI bus that handles the card itself. The processing load used to get data through these components is relatively light and does not use much memory or hard disk space.

Firewall

Firewall servers usually live and breathe in the same environment as routers. A firewall's purpose is to repel and prevent nasty security related intruders from penetrating your network computers and causing harm. Specifically, we are talking about hacker activity. Basically, firewalls function as a force field that prevents all unsafe communications from coming into the network. It is possible to configure specific firewall bypasses in order to allow legitimate and safe traffic into the network; however, any bypasses can also be considered security risks, and the balance between security and accessibility needs to be considered. Firewalls can be found as software servers, standalone devices, and also within router devices. Because a firewall exists at the point where an external and internal network meet, many routers are configured with additional software to perform firewall functions.

Proxy

Proxy servers are also Internet related servers whose primary job is to essentially intercept all Internet-bound traffic within a local area network. What happens after outbound traffic is caught is highly dependent upon the configuration and features of the proxy server. If caching is installed, the server copies and stores frequently requested or specifically configured Web sites. Depending upon configured security parameters, the proxy server can grant or deny Internet access based on the user making the request or on the Web site that is being requested. Because both firewalls and proxies function at the point where an external and internal network meet, it is not unusual to see a router device programmed with additional proxy and firewall software in order to handle these additional security features.

Generally, a company installs a proxy server if it wants to perform any of the following tasks:

➤ Grant or deny Internet access on a user-by-user basis

➤ Log all Internet usage

➤ Reduce Internet bandwidth usage

➤ Increase Internet access speeds

Internet access requires a TCP/IP configuration on the client operating system. It is possible to restrict Internet access by neglecting to configure the OS with a default gateway, which is certainly a poor man's way of handling things. There are, however, significant drawbacks to using a proxy server to restrict Internet access because current Dynamic Host Configuration Protocol (DHCP) server technology is not user-specific. DHCP, as described in more detail in the "DHCP" section later in this chapter, provides TCP/IP configurations to client computers. Unfortunately, DHCP cannot serve a single gateway to one user and a different gateway address to a different user. In addition, it lacks the increased bandwidth that you would see with caching services and the logging that really comes in handy when dealing with employee performance issues.

Software-based proxy servers usually require more RAM than your average file and print server because they keep active and running logs on all Internet activity and cached Web pages. Increased hard disk space might also be necessary depending upon the configuration and size of any caching abilities on the proxy server.

Remote Access

Remote access servers, in the strictest sense, allow users to connect to a corporate network and utilize network resources within that network from a remote location. Traditionally, Remote Access Services (RAS) are synonymous with dial-up networking via modem because Windows provides a built-in dial-up interface with Windows 95, 98, NT, and 2000. Technically, RAS servers can also be virtual private networking (VPN) servers, which allow remote access via the Internet rather than a modem. Modem-based RAS servers are natively supported within Windows NT, 2000, and Novell NetWare. All of these NOSs support more than just a few concurrent RAS connections. Unfortunately, most PCs do not know how to handle more than two concurrent connections, so modem banks, or external RAS servers such as Shiva, were created to help out. Add-on software not only handles driver initialization and support, but also adds extra features above and beyond those provided by Windows and NetWare.

Native Windows and NetWare RAS security is handled in parallel with the NOS authentication. When a user dials in to native RAS, it authenticates the user onto the wire and into the network at the same time.

External RAS device security is handled in series with the NOS authentication. When a user dials in to an external RAS device, it authenticates the user into its own system based on its own database or on a replica of the NOS database. Once the initial authentication occurs, it gets the user in the door and on the wire. The RAS device then hands the user over to the NOS for the authentication that allows the user to access network resources. This is when login scripts and startup applications are launched.

Remote access servers usually require little or no additional RAM aside from what you would see in a file and print server. The same applies for hard disk drive (HDD) space. This is because the RAS server activity never goes higher than the number of analog ports or concurrent connections that are installed on the server. With such a wonderfully fixed ceiling of activity, you do not need to concern yourselves with additional RAM or hard disk space simply because RAS usually performs connection services and limited authentication. All other functions are passed off to the NOS.

Application Servers

Application servers are relatively new in the PC server marketplace. The first PC servers were simple file and print servers that only handled user authentication, access, and I/O services for files and printers. As soon as people realized that files could be stored on the network, they began to wonder if it was possible to have active applications reside on the network in much the same way that mainframes do. They were not talking about simply installing an application on a server and having multiple users access it. They were talking about having a living application on a server where the server is integrated with the application, and the server performs independent functions on behalf of the application.

As a rule of thumb, application servers provide a broader range of features and capabilities than an application that's shared on a network or installed on a single user's computer. These additional features eventually created an increased demand for application uptime and availability, which eventually translated into different hardware configurations for applications:

➤ A *dedicated application server* is a single server that runs a single application.

➤ A *distributed application server* is a single server that handles a piece of an application.

➤ A *peer-to-peer application server* is a server that is a member of a pack of servers all running and sharing the same instance of an application. All servers participate on an equal footing, which is where the term peer-to-peer comes into play.

Cluster

As mentioned in Chapter 11, server clustering is actually a type of multiprocessing configuration where applications detect CPU utilization and delegate tasks across a cluster or pack of computers. Clustering usually requires specialized software to handle the task, and quite often that software is intimately linked with a specific application server package. An example of a clustered system would be a group of computers that handle client triggered processing based on a group of database queries and rules. Whereas a single server might receive the initial request, the cluster/application software can delegate pieces of the processing to other CPUs within the cluster if their CPU utilization is less. It is easy to get confused between clustering and load balancing. Keep in mind that clustering is essentially sharing CPU power, and load balancing is sharing application functionality as well.

Email

Email servers are probably the most popular application server on the market. Just about every company that uses computers also uses email in order to simply function in today's world. Email applications like Microsoft Exchange and Lotus cc: Mail and Notes added many features beyond the simple email products. These additional features include scheduling, calendars, task management, publicly shared folders, and personal and public forms and forms management as well. Running all of these features can require a pretty powerful piece of server hardware.

Database

Database servers are probably the second most frequently utilized application servers on the market. Databases are essentially places to store information. There are many types of databases; however, it's a good bet that any database running on its own server is using a relational database structure. Database architecture is not covered in the exam; however, it's beneficial to know that relational databases are faster and more efficient than flat databases. Popular database servers range from Informix to Oracle to SQL Server.

Client/Server

For quite awhile, client/server applications have been something of a mystery as to what they are and what they do. Most client/server applications are also database applications, and it's difficult to understand how a relational database application differs from a client/server database application. Actually, the difference lies in how communications occur.

When database applications started becoming popular, the computer industry started to realize that the demands on the hardware supporting database applications increased beyond the capability of the existing hardware. Application clients were booting into their respective operating systems to access an application server, and the server was responsible for absolutely everything associated with the application, from client settings to user interface to query building and data services. Client computers were only working to translate instructions from the server appropriately and maintain the networking connection. Server clustering was still a very expensive, somewhat unstable, and almost unknown technology. The natural evolution was to attempt to offload some of the processing functions from the server to the client in order to reduce not just server processor utilization, but also network bandwidth. The end result had the added benefits of increased speed and productivity and was an alternative to installing the application exclusively either on the server or on the user's machine.

As a general rule, client/server applications are split so that the server handles the database management, overhead, and database services, whereas the client handles the user interface and any additional processes that can be performed exclusively by the client machine, such as building queries.

Fax

Similar to print servers, fax servers broadcast themselves to client computers as print devices. When users want to fax a document, they print the document to a specifically installed printer driver, which routes the print job to a fax server device or fax application residing on the computer or server. Some fax servers also have the ability to receive incoming faxes and route them to the appropriate email box or drive location. For users who frequently utilize fax services, this is a huge improvement in productivity, paper, and time. Normally a user would need to print a document, fill out a fax cover sheet form, and find a fax machine to fax the document to the recipient. The situation is more time consuming if the user needs to fax the same document to multiple recipients. Fax servers eliminate all of these annoyances by allowing a user to print the document to the fax driver, which produces a cover sheet form to fill in on the computer. Once the cover sheet is complete, the user is prompted to enter the recipient's information either from a database, some other application, or directly into the program. The document can also be flagged for delivery to multiple recipients. After the user completes the cover sheet and chooses the recipients, the fax server sends the fax.

The fax server utilizes one or more analog phone lines to complete the fax process. If more than one fax is waiting to be sent, it is usually placed in a queue for the next available analog line for outbound faxes. Most decent fax servers offer automatic failure retry and logging features to properly provide fax services. These are great features, as they truly allow the user to fax a document and forget about it. Usually, if the document fails to fax properly after several retries, the fax program either notifies the user of the failure or places an entry in a log file that indicates the reason for the failure.

Fax servers that utilize analog lines attached to a server usually require additional hard disk space in order to handle temporary fax files and fax logs. Additional RAM is not necessary because these types of servers do not perform heavy-duty I/O.

SNA

All you really need to know about Systems Network Architecture (SNA) servers for the exam is that SNA equals mainframe. Well, this is not precisely true, so let me explain. Mainframe applications are still very much in use, are very powerful and reliable, and quite often encompass a valuable set of features. Many companies maintain numerous mainframe applications and still roll out and implement PCs in their network. SNA is the de facto protocol for communicating with mainframes. SNA was originally developed by IBM, but is frequently used to connect to non-IBM mainframes.

Web

Web servers have gained tremendous popularity since Windows NT/2000, NetWare, and Linux started shipping Web servers with their products. The features of these Web servers allow smaller companies to experiment and dabble with the idea of creating a business Web presence. Coupled with the Internet explosion and the timing of these on-board Web features, the increase in the use of Web servers has been outstanding. The concept of an intranet where central-ized information could be made available to multiple OS clients in an easy Web-based manner also added to the expanded use of these servers.

There are two different types of Web servers:

➤ *Static Web servers* usually contain flat HTML code that can change as often as necessary. Quite often a front-end server box can handle the kinds of Web traffic that is sent to static Web servers. Front-end server computers are not designed to be scaleable, but they can be designed for redundancy in order to enhance computer uptime. System uptime on static Web servers is usually less of an issue than on dynamic Web servers because e-commerce, database, or form functions do not come into play.

➤ *Dynamic Web servers* are different from static Web servers in that they per-form more advanced functions in order to allow the Web user to experience different effects and features. Dynamic Web servers usually run scripts, executables, Java, Perl, and any number of other video-based eye candy for a Web site. Dynamic Web sites are more interactive than static Web servers, and they usually require more RAM than static servers. In some cases, addi-tional hard disk space is required for e-commerce or other database related Web applications.

Most Web servers also offer File Transfer Protocol (FTP) and Gopher services in conjunction with Hypertext Transfer Protocol (HTTP) services. Both FTP and Gopher are different ways to retrieve information from a server. The inter-face for retrieving this information is completely text-based and very much de-pendent upon command-line utilities, which you do not really need to know for the exam. What you do need to know is that realistically, the infrastructure re-quired to support these additional protocol/connection methods is very similar to standard HTTP, so the additional overhead required is very small. In addition, FTP and Gopher do not support active or dynamic elements; so additional RAM and HDD space is completely dependent upon the usage of these services.

Resolution and Protocol Servers

Resolution and protocol servers assist and promote the network itself. They do not necessarily make it easier to print or open network resources. They make it possible for you to access more network resources differently.

Domain Name System (DNS)

The Internet would not exist without DNS or something like it. We touched on TCP/IP briefly in the previous sections, but let's make sure you understand how very important DNS is.

Back in the days when NetWare was the only major PC-based NOS in the market, it was not necessary to know what every computer's name was because all of the computers talked to a primary server and that was about it. Computers did not have names because the server never needed to talk to the computer, and regular desktop computers did not share local data, so there was no reason to name them.

When Microsoft introduced Windows for Workgroups, things changed. Suddenly, networked computers needed names because they now had the capability to share information on the network. Think about it: It is hard to look at someone's file if you do not know who they are, where they are, or what they look like. So, computers had to be given names. These names were called NetBIOS names. So if you needed to look at someone else's file, you could use a name like "Charlie," "Media," or "Server."

Once users became accustomed to sharing and accessing information on a first-name basis on a local area network, they began to realize that they could share information across multiple local area networks grouped together into a wide area network. The problem encountered at this point was analogous to trying to locate a file belonging to "Charlie" in a roomful of strangers. There was always a chance that other Charlies were on the network. Although users might be able to adapt to the situation and ultimately find the right "Charlie," computers did not know how to do this intuitively. People might know additional criteria about "Charlie," which would enable them to locate the right guy, but computers only had a name. If more information could be added to the identity of each computer, the computer would be much more likely to find the correct "Charlie" and access the file. It turns out that the government (among many other companies and authorities) had already figured out that the solution to this problem was to assign an ID number to each computer instead of a name, and do it in such a way that there would be no other computer on the face of the earth with that exact number. Computers could then be sure that they were accessing the correct files. The ID number used was called a TCP/IP address. This identification scheme all evolved into a basic communications system. Computers talked to other computers by addressing each other using their TCP/IP addresses and talking in a protocol that basically put the "to" and "from" information at the end of every word. This protocol ensured that multiple conversations could occur in the same place without losing information in all the noise. Because TCP/IP addresses were unique to each computer, TCP/IP became the de facto protocol used for Internet communications.

The problem with calling computers by a TCP/IP address was that humans could not easily remember numbers, but they could remember names. So a solution was needed that would combine the uniqueness of numerical TCP/IP addresses with a naming system easy enough for humans to remember. That solution was DNS. Names for computers were created in a hierarchical manner where the final computer name was a compound name containing what could be the NetBIOS name of the computer along with the domain or parent network's name as well as other parent domain names. This type of compound computer name was called a Fully Qualified Domain Name (FQDN).

Computers now have TCP/IP addresses, and they talk in TCP/IP because they like dealing with numbers. And people have FQDNs to recognize servers because they like dealing with names. However, the problem then becomes the issue of taking an FQDN and figuring out which TCP/IP address it belongs to. This is exactly what DNS does, which is the point of this section. DNS handles FQDN to TCP/IP address resolution. DNS enables your computer to figure out that **www.yahoo.com** is the same as 64.58.76.179, and that **www.comptia.com** is the same as 207.254.119.234. Simply put, you could not cruise the World Wide Web without the DNS infrastructure in place.

Imagine a situation where you are in charge of the Web presence for your company. You have created a Web site and have hosted it at a local Internet service provider (ISP) office, but you now need to move your Web site to a different ISP. The Internet authorities that maintain the unique TCP/IP addresses also maintain master DNS databases that have the DNS names resolved to IP addresses for every major domain name on the Internet. These master DNS databases are in turn read by every major Internet player and ISP in the industry. That information in turn trickles down to DNS servers at companies and corporations. When you move your Web site to a different ISP, the FQDN might not change, but the server's TCP/IP address will change. Your new ISP notifies the Internet authorities of the change, and those changes are filtered through the Internet in a matter of minutes, hours, and days.

Not only is DNS important for external or Internet communications, but Unix has relied on DNS for its own network communications for years. Windows NT and NetWare do not require DNS. However, Windows 2000 now requires DNS because Microsoft has finally decided that FQDNs are very similar to NetBIOS names, and it has figured out a way for them to appear to be the same to the user.

DNS servers in small companies do not require much overhead in terms of memory or HDD space because they only keep local network information (which is a whole different administrative can of worms) and refer everything else to its forwarding DNS server. Larger companies and those utilizing Unix will see a greater use of DNS along with a definitive hierarchy for administration and configuration.

Large DNS setups usually require a lot of RAM, especially if they are queried often for name resolution. Additionally, certain versions of DNS servers require a great deal of administrative handholding, so this might be a factor when choosing a DNS solution for a company.

Windows Internet Naming Service (WINS)

In the previous section, we briefly discussed NetBIOS names. Similar to TCP/IP, computers can communicate with each other on a local area network by using their NetBIOS names and talking in a NetBIOS or (in the case of Microsoft) NetBEUI protocol.

Computers will, if given the choice, choose to call each other by numbers rather than names. If the TCP/IP protocol is in place on a network, a WINS server can be used to resolve NetBIOS names to TCP/IP addresses on computers. With the exception of Windows 2000, Microsoft networks still use NetBIOS names to communicate between computers on a local area network. Many network applications also utilize NetBIOS naming schemes to communicate between computers because NetBIOS names are easier to remember than TCP/IP addresses. As Windows 2000 becomes more popular, you will see a slow decline in NetBIOS names because Windows 2000 references computers by their FQDN. Users still call computers by what appears to be their NetBIOS names, but in reality, Windows 2000 automatically translates those names into FQDNs on behalf of the user, and all communications proceed with FQDNs instead of NetBIOS names. As the slow decline in NetBIOS traffic occurs, you will also see a reduced need for WINS resolution and servers.

WINS servers require more RAM than standard servers because they are dynamic services that are constantly on the lookout for more names to resolve.

Dynamic Host Configuration Protocol (DHCP)

In the real world, if you have to choose one server out of the three network servers discussed, always choose DHCP. A DHCP server is probably the single greatest administrative timesaver to come along since autoexec.bat. In the previous sections, we discussed how TCP/IP addresses must be unique in order to ensure that communications flow smoothly. Well, servers aren't the only computers that need a TCP/IP address in order to maintain uniqueness. Any client or computer that wants to talk to a server running the TCP/IP protocol must also be running the TCP/IP protocol and have its own unique TCP/IP address. Additional TCP/IP configuration information is also necessary in order for a computer to access the Internet (default gateway setting) and find computers running on the Internet (DNS resolution). This information needs to be entered into every computer. Also, IP addresses change occasionally when computers leave or join the network or just in the process of natural evolution. Thus, the administrator must maintain a list of every IP address assigned to every computer on the network and make sure that no two numbers are alike. When the network changes, it sometimes becomes necessary to reconfigure the TCP/IP settings on every computer in the network. If you consider a network that contains thousands of computers, you can imagine that this might be a somewhat unpleasant task.

Enter DHCP, a server application that serves IP addresses and IP configuration information to computers on the network. Instead of manually maintaining a unique list of IP addresses, DHCP does this for you. Additionally, there's enough flexibility to maintain static IP addresses for servers and workstations where it is necessary without interfering with DHCP services. With the right DHCP configuration, you will rarely need to deal with manual or static IP address configurations again.

Practice Questions

Question 1

> You are the administrator of a server that currently resides in a computer room with a printer physically attached to it. Other personnel in the company need access to the printer, which prevents you from locking the computer door. How can you increase security of the server and at the same time allow users to access the printer?
>
> ○ a. Place a guard outside the door.
>
> ○ b. Route the users to a different printer.
>
> ○ c. Install a NIC on the printer, move it out of the computer room, and connect it to the network.
>
> ○ d. Give only designated personnel access to the computer room.

Answer c is correct. Installing a network card on the printer and taking it out of the computer room allows the server to maintain its control over the printer and still allow users to access the device. Answer a is incorrect because this is an inefficient use of personnel. Answer b is incorrect because there might not be another printer to route the users to. Answer d is incorrect because the question states that you cannot lock the computer room.

Question 2

> What is the difference between a gateway and a bridge?
>
> I. There is no difference.
>
> II. A bridge links different applications, whereas a gateway links only different network types.
>
> III. A bridge links different network types, whereas a gateway links different applications.
>
> IV. A bridge is strictly hardware, whereas a gateway can be both hardware and software.
>
> ○ a. I and III
>
> ○ b. II and IV
>
> ○ c. I and II
>
> ○ d. III and IV

Answer d is correct. A bridge is strictly a hardware solution that links different networks together, and a gateway can link different applications and also link different networks together by performing the same function as a bridge with added software components to do protocol translation. Answers a and c are incorrect because there is a difference between a gateway and a bridge. Answer b is incorrect because a bridge does not link different applications.

Question 3

> What server functions are often found on the same device? [Check all correct answers]
>
> ❏ a. DHCP
>
> ❏ b. Proxy
>
> ❏ c. Router
>
> ❏ d. Firewall

Answers b, c, and d are correct. All three of these servers focus on communications at the point where the LAN joins the WAN or Internet, so it makes sense to have all three of these servers run on the same machine. Answer a is incorrect because having DHCP reside on any of these servers could be a security threat. Anybody who managed to find a way to burst through a proxy, router, or firewall could gain access to all of the computer names and addresses on the network.

Question 4

> What server type is used to allow communications with a mainframe?
>
> ○ a. DHCP
>
> ○ b. SNA
>
> ○ c. WINS
>
> ○ d. FTP

Answer b is correct. SNA was developed by IBM in order to facilitate the communications between PCs and mainframes. Answer a is incorrect because DHCP serves IP configuration information. Answer c is incorrect because WINS resolves NetBIOS names to IP addresses. Answer d is incorrect because FTP is a network file transfer protocol.

Question 5

Which network server would resolve the following name: blue.southcampus.
gadgetsrus.com?

○ a. WINS

○ b. ARP

○ c. DNS

○ d. DHCP

Answer c is correct. The name blue.southcampus.gadgetsrus.com is an FQDN
that is resolved by DNS. Answer a is incorrect because WINS resolves NetBIOS
names. Answer b is incorrect because Address Resolution Protocol (ARP) is a
protocol not a server. Answer d is incorrect because DHCP does not perform
name resolution.

Question 6

Which network server would resolve the following name: blue?

○ a. WINS

○ b. RAS

○ c. DNS

○ d. FTP

Answer a is correct. Blue is a NetBIOS name. Answers b and d are both incorrect
because they do not perform name resolution. Answer c is incorrect because DNS
only resolves FQDNs.

Question 7

Which of the following is not an example of an application server?

○ a. Gateway

○ b. Fax

○ c. Email

○ d. SNA

Answer a is correct. A gateway is a network server type. Answers b, c, and d are incorrect because fax, email, and SNA are all application servers.

Question 8

You need to monitor users' Internet activity. Which server can you use?

○ a. Gateway

○ b. Router

○ c. Firewall

○ d. Proxy

Answer d is correct. A proxy server can maintain a log of Web sites that users connect to. Answer a is incorrect because a gateway is a hardware and software solution that links either networks or specific applications to each other. Answer b is incorrect because a router links different networks together and routes data between the networks based on protocol criterion. Answer c is incorrect because a firewall keeps external traffic from penetrating a local area network.

Need to Know More?

 Craft, Melissa, Mark A. Poplar, David V. Watts, and Will Willis. *Network+ Exam Prep.* Scottsdale, AZ: The Coriolis Group, 1999. ISBN 1-57610-412-5. This book contains information about protocols and protocol servers.

 Zacker, Craig and Paul Doyle. *Upgrading and Repairing Networks.* Indianapolis, IN: Que Corporation, 1996. ISBN 0-78970181-2. This book is a great neutral reference for server types and applications.

 http://channel.intel.com is a server encyclopedia that contains a wealth of server type information.

 www.internet.com is similar to pcwebopedia.com. This site is an excellent source for information dealing with networking, PCs, and servers.

 www.microsoft.com provides a useful overview of clustering technologies and how they apply to Windows NT.

 www.novell.com contains a white paper, "SFTIII for NetWare," that provides information about the NetWare equivalent to clustering and load balancing. SFT is a complete system mirroring solution and does not currently span more than two systems.

 www.pcguide.com, a site developed by Charles M. Kozierok, contains a wealth of information on many IT topics.

 www.pcwebopedia.com is an excellent reference site for basic definitions as well as industry links for more information.

Network Operating Systems

Terms you'll need to understand:

✓ NOS
✓ Protocol
✓ Server
✓ Client
✓ Peer-to-peer
✓ GUI
✓ Domains

✓ Directory Services
✓ File and Print Services
✓ Tree
✓ Authentication
✓ CLI
✓ User
✓ Group

Techniques you'll need to master:

✓ Differentiating among types of operating systems
✓ Identifying network communications
✓ Working with protocol stacks
✓ Explaining user and group administration

✓ Installing an operating system
✓ Starting up and shutting down procedures

There is a saying that the hardware is only as good as the software. In the case of networks, this is actually a fifty-fifty split in my opinion. If either one is bad, your network is just a collection of cabling and electronics. For this reason, you need to have a Network Operating System (NOS).

Some people might think that there is no difference between a standard operating system like Windows or MacOS and a NOS. This could not be further from the truth. Although they may share the same interface and same basic look and feel, a NOS has more functionality and requires more system resources than a standard operating system. Directory systems, protocols, encryption, file maintenance, user information and configuration, and so on are just a few of the additional "overhead" features that a NOS will handle.

NOSs come in many different flavors. There are no-frills command-line interfaces like the many varieties of Unix and Linux, and there are the graphic user interface (GUI) models like the Microsoft Windows family, Novell's NetWare, and IBM's OS/2 Warp. No matter which one you choose, you will have to know the purposes they serve.

A NOS's main goal is to connect clients together and enable a server to share file and print functions with those clients. This is where the term client/server network originated. There are a few exceptions to this rule, but generally a standard operating system exists primarily for a single PC. NOSs exist so that data can be transferred from one machine to another without using "sneaker-net." Sneaker-net is the old standby of taking a file, placing it on a disk, and then walking that disk over to the computer that needs it.

Most modern networks are based on the client/server model. Once you have a NOS installed on the server, you can begin file and print sharing, communications, shared applications, user and group administration, and more importantly Internet access.

Note: It is important to understand that NOSs are software based and can run on many different hardware platforms. One of the benefits of having several NOSs to choose from as well as hardware platforms is that you can customize your network's environment to satisfy your business goals.

It is obviously beyond the scope of this book to cover all the nitty-gritty details of each NOS, so we will not even attempt to do so. There are excellent certification programs that provide more in-depth knowledge of these NOSs: Microsoft's Microsoft Certified Systems Engineer (MCSE), Novell's Certified NetWare Engineer (CNE), several brands of Unix, and forms of Linux like Red Hat and Caldera are just a few of the many available. In this chapter, we provide an overview of each NOS as well as their startup and shutdown procedures.

For the Server+ exam, you will be expected to know several NOSs. By the time you finish this chapter, you should have a good understanding of the following NOSs:

➤ Windows NT

➤ Windows 2000

➤ NetWare 3.x, 4.x, and 5

➤ Unix

➤ Linux

➤ IBM OS/2

Windows NT

More people use Microsoft's Windows operating system than any other. So it came as no surprise when Microsoft introduced a network operating system called Windows 3.11 or Windows for Workgroups. It was not taken very seriously, but Microsoft remained undaunted and eventually released Windows NT 3.1 in 1993 to compete with networking giants like Sun, Novell, and IBM. It had the same look and feel as Windows 3.1, but was intended for the networked environment. As a NOS it had its pluses and minuses. One of the biggest minuses was the nonconformity to industry standards. Another was the lack of hardware support at the time. However, its easy to use interface and 32-bit system made it hard to overlook as more and more people in the early- to mid-1990s moved from both ends of the spectrum (mainframes and peer-to-peer networks) to the middle with client/server networks. Windows NT 3.1 went through several renditions before stopping at Windows NT 3.51.

When Windows NT 4.0 was introduced in 1996, the world sat up and took notice. Coinciding with this release was the introduction of Windows 95/98, which made the world adopt a GUI platform. Windows NT is known for its intuitive interface, multitasking abilities, and compatibility with a host of applications. In fact, the Microsoft Windows family has more software written for it than most other operating systems. This makes it a good choice for administrators looking for a product with wide acceptance. Do not underestimate Linux, however, because it is quickly catching up in the software application market.

Major Features

Microsoft Windows NT 4.0 is a popular NOS. Although regularly snickered at by hardcore computer enthusiasts, Windows NT 4.0 makes up a majority of the local area networks (LANs) found in today's offices. There are two versions of the software: Workstation and Server. (As an interesting tidbit of trivia, NT is an acronym for New Technology.) Windows NT offers full support for almost every type of topology and network protocol that is in use in LAN environments. Windows NT also offers a lot of WAN connectivity as well with its remote access server application.

Windows NT 4.0 offers multiprocessor support and multitasking for servers running this NOS. Multitasking allows server-based processes to share CPU time so that more people can print, access files, backup data, and so on at the same time.

The use of the GUI interface also makes it easier for administrators to learn the system and implement some of its capabilities faster and more efficiently. When you have the entire network in front of you on the screen, you can quickly complete the task at hand.

Windows NT 4.0 uses a 32-bit shell, which can cause problems with 16-bit applications. Additionally, Windows NT 4.0 is not as scalable as some enterprise administrators would desire. We will discuss these and other issues with Windows NT 4.0 throughout the chapter.

Because of the wide variety of networks, it is imperative for a NOS to be able to integrate with other operating systems. Windows NT 4.0 can integrate with Unix, Linux, NetWare, and OS/2. It does this by supporting the different protocols like Novell's IPX/SPX, TCP/IP, and NetBEUI. TCP/IP is the universal language of the Internet, which makes for easy translation when communicating with other NOSs.

Logical Organization

When operating in a Windows NT 4.0 world, there are several logical concepts that need to be mastered in order to understand how people and computers are organized. Windows NT 4.0 uses what is known as a *domain* (shown in Figure 9.1) to organize objects on the network. A domain is quite simply a security boundary that contains resources and users. Because a domain is logical in nature, a computer or user does not have to be physically in one place or another to belong to the domain. Domains go beyond physical boundaries. However, they are logical boundaries that allow you to give or deny access to resources on your network. Resource access across these logical boundaries is accomplished with objects known as *trusts*. Figure 9.1 shows a logical grouping of three domains with two trusts. These trusts allow users in Domain H to access data (with the appropriate security permissions) located in Domain G. Likewise, users in Domain I can access data in Domain G. Users located in Domain H, however, are not able to access resources located in Domain I.

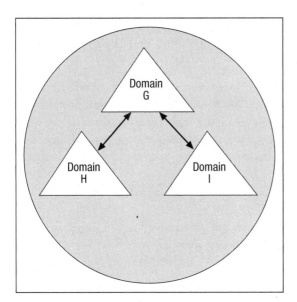

Figure 9.1   Logical multidomain structure.

The physical devices that contain these domains are called *domain controllers*. A domain controller is a server that has more processing power, memory, and hard drive space than a workstation. Servers running as domain controllers generally have backup equipment installed to ensure a long period of uptime. In the Windows NT environment, it is not necessary for a server to be a domain controller, but a domain controller can only be installed on a PC running Windows NT 4.0 Server. A server that is not a domain controller is called a *member server*. These servers generally supply resources or contain data and services for the network.

In a domain, there is one Primary Domain Controller (PDC) that contains all of the user and resource information for that domain. There can be only one PDC, but there can be many Backup Domain Controllers (BDCs) for a domain. The BDC contains a backup copy of the database contained on the PDC for fault tolerance. If a PDC goes down, you can promote one of its BDCs to a PDC. This ensures that your network remains up and running in case of a hardware failure.

Each user and computer in a domain is registered on the PDC. This database of information is called the Security Accounts Manager (SAM) database. As mentioned before, this database is replicated to the BDCs from the PDC. You cannot update a BDC. An administrator can only add computers or users to the PDC, which then replicates that information to its backups. The BDC can authenticate users on the domain if the PDC is down for maintenance or repair, but remember that new users or computers cannot be added at this time as only the PDC can make those additions.

A workstation in the Windows NT 4.0 environment can be anywhere physically and belong to a domain. However, you need to have the workstation close to a domain controller to authenticate in a quick and efficient manner. If you place workstations in a domain far away from the domain controller across slow network connections, you might not be able to log on to the domain during peak network traffic.

System Requirements

Windows NT 4.0 as a NOS requires a higher amount of processing, memory, and disk management than your ordinary operating system. Table 9.1 lists the recommended hardware requirements for Windows NT 4.0.

Windows NT 4.0 does not support Plug-and-Play as does its look-alike Windows 95/98. All equipment that you want to install on a Windows NT 4.0 machine should be listed on Microsoft's Hardware Compatibility List (HCL). You can find this list on the Microsoft Web site. Verifying that your hardware is on this list is highly recommended before trying to install Windows NT 4.0 on your server. You could be in for a rude awakening if your equipment is not compliant. You also need to know that there are many hardware items that work fine with Windows NT 4.0 although they are not on the HCL list, but if you want assured (and supported) functionality, it is best to find something that is on the HCL list.

Another bone of contention for administrators is the lack of Universal Serial Bus (USB) support in Windows NT 4.0 Server. USB is used to chain several serial

Table 9.1 Hardware requirements for Windows NT 4.0.		
Hardware	**Minimum**	**Recommended**
CPU	Intel 486 or comparable	Pentium or RISC-based
Internal RAM	16MB	64MB–128MB
Disk space	110MB free on a SCSI or IDE drive	1GB for domain controllers; more for resource servers
Network interface	One supported NIC	Depending on the role of the server; more than one is supported
CD-ROM	Not required	Recommended
I/O devices	Keyboard and mouse	Other pointing devices are supported
Floppy disk support	3.5-inch floppy disk	

devices together, which makes it vital when you have a scanner, digital camera, mouse, keyboard, Zip drive, and other peripherals you want to add to your computer. This is fixed in Windows 2000, which is discussed in its own section later in this chapter.

Windows NT 4.0 utilizes a 32-bit addressing scheme, which means it is twice as fast as a 16-bit system. Addressing is the flow of information through the CPU in order to perform tasks or processes. Changing from 16- to 32-bit addressing is basically like widening a highway: When you have more room on the highway for bits of information to pass through, it can improve your NOS's operating performance.

The other big factor in computing is memory. Windows NT 4.0 allows you to install over 256MB of memory in your servers. The more memory you have, the faster your computer can run. The internal memory or RAM is where the information is stored temporarily as it is being processed. The more memory you can place in your computer, the more applications you can run simultaneously. The 32-bit processing extends to the memory as well. Every process can be placed into its own 32-bit area of memory. This prevents processes from crashing into each other as they are operating.

Microsoft has also allowed for several types of *disk file systems* to be supported in Windows NT 4.0. Disk file systems are the methods by which data is stored on hard drives. Those supported in Windows NT 4.0 include file allocation table (FAT), FAT32, New Technology File System (NTFS), and High Performance File System (HPFS). HPFS is the file system of choice for OS/2 systems. You are most likely to find FAT, FAT32, or NTFS on a Windows NT server.

FAT has been around for years. It was designed back in the 1970s to support the new minicomputer and PC industry. When designing FAT, engineers decided to place data in different areas on the disk. Because of the cylindrical nature of the disk, these areas were called allocation units or clusters. These clusters were combined into partitions. Information about these clusters and partitions are contained on the FAT table that is placed at the beginning of a partition.

FAT has many limitations including partition size, eight character names, 16-bit fields, no security, and is easily fragmented. To fix some of these issues, *FAT32* came into being. FAT32 allows up to 256 characters for file names, and you can support more than the 4GB partition size of FAT. Up to 2TB (2,000GB) can be contained on one partition with FAT32. FAT32 also allows for compression and is less fragmented. It is a great improvement over the old FAT system; however, it still does not provide for much security.

When creating Windows NT 4.0, Microsoft developed NTFS. The days of DOS had waned and the developers in Redmond knew they needed something more robust for their new NOS. NTFS allows for large partition sizes (up to 16 exabytes), large filenames, file and folder access control, and extensible volumes. NTFS version 5 also allows for encryption through the Encrypting File System (EFS). NTFS enables you to compress files to save disk space, which is vital in most server environments. Probably the most important feature of NTFS is the ability to assign permissions to files and folders. Administrators can allow or deny people permission to read, write and modify files, as well as more granular permissions that equate to a more fully-featured, secure system. This provides a very secure environment and prevents inadvertent deletion of vital files. Although NTFS can recognize FAT, FAT cannot recognize NTFS partitions unless you use a third-party utility. Some people recommend that you keep a FAT32 partition if you want to boot between operating systems. For a server, this would never be something you would want to do.

When installing the Windows NT 4.0 NOS, you have to be careful to plan the the roles of your servers. There are several areas that you need to consider.

➤ What will you call the server?

➤ Which domain will it belong to?

➤ What services will you place on it?

➤ What type of network topology should you run?

➤ What type of server will this be?

The name of the server should reflect the type of service it provides or the physical/geographical location it occupies. If it is an email server, you might call it MAIL1. If it is located at the corporate headquarters in Chicago, you might call it CHICORP1. You can only use 15 characters in the description and the name cannot include symbols.

Before you place a database application, mail server, Internet proxy, and remote access server on one machine, make sure you understand the resources that will be taken up by these services and applications.

Are you on a Token Ring network? Ethernet? What types of protocols do you require to connect to your network? All of these issues should be ironed out before you install the NOS.

Make sure you know what type of server this will be. If it is a domain controller, you need to make sure that you have the PDC online. Also, look at how many domain controllers you have running. Sometimes it makes more sense to install a new member server instead.

Startup/Shutdown

It is very easy to integrate with Windows NT 4.0. With its GUI interface and intuitive administration, you can be up and running fairly quickly.

When a server running Windows NT 4.0 boots, you will eventually see the logon screen. On the screen is a Microsoft Windows NT 4.0 logo with the instructions to press Ctrl+Alt+Del to logon. By pressing these three keys, you will bring up the logon box. Enter your username, domain, and password in the corresponding fields.

On a PDC, you can only enter the administrator account to gain access to the server. On a BDC or member server you can log on with any authorized user for that domain. The password is case-sensitive, so you need to make sure the Caps lock key is not turned on when you attempt to log on to the system. Remember that if you are attempting to log on to the local machine account, you will not have access to the domain resources. Only by providing the domain name and global user account/password will you gain access to the domain.

Note: More than likely, you will want to change the name of the administrator account as this will help add a layer of security to your server. You cannot delete the administrator account, but you can rename it. Do not name it after your Senior Network Administrator. Although flattering, it is pretty easy to guess. With the name of the account, a hacker is halfway to gaining access to your network.

To shut down a Windows NT 4.0 server, you have two options. The first is to click on the Start menu and select Shut Down. This brings up a dialog box that asks you whether you want to log off, restart, or shut down. By selecting Shut Down, the server will end the services one by one and turn the computer off if it supports a soft power off. Otherwise you will see a screen that says, "It is now safe to shut off your computer." If you log off instead of shutting down, the services will continue to run in the background, but the interface will be shut down. This allows you to keep your server secure without losing the services of your machine. The Restart option powers down the machine, and then restarts back to the Ctrl+Alt+Del screen.

The other option is to press Ctrl+Alt+Del when the interface is running. It brings up a dialog box that gives you the option to lock the computer interface, log off the machine, shut down, restart, and start Task Manager. Task Manager is a utility that allows you to view the processes and applications that are running and turn them off if they are refusing to respond. You also have a Performance tab that shows memory and processor usage. You can choose Shut Down from this dialog box, and it will accomplish the same procedure as clicking on the Start menu.

Windows 2000

Microsoft originally had the title of Windows NT 5.0 planned for its upgraded and improved NOS. When the name changed to Windows 2000, people realized what they had only suspected before; this was going to be a *new* NOS.

Windows 2000 is not the latest service pack for Windows NT 4.0. In fact, at this writing, Microsoft has decided not to release Service Pack 7 (SP7) for the Windows NT 4.0 NOS. Instead, Microsoft is throwing its weight behind Windows 2000 and will not continue to improve upon its "old" New Technology.

Windows 2000 was a big step for Microsoft. After spending some time listening to the complaints and suggestions of network administrators, the company decided to create a scalable, robust NOS that would be able to handle the rigors of the new millennium and its Internet-driven computing world.

Many of the upgrades and improvements have been tossed around at the Redmond offices since the early 1990s, and with Windows 2000, you get to see the results. NTFS version 5, reallocation of Control Panel tasks, simplified management, increased security, and increased hardware support makes this a very powerful NOS. Probably the biggest change from Windows NT 4.0 to Windows 2000 is Active Directory Services (ADS). ADS is a *directory service* based on the X.500 data model. In a nutshell, ADS is a logical repository of information about objects on your network. You can find just about anything you are looking for by searching the AD database.

Increased hardware support also gives network administrators some relief. Plug-and-play makes its appearance in Windows 2000, and with Microsoft approved drivers on the HCL, you will be able to get most obscure equipment to run properly.

Overall, there are some great improvements in the Windows 2000 NOS. However, with the release of a new NOS comes some security hole issues as well. Out of all of the current NOSs, Windows 2000 is the latest, with plans to release Windows XP at the end of 2001. Microsoft is definitely making a play to be (or remain) a dominant force in the networking world.

Major Features

The most important improvement of Windows 2000 over Windows NT is its directory service: Active Directory (AD). This concept is not new as you will see when we discuss Novell's NetWare, however it is a step in the right direction for Microsoft. AD is based on industry standards and communicates with other directory services that utilize the X.500 data protocol. AD uses the X.509 protocol, which allows it to communicate with Novell's NetWare Directory Services (NDS) and Unix's Network File System (NFS). AD uses Lightweight Directory Access

Protocol (LDAP) queries, uses TCP/IP, utilizes DNS naming conventions, and is a multimaster replicated database. Gone are the days of PDCs and BDCs in Windows 2000. Instead, all domain controllers are peers of each other. This provides fault tolerance and redundancy throughout the entire network. Unlike Windows NT trusts, Windows 2000 trusts are transitive in nature and dynamic. This means that users in Domain I shown in Figure 9.1 are able to access (again, with the appropriate security permissions) data located in Domain H via their mutually associative trust to Domain G.

Overall, Microsoft has made it easier to install, upgrade, and repair Windows 2000. Users of Windows 95/98 with Internet Explorer 4 are able to use the Windows Update service to get hot fixes downloaded to their PCs without needing to constantly keep an eye on the Web site. This service is now available for Windows 2000 as well. With Remote Installation Services (RIS), network administrators can install Windows 2000 on desktops quickly and easily. Any computer that has a Pre-Execution boot (PXE pronounced "pixie") compliant network interface card can install Windows 2000 automatically when it starts up the first time. For large networks, this considerably decreases rollout time.

There are four basic flavors of Windows 2000:

➤ Professional

➤ Server

➤ Advanced Server

➤ Data Center Server

There are several other types of Server products, but for the exam and sanity purposes we will refer only to these four versions.

Windows 2000 Professional is the replacement for Windows NT 4.0 Workstation. Special attention has been paid to the mobile workforce that is growing exponentially. Professional works well with laptops as it has improved upon the Advanced Power Management (APM). The new Advanced Configuration Power Interface (ACPI) helps create power schemes to get the most power from laptop batteries. Also included in the Professional version is a limited version of Internet Information Server (IIS) 5.0.

Windows 2000 Server is where you encounter AD, which is the foundation of the Windows 2000 NOS. To create a domain controller in a Windows 2000 network, you need to be running Windows 2000 Server. As in Windows NT, you can choose whether the server running Windows 2000 Server will be a domain controller or a member server, but the beauty of it is that you do not have to make this choice until after the NOS is installed. The upshot of this is that you do not need to reinstall the operating system if you promote or demote a domain controller (DC), because all domain controllers are the same. If you need to create a DC or even change a DC to a member server, all you need to do is run a program and then reboot. In Windows 2000 Advanced Server, you have the same services as Server but with increased hardware support. Advanced Server can handle up to eight CPUs and 32GB of memory in each server. In addition to the increased hardware support, Advanced Server can utilize load balancing through clustering. Clustering allows multiple servers to act like one server. If one fails, the others can pick up the load and ensure uninterrupted service to clients. This is an excellent feature to have in highly utilized networks.

Windows 2000 Data Center is the largest operating system that Microsoft has produced to date. With support for 32 processors and 64GB of memory per server, Data Center Server approaches the small mainframes in computing and processing power. Data Center Server is not sold in stores like the other NOSs. To obtain Data Center Server, you need to buy a large server from one of the big manufacturers such as Dell, Intel, Compaq, Hewlett-Packard, and so on.

Hardware

Table 9.2 lists the minimum hardware requirements for Windows 2000 Server.

A nice thing about Windows 2000 is that you can check beforehand whether a server is able to handle the NOS. Place the Windows 2000 installation CD into the drive, go to the /WINNT32 folder, and type the command **checkupgradeonly**. Windows 2000 Server uses hardware detection and plug-and-play to determine the ability of the server to handle the NOS.

One of the biggest advantages that Microsoft is touting about the Windows 2000 Server family of products is its ability to interface with large amounts of

Table 9.2 Minimum hardware requirements for Windows 2000 Server.	
Hardware	**Minimum**
CPU	Pentium 133
Hard drive space	1GB
Internal memory	128MB
Floppy drive	3.5-inch floppy drive
Monitor	VGA
I/O devices	Keyboard, mouse
Other drives	CD-ROM
Network interfaces	At least one network interface card

hardware. Using the plug-and-play system that was initially used in Windows 95 and improved upon in Windows 98, Microsoft makes it a whole lot easier to get equipment to communicate and work with Windows 2000.

One of the major issues Windows NT 4.0 ran into was the lack of USB support. In Windows 2000, you have USB support plus greater PCMCIA support as well. As mentioned earlier, this makes it very friendly for laptop computers. In fact, I typed this chapter on my laptop using a USB mouse hookup so that I could hook up a serial interface camera to download digital photos. It worked like a charm.

Once you change a Windows 2000 Server machine into a domain controller, AD will be stored on its hard drive. Certain features of AD actually require that the disk be using NTFS. This file system is optimal for the server's environment in several ways:

➤ Disk quotas

➤ Encryption

➤ Distributed File System (DFS)

NTFS allows you to control access to files and folders using a discretionary access control list (DACL). Because you can control access to the files and folders, you can also control how much disk space a user can have. Disk quotas allow you to set predetermined limits on how much hard drive space each user can fill. This is useful to prevent overloading a drive and causing it to crash.

One thing to note is that Windows 2000 Server uses NTFS 5, which is different from previous versions in Windows NT.

Another feature of NTFS is the use of DFS to share information around the network in folders that appear to be in one location. This allows everyone to see one file folder hierarchy that is actually spread across the entire network. With users confused by shared drives, folders, passcodes and accounts, it is nice to just click on a folder and be able to access the resources without trying to search through thousands of folders to find the right file.

Startup/Shutdown

Starting Windows 2000 is almost identical to starting Windows NT 4.0. When a server running Windows 2000 boots, you will eventually see the logon screen. On the screen is a Microsoft logo with the instructions to press Ctrl+Alt+Del to log on. By pressing these three keys you will bring up the logon box. Enter your username, domain, and password in the corresponding fields. Most of the time the information will be already in place except for the password.

As in Windows NT 4.0, you cannot log on locally to a domain controller. Because it is part of ADS, you must log on with your domain and password.

To shut down a Windows 2000 Server, you have two options. The first is to click on the Start menu and select Shut Down. This brings up a dialog box that asks whether you want to log off, restart the computer, or shut down. By selecting Shut Down, the server will end the services one by one and turn the computer off if it supports a soft power off. Otherwise you will see a screen that says, "It is now safe to shut off your computer." If you log off instead of shutting down, the services will continue to run in the background, but the interface will be shut down. This allows you to keep your server secure without losing the services of your machine. The Restart option powers down the machine and then restarts back to the Ctrl+Alt+Del screen.

The other option is to press Ctrl+Alt+Del when the interface is running. It brings up a dialog box giving you the option to lock the computer interface, log off the machine, shut down, restart, and start Task Manager. Locking the interface merely hides the desktop and requires you to press Ctrl+Alt+Del and enter your password to continue working. All of the services and even open applications continue to run while this is in place. Task Manager is a utility that allows you to view the processes and applications that are running and turn them off if they are refusing to respond. You also have a Performance tab that shows memory and processor usage. You can choose Shut Down from this dialog box, and it will accomplish the same procedure as clicking on the Start menu.

NetWare

Back in the early 1980s, Unix ruled the networking world. However, it did not really supply the file and print services that the new LANs were requiring. In the 1970s, a little company called Novell was developing the Z-80 computer. In 1983, when IBM created the XT personal computer, it was the first to have an internal hard drive. Novell introduced a product that same year called S-Net. This enabled the hard drive to have file-sharing capabilities and was attached in a star configured cabling system. Microsoft was still just an idea in Bill Gates's head, and people were using personal computers called TRS-80, VIC-20, PET, and Apple II. Because of its ability to enable users to share resources across a network, Novell quickly became the leader in networking. In 1986, Novell introduced NetWare/86.

It has been a long time since 1983 when NetWare was first introduced to the computing world, and NetWare 5.x is currently used to help run many networks. One thing that sets NetWare apart from Windows NT is that there are still people using NetWare 3.x because of the reliability of its environment. NetWare

386 3.0 was introduced right before 1990 to take advantage of the new Intel 386 microprocessor. It was a full 32-bit NOS that added security, performance, and large amounts of users and data handling.

In the mid-1990s Novell introduced NetWare 4.x (which includes 4.0, 4.1, and 4.11). With these versions, Novell produced its first true GUI to help administrators that were familiar with Windows products. This was also the first version (4.11) to fully support IP address management, Web hosting, and FTP hosting. Probably the most important feature was the addition of NDS. Like Windows 2000's AD and Unix's NFS, Novell's NDS was designed with a X.500 hierarchical tree structure.

Novell released NetWare 5 in 1998 after totally rewriting the core NOS and making TCP/IP a native protocol alongside its proprietary IPX/SPX. Another big win for Novell was the addition of Oracle8 for NetWare, which added a database capability to all of the applications on its networks.

As mentioned before, greater detail about NetWare will not be covered; however, we will provide an overview of the three most popular versions 3.x, 4.x, and 5. More emphasis will be placed on NetWare 5 as it is the current NOS.

Major Features

Novell bases its network design on *pervasive computing*, which is a strategy that links users to corporate information through the use of computers, pagers, cellphones, wireless, and so on. In a nutshell, information should be available to someone anywhere, anytime. Within this strategy are three areas:

➤ Network Services

➤ Access

➤ Applications

Network services are the tools that a user utilizes to access the information. This can be accomplished through telephony, file, print, management, NDS, and security services. These services should be platform independent (i.e., these services should be able to run on any manufacturer's system).

Access should be easily granted whether you are using a desktop or laptop computer, telephone, or even a television. All applications that work in a NetWare environment should provide access to the network and resources that users need.

As you can see, this is part of the reason for NetWare's success, making products that work with many different kinds of applications and platforms. With NetWare 5, Novell has taken this strategy to a new level. Although it is losing ground to Microsoft, Novell is still a dominant player in the enterprise networking arena.

NetWare, like its Microsoft counterparts, also suffers in certain areas. Many of the services are simply provided as add-ons and lack common installation, management interfaces, and security infrastructure. But this is one robust NOS that should not be taken lightly.

Logical

One of the most important introductions into NetWare's architecture is NDS. This directory service provides a system for managing multiple servers and their resources. All of the computers, users, printers, disk drives, file folders, and so on are contained in NDS. You could almost call it the "Yellow Pages" of the network except that it stores more information than just a person's name, address, and phone number.

NDS was introduced in NetWare 4.0. Prior to version 4.0, users, groups, and other information were contained in the Bindery.

 If you see the word Bindery in conjunction with Novell, the reference is to NetWare 3.x or earlier.

The basic foundation of NDS is quite simple, but as you grow the organization it can become increasingly complex. NDS design is beyond the scope of this book, but there are volumes of materials that discuss the intricate details of NetWare administration.

When you install the first instance of NetWare 4.x or later, the first instance of NDS is installed as well. This is called the root. NDS then builds an upside down tree as more and more objects are added to its database. Each of these objects has options. These options are defined in the NDS schema. Like the schema in Windows 2000 ADS, it can be added on to or "extended." When a new object is added to the schema, the NDS directory then has to replicate the information to all of the NDS replicas.

As mentioned earlier, NetWare comes with core services that are amplified with utilities and applications. Some of the important ones include:

➤ *Novell Installation Service (NIS)*—This common utility allows you to install Novell products in a consistent manner. It is GUI based.

➤ *NetWare 5 GUI Console*—The server console is managed using a GUI interface reminiscent of Unix's X Windows. Known as ConsoleOne, administrators can utilize such features as applet launching, local volume browsing, basic management, and graphical server monitoring as well as server-based remote console functions.

➤ *Novell Storage Services (NSS)*—NSS is a new file system developed to help manage the huge enterprise needs of file storage. Currently it only supports CD-ROMs and hard drives.

➤ *Oracle8 Database*—NetWare 5 includes a five user version of Oracle 8.0.3 ORDBMS. This version uses NDS to provide transparent authentication to any Oracle server on the network. Each database can be configured for single sign-on and privilege management through NDS.

NetWare 5 also includes extensive data protection features, security, and support for Windows NT servers through the use of NDS for Windows NT. NetWare does a great job of integrating into networks that are serviced by multiple NOSs.

Hardware

To install NetWare 5, you must meet the hardware requirements listed in Table 9.3.

One of the essential ingredients for NetWare is memory. Because NetWare uses NetWare Loadable Modules (NLMs) to run its range of programs and applications, you need enough memory to handle these processes. The more NLMs, the more memory you need to add to your system.

NetWare 4.x and 5 support multiple processors in each server. Up to 32 processors may be installed on any one server. This can provide improved performance for your applications and the core NOS itself. You will find that as you grow your network, the heavy duty processing can become a bottleneck in your system. However, be forewarned that you should have these multiple processors installed at the manufacturer as it can become a nightmare trying to upgrade processors on a system already running a full-blown NOS.

Table 9.3 Hardware requirements for NetWare 5.	
Hardware	**Minimum**
CPU	Intel Pentium or equivalent
Internal RAM	64MB (128MB if you are running Java applets)
Hard drive space	600MB
Network interface	NIC card that supports your topology
CD-ROM	ISO 9660 formatted
I/O devices	Keyboard (mouse or other pointing device if you use the GUI interface)
Other drives	Floppy 3.5-inch drive to aid with installation

Although NetWare 4.x was unable to utilize virtual memory, NetWare 5 can. Virtual memory allows for a process known as paging. Memory on the hard drive is swapped with memory in RAM. This is appropriately called "swapping." Think of it as having runners that take full boxes out of a warehouse when room is needed for new boxes. If the warehouse needs the old boxes, runners will swap out some of the existing boxes for the old ones. The same holds true in virtual memory (also known as paging). Space on the hard drive is reserved for extending the memory from the internal RAM. If the system requires more RAM than what is physically installed, pieces of inactive memory will be placed on the hard disk in this virtual memory space. If the memory is needed again, it is swapped out for the other. Remember that swapping can cause problems if your paging file is lost or corrupted. It can also be a headache when you use virtual memory a lot. Access time and processor time are slowed down because of the time needed to swap information in and out of internal memory.

The NetWare file system is not like any file system used in Windows NT or Windows 2000. The traditional NetWare filing system consists of servers that have one or more volumes. The first volume on each individual server is called SYS. Each volume thereafter is called VOL1, VOL2, and so on. You can change the names if you desire. Each volume has its own directory system.

Volumes appear as objects in the NDS tree. NetWare 5 servers can support up to 64 volumes. Remember that the first volume is called SYS and contains the NetWare system and public files. Physically, volumes are divided into volume segments that can be stored on one or more hard drives. Logically, the volumes are divided into folders and subfolders.

One of the issues that administrators had with NetWare's traditional filing system was its lack of scalability. Using a 32-bit interface forced administrators to keep their file sizes to 2GB of data. In today's world of multimedia, video, and audio, this is not sufficient. Administrators and users were also limited to 64 volumes per server.

Novell Storage Services (NSS) was introduced to help alleviate these limitations. NSS is an optional file system than can be installed on a NetWare 5 server. It is fully compatible with the traditional file system. A few highlights of NSS include:

➤ Faster volume mounting

➤ Larger file size; up to 8TB per file

➤ Trillions of files in a single directory

➤ Allowance of up to eight partitions per disk

➤ Unlimited volumes per partition

There are a few gotchas to NSS. NSS cannot create a SYS volume, so it needs the traditional filing system to do so. NSS, sadly, does not support any RAID implementation (software based), so there is little performance enhancement or fault tolerance available. One nice feature though, is the ability for NSS to find any free space available on the network and make use of it.

Startup/Shutdown

To start a server with NetWare, you first need to boot to a DOS prompt and verify that you are in the NWSERVER directory. If you are not, move to that directory. Once in the directory, type "server.exe". You can also include this command in the autoexec.bat file so it automatically runs when the server starts. The server console appears with the name of the server and a flashing cursor. As with a DOS prompt, you issue commands to the operating system from the server console. The console is very similar to a workstation connection. From the console, you can start the GUI interface ConsoleOne. For NetWare administrators, you would access ConsoleOne from a client computer running the Microsoft Windows interface.

To shut down a NetWare server, type "down" at the console prompt. The **down** command closes the filing systems and saves all data in cache memory to disk. The directory and file allocation tables are also properly updated. The filing system will not be accessible to other servers on the network, so be aware of this. You should also add a broadcast message that is sent across the network warning users and administrators that the server is shutting down.

Unix

Many years ago, with the arrival of the minicomputer, AT&T's Bell Laboratories needed an operating system to run on these multiuser systems. As a result, Unix was born in 1969. TCP/IP as yet was not available, and Defense Advanced Research Projects Agency (DARPA) controlled the Internet. In fact, it was Unix that helped create the TCP/IP protocol stack.

Unix is very complicated to understand, and it has a very interesting history, which we will not go into. Suffice it to say that after AT&T offered the Unix version known as System V (Bell Lab's version) for a minimal licensing fee to everyone, researchers at the University of California Berkeley began to improve it and added TCP/IP to the system. In fact, one of the first versions of Unix, BSD, was created at the university.

By the time AT&T was broken up in 1983, the Unix operating system had become a cause known as Open Source. Eventually AT&T sold its rights to Unix and the rights changed hands several times up to the early 1990s. Finally, the

Santa Cruz Operation (SCO) and The Open Group (TOG) gained the rights to Unix. To make it impossible for anyone to get Unix and try to "rule the world," the rights to the code are now owned by SCO and the naming rights are owned by TOG. In order to develop a Unix-like system, you must go through a verification process. This process prevents anyone from gaining overwhelming market share. You must first pass muster on the code from SCO, and then pass TOG's verification test before being called Unix. Licensing fees are paid to the organizations for these rights. These versions of Unix are called Proprietary Unix. Companies like Sun Microsystems and Hewlett-Packard have developed their own versions: Solaris for Sun and HP-UX for Hewlett-Packard.

If you just want to create your own operating system with the Unix code, you are able to do so at no charge. It is when you want to make it available and charge people for it that the verification process kicks in. This is a very simplified explanation of the Open Source movement. The copyright included in these open source versions requires that any changes to the code be made available to everyone else. One of the most popular open source versions is Linux, which is discussed in the "Linux" section later in the chapter. Other versions are GNU, FreeBSD, and AIX.

We will mostly discuss the general abilities and features of Unix, but understand that each different flavor gives you some advantage or another. Knowing what you need and either buying it or writing it makes the choice easy for an administrator.

Major Features

All brands and flavors of Unix hold some common features:

➤ Background processing

➤ File systems that allow you to "mount" drives

➤ Thousands of subsystems

➤ Interface support for all major hardware

➤ GUI interfaces

➤ Access to the source code

➤ TCP/IP protocol stack

➤ Ultimate scalability

The most common element in Unix is the TCP/IP protocol stack. Born out of the Unix programming world, TCP/IP allows computers in all NOSs to communicate in a secure, logical, connection/connectionless state. Because the Internet was originally part of DARPA, TCP/IP is the language of the Internet. Unix is the most widely used operating system by Web and Internet users. A full 80 percent of Web servers are using some form of Unix. In fact, the servers with the most "uptime" and least downtime are running FreeBSD.

Unix primarily uses a text-based command-line interface (CLI), which is similar to a DOS prompt. However, several GUIs are available to users more comfortable with that environment. The most popular is X Windows followed closely by Motif. If you are comfortable with a Microsoft Windows environment, use one of these GUIs. If you like the challenge of a black and white blinking cursor begging for you to type something, then the CLI is for you.

Logical

Users can be organized in Unix using user accounts known as UIDs and group accounts called GIDs. When you create your Unix network, you create the root account first. Also known as superuser, root has the power to do anything in the Unix environment. He/she can override file permissions and change just about anything. It is similar to Enterprise Administrator in Windows 2000.

Unix is controlled by configuration files located in the /etc directory. For example, the /etc/passwd file contains user information. Other files and directories can include /usr, /sbin, /boot, /var/log/messages, and /lib. Notice that unlike the \\server1 type of access in Windows NT, the Unix system uses the forward slash.

Unix systems work with Macintosh, Windows, and NetWare clients using a file and print service, such as Samba. Many other open source programs can aid in this merging of networks. Unix works well in a hybrid networking situation.

One factor that separates Unix from other NOSs like Windows 2000 is its use of resources. In Unix, you must run applications to access resources—a sort of direct connection. This is more advantageous than trying to access resources over the network. It is like being directly connected to the resource. Think of a dumb terminal attached directly to the mainframe. With Unix, you control the resource at its source and view the changes made. Other NOSs bring the resources to you across the network.

In regard to security, Unix is superior to other NOSs. Because the code has been written, rewritten, and tested vigorously, it is very robust and very secure. The Department of Defense (DOD) gave it the Orange Book certification. This certification is not easy to obtain with the high security needs of the DOD.

Hardware

There really is no piece of hardware that does not like Unix. As mentioned previously, the code is very robust and secure. In addition, with the proprietary forms of Unix, you know that the equipment it is installed on has been thoroughly tested with the brand of Unix installed. For example, you know that your Sun SPARC server running Solaris 7 should not have any problems with hardware compatibility. This gives quite a few administrators peace of mind and a network with less downtime due to hardware and software conflicts.

There are few differences between the server versions of Unix and the workstation versions. Unix is modular and is set up with the utilities that it needs to perform server type functions.

The minimum hardware requirements for today's flavors of Unix are listed in Table 9.4.

As is true in most of the modern NOSs, there are minimum stated requirements and recommended requirements. Choose the recommended requirements to ensure that your system remains in good working order. Preventing downtime is usually due to having reliable equipment and plenty of working room (i.e., memory, CPU power).

Multiprocessing is supported in almost all versions of Unix. Some are even experimenting with *asymmetric multiprocessing* where processors do not have the same manufacturer or clock speed (for example, an Intel Pentium III with an AMD Athlon 1.3 GHz chip). Most multiprocessing done today is *symmetric*.

The file systems currently in use by Unix brands are diverse to say the least. One type is the Network Information Services (NIS), which allows the database to be extended across multiple servers using the TCP/IP protocol. Another popular

Table 9.4 Minimum hardware requirements for Unix.	
Hardware	Minimum
CPU	Intel 486, Pentium
Memory	16MB RAM
Hard drive space	150MB to 300MB (depending on utilities)
Network interface	Any that are found on the vendor's HCL
I/O devices	Keyboard
Other drives and devices	One 3.5-inch floppy drive

file system is the Network File System (NFS), which is used by Sun's Solaris system. Once again, the X.500 data model is in place providing a hierarchical approach to organizing objects in a database. NFS can query Novell's NDS and Microsoft's ADS using LDAP. This allows you to integrate even further with the hybrid systems.

Startup/Shutdown

To start a Unix server, you need to use the Login command. If you have an account and are authorized, you will be able to enter the system. You can also launch the GUI, like X Windows or Motif, at this point.

To shut down a Unix server, type:

```
Shutdown now -g - 0
```

The **Shutdown** command brings the system down in a secure way. All logged-in users are notified that the system is shutting down, and any other logins are blocked. It is possible to shut the system down immediately or after a specified delay. All processes are first notified that the system is shutting down. The information is saved to disk, and the server shuts down.

Linux

When the open source movement was becoming popular, a Finnish scientist by the name of Linus Torvalds, dissatisfied with the need to be verified by the license holders of the Unix source code, developed Linux. When he finished Linux, he posted it on the Internet for all to use freely. His only request was that programmers and designers would take his beginnings and create a stable, robust operating system. Soon Linux was being embraced by larger corporations.

The three major vendors in the Linux world are Red Hat, Caldera, and Slackerware. Others, like Mandrake, are popular as well, but do not have the support that the major vendors do.

Linux is easy to work with if you are familiar with Unix. In fact, it is probably easier to learn for beginners because of its recognition of the latest technologies that have been introduced over the past 10 years. The information presented in the Unix section holds true for Linux as well except for some changes here and there.

Major Features

One big advantage with Linux that makes it attractive to many people is that Linux is free. Linux also offers a true server networking environment as well as a peer-to-peer scenario. Linux is:

➤ Multitasking

➤ Multiuser

➤ Multiplatform

As an NOS, Linux is becoming more popular because of its ability to offer multitasking environments like Windows, NetWare, and OS/2. One aspect of networking in the server environment is the capability to do many things at one time. This is the basis of multitasking and is vital to the success of a server and the network.

Linux borrows its file structure from Unix. The root is the beginning of the hierarchy followed by container objects called directories. In these directories are contained the applications and services. In particular, the /boot directory contains the main Linux kernel and initialization files. Any time you create a user, a /home directory is established for that user. For example, if *dougb* needs to be added to the directory, dougb's user account will reside in the /home/dougb directory.

The file system is known as ext2, as it is the second of the extended file systems created from scratch for Linux. This file system supports both local and remote systems. It is also important to remember that Linux recognizes and supports (through added services) OS/2's HPFS, and Windows NTFS, FAT-32, and the older FAT for DOS. Because of this support, you can map shares across the entire network, and Linux will recognize them.

Linux supports the same installation requirements as Unix. See Table 9.5.

Table 9.5 Minimum hardware requirements for Linux.	
Hardware	**Minimum**
CPU	Intel 486, Pentium
Memory	16MB RAM
Hard drive space	150MB to 300MB (depending on utilities)
Network interface	Any that are found on the vendor's HCL
I/O devices	Keyboard
Other drives and devices	One 3.5-inch floppy drive

Remember that you need to be careful when planning for your servers using Linux. There are several considerations to take into account, not the least of which is how many services and utilities you are going to run.

Startup/Shutdown

The methods to start up and shut down Linux will vary slightly between versions, but the overall methods are quite similar to Unix.

Some things to remember:

➤ Save all your work and close all running applications.

➤ Broadcast a message to clients informing them that they should save their work and provide a specific time when the server will be shut down.

➤ Remotely shut down your servers manually (with the right permissions) by application or by script.

Login is used when signing onto a system. It can also be used to switch from one user to another at any time (most modern shells have support for this feature built into them, however). If an argument is not given, **login** prompts for the username. If the user is *not* root, and if /etc/nologin exists, the contents of this file are printed to the screen, and the login is terminated. This is typically used to prevent logins when the system is being taken down. If special access restrictions are specified for the user in /etc/usertty, these must be met, or the login attempt will be denied and a **syslog** message will be generated. If the user is root, the login must be occurring on a tty listed in /etc/securetty. Failures are logged with the **syslog** facility, which is also used to report any successful root logins. After these conditions have been checked, the password is requested and checked (if a password is required for this username). Ten attempts are allowed before **login** dies, but after the first three, the response starts to get very slow.

The **shutdown** command brings the system down in a secure way. All logged in users are notified that the system is shutting down, and login for users is blocked. It is possible to shut the system down immediately or after a specified delay. All processes are first notified that the system is shutting down. This gives programs like /vi the time to save the file being edited, mail and news processing programs a chance to exit cleanly, and so on. **shutdown** does its job by signaling the *init* process and asking it to change the runlevel. Runlevel **0** is used to halt the system, runlevel **6** is used to reboot the system, and runlevel **1** is used to put the system into a state where administrative tasks can be performed; this is the default if neither the -h or -r flag is given to **shutdown**. To see which actions are taken on halt or reboot, see the appropriate entries for these runlevels in the file /etc/inittab. If the file .hushlogin exists, a "quiet" login is performed (this disables the checking of mail and the printing of the last login time and message of the day). Otherwise, if /var/log/lastlog exists, the last login time is printed (and the current login is recorded). Random administrative tasks, such as setting the UID and GID of the tty are performed. The **Term** environment variable is preserved, if it exists (other environment variables are preserved if the -p option is used). The **HOME, PATH, SHELL, TERM, MAIL,** and **LOGNAME** environment variables are then set. PATH defaults to /usr/local/bin:/bin:/usr/bin:. for normal users. The file with the user's name in /usr/spool/mail will be checked and a message printed if it has nonzero length. The user's shell is then started. If no shell is specified for the user in /etc/passwd, then /bin/sh is used.

Practice Questions

Question 1

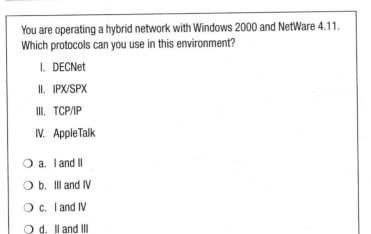

You are operating a hybrid network with Windows 2000 and NetWare 4.11. Which protocols can you use in this environment?

I. DECNet

II. IPX/SPX

III. TCP/IP

IV. AppleTalk

○ a. I and II

○ b. III and IV

○ c. I and IV

○ d. II and III

Answer d is correct. IPX/SPX and TCP/IP are both supported by Windows 2000 and NetWare. Answer a is incorrect because DECNet is not a protocol. Answers b and c are incorrect because AppleTalk is a protocol used to connect Apple and Macintosh computers.

Question 2

What is the appropriate shutdown procedure for a Unix server?

○ a. Use the X Windows shutdown menu

○ b. Type "turnoff" at the command prompt

○ c. Type "shutdown -g -0" at the command prompt

○ d. Press Ctrl+Alt+Del

Answer c is correct. Type "shutdown -g -0" at the command prompt. Answer a is incorrect because not all versions of Unix come with an X Windows shell. Answer b is incorrect because there is no shutdown command called turnoff. Answer d is the first step in shutting down a Windows NT server.

Question 3

You are a network administrator for a small company that needs to create a client/server network at its new branch office. When you interview the new manager there, she tells you that you cannot buy any new equipment, but you can install whichever NOS you would like. All of the computers are Pentium 90 machines with the exception of two Pentium 133 MHz desktops. Each machine has 16MB of RAM and 6GB hard drives. Which two NOSs could you install in this situation?

   I. Windows 2000

   II. NetWare 5

   III. Windows NT

   IV. Linux

  O a. I and II

  O b. III and IV

  O c. I and IV

  O d. II and III

Answer b is correct. You could install Windows NT and Linux. Answers a, c, and d are incorrect because both NetWare 5 and Windows 2000 have higher memory requirements for this scenario.

Question 4

Which NOS supports plug-and-play?

  O a. NetWare

  O b. Unix

  O c. Linux

  O d. Windows 2000

Answer d is correct. Windows 2000 supports plug-and-play. Answer a is incorrect because NetWare requires that an NLM be installed prior to recognizing a piece of hardware. Answers b and c are incorrect because Unix and Linux only support limited plug-and-play features during the installation phase of the program.

Question 5

Which NOS supports up to 32 CPUs?

○ a. Windows 2000

○ b. NetWare

○ c. Unix

○ d. Linux

Answer a is correct. Windows 2000 Data Center Server supports up to 32 CPUs. Answers b, c, and d are all incorrect because although all of these operating systems support multiprocessing, none support up to 32 CPUs. Part of the reason is because Windows 2000 Data Center Server requires specialized hardware to run 32 CPUs.

Question 6

Which NOS uses the ext2 file system?

○ a. Windows 2000

○ b. NetWare

○ c. Unix

○ d. Linux

Answer d is correct. Linux uses ext2. Answer a is incorrect because Windows 2000 supports FAT, FAT32, and NTFS. Answer b is incorrect because NetWare supports NFS. Answer c is incorrect because generic Unix supports NIS.

Question 7

You just installed an NLM on your NetWare server, and you need to safely restart the server in order to complete installation. How do you do this?

○ a. Ctrl+Alt+Del, restart

○ b. Shutdown, Ctrl+Alt+Del

○ c. Down, exit, server

○ d. Down, exit, Ctrl+Alt+Del

Answer c is correct. Once a NetWare server is downed to the DOS level, you can type the word "server", press Enter, and the server will initialize. Answer a is incorrect because this is the restart procedure for Windows 2000. Answer b is incorrect because this is the process for Linux. Answer d is incorrect because this will reboot the computer and then initialize the NetWare server.

Question 8

A hard drive has failed on your NetWare server, and you need to shut it down in order to replace the drive. How do you do this?

○ a. Ctrl+Alt+Del, shut down

○ b. Shut down, power it off

○ c. Down, exit, server

○ d. Down, exit, power it off

Answer d is correct. Once the server is downed and exit reaches the DOS prompt, you can safely power it down. Answer a is incorrect because this is the shutdown process for Windows 2000. Answer b is incorrect because this is the procedure for downing a Linux server. Answer c is incorrect because the **server** command will reinitialize NetWare.

Question 9

Which of the following GUIs is run by Unix?

○ a. ConsoleOne

○ b. File Manager

○ c. X.500

○ d. X Windows

Answer d is correct. X Windows is a GUI that can be run on a Unix box. Answer a is incorrect because ConsoleOne is the interface for NetWare. Answer b is incorrect because File Manager was the interface for Windows NT 3.51 (which is not covered on the exam.) Answer c is incorrect because X.500 is a directory service protocol, not a GUI.

Need to Know More?

 Craft, Melissa, Mark A. Poplar, David V. Watts, and Will Willis. *Network+ Exam Prep*. Scottsdale, AZ: The Coriolis Group, LLC, 1999. ISBN 1-57610-412-5. This book contains in-depth information on RAID.

 Dean, Tamara. *Network+ Guide to Networks*. Course Technology, Boston, MA, 1999. ISBN 0760011451. This book contains information on NOSs.

 Dyson, Peter John. *Dictionary of Networking, 3d ed*. Sybex, Inc., Berkeley, CA, 1999. ISBN 0782124615. This book contains general networking terms and definitions.

 Minasi, Mark, Christa Anderson, and Elizabeth Creegan. *Mastering Windows NT Server 4, 4th ed*. Alameda, CA: Sybex Network Press, 1997. ISBN 0-78212067-9. This book is an ideal administrator's companion for Windows NT 4, covering mostly basic to intermediate content. It includes several advanced topics as well, such as Microsoft RAID support and installation.

 Zacker, Craig and Paul Doyle. *Upgrading and Repairing Networks*. Que Corporation, Indianapolis, IN, 1996. ISBN 0-78970181-2. This book is a great platform neutral resource on which NOSs to choose for which applications. Features, benefits, and drawbacks are also included.

 http://pla-netx.com/linebackn/guis/guitimeline.html by Nathan Lineback provides an impressive picture history of GUI evolution.

 www2.linuxjournal.com from Specialized Systems Consultants in Seattle, WA, hosts the Linux Online Journal, which contains a wealth of Linux industry support, configuration, programming, and background information.

 www.novell.com is a good source of information about ConsoleOne.

 www.pcguide.com, a site by Charles M. Kozierok, is similar to TechRepublic and contains a wealth of information on many IT topics.

Troubleshooting

Terms you'll need to understand:

✓ NIC

✓ Hub

✓ Switch

✓ BIOS

✓ CPU

✓ NOS

✓ Controller

✓ Wake-on-LAN

✓ PING

✓ DHCP

✓ OS

✓ TRACERT

✓ SNMP

✓ RMON

✓ POST

✓ RAID

✓ Crosstalk

✓ WINS

Techniques you'll need to master:

✓ Troubleshooting server BIOS problems

✓ Troubleshooting server hard drive problems

✓ Troubleshooting network problems

✓ Troubleshooting CPU problems

✓ Troubleshooting memory problems

✓ Distinguishing between a hardware problem and a software problem

Troubleshooting 101

Troubleshooting is perhaps one of the most difficult and complex topics to teach. Many people say that certain people just have a talent for it, and others do not. Other people say that solid troubleshooting skills come with experience, yet experience does not grow without troubleshooting. The goal of this chapter is to teach you troubleshooting in such a manner that not only will the material on the exam be covered, but hopefully you will also gain some insight into the "gentle" art of troubleshooting.

By definition, troubleshooting is what occurs when there is a problem to be solved. Many times the nature of the problem is directly linked to the symptom. For example, a few years ago, there was a popular technical support email story being spread around that described a technical support call. The technician received a call from a user indicating that his monitor had gone blank. The technician proceeded to troubleshoot the problem over the phone, making sure that the monitor was switched on, tracing the data cables, making sure that power was plugged in, and so on. The technician had pretty much decided to have the client reboot the computer in order to start fresh and proceeded to instruct the user over the phone in the mutually blind process of finding the on switch. That was when the user informed the technician that it was very dark in the room because there had been a power outage. Although this is a great example of the symptom pointing directly to the cause, those of you with some experience can at least see how easily the technician was misled by the assumption that the user knew that the computer would not work (let alone the monitor) if the power was out.

Server systems issues are completely different situations to deal with when troubleshooting problems. There are several reasons for this:

➤ A server usually has more complex hardware than the average desktop computer.

➤ Servers are connected to many different systems that can fail and impact server functionality in several ways.

➤ By and large, servers are subjected to more wear and tear in a single day than most desktops see in a month. Servers are utilized more than desktops and thus are more prone to failure. Even when fault tolerance is involved, issues often just simply arise.

➤ Servers are "high-profile" devices—if anything goes wrong, a large number of people are likely to notice and blame it on a networking or server issue out of sheer ignorance.

➤ On the other hand, a single issue that appears to be a desktop problem can in reality be a server problem.

It is because of these issues that quite often the symptoms of a problem do not directly point to a server hardware issue. To the contrary, frequently a software issue can appear to be hardware, and a hardware problem can be masked by a plethora of software annoyances.

This is when most technicians end up investigating the software and OS world, trying to determine if the issue truly is a hardware issue or rather a software, virus, or even a simple configuration problem. This is also the reason, despite the "vendor neutral" status of the Server+ exam, CompTIA and the supporting vendors want to ensure that you know enough about servers, and everything on and connected to them, to be able to make the call between a hardware and software problem. Most employers recognize that it can be difficult to think straight in "emergency" situations, such as when a server goes down. Passing the Server+ exam will help ensure employers that you have the knowledge and ability to find and fix problems under pressure. Employers also have firsthand experience in witnessing hardware and software people pointing fingers at each other during a crisis. Having a server hardware technician on board who knows how to handle crises by delving into both software and hardware issues is an asset they look for.

The Scientific Method

Novice technicians often ask questions first and think later. With some experience, you will be able to form ideas and conclusions on the fly as you ask questions. Eventually, you should be able to narrow down the causes of an issue before making any changes to the hardware or software.

Just as in fourth grade science class, the scientific method is paramount in solving problems, even those that are not science related. The whole scientific method is based on the process of elimination, eliminating possible problems until you determine the true source of a problem and can subsequently solve it. To recap the scientific method, here is how it works:

1. Gather information.

2. Draw a conclusion.

3. Test your conclusion.

4. Use test results to modify your conclusion.

5. Test again.

6. Continue the process until a solution is met.

These steps did not make sense while we were in school, but it makes ultimate sense when troubleshooting problems and figuring out the "whys" of the world. Let's discuss this process in detail, as it is valuable in the overall methodology of troubleshooting. And don't forget: just as in science class, it is a good idea to document everything you have done so that you don't lose track of what is going on and what needs to be done.

Gather Information

The Server+ exam covers issues that do not appear to be truly server related. One reason for this is that in the real world, anything that is perceived as a server issue is a server issue—even when it is not. The Server+ exam does not quiz you on desktop troubleshooting, but it does ask questions that essentially span an associative radius that could be drawn around a server. These questions may touch on subjects just enough for you to be able to claim the issue as a server hardware problem, or diagnose it as a server software or desktop issue.

The first step in troubleshooting is to assess the situation. Look at the environment and take some mental notes. If there is a proverbial path of breadcrumbs, follow it. The troubleshooting process begins with an open mind. Be very careful not to focus too deeply on the symptom, but rather look at the entire picture to get an idea of the scope of the problem you are dealing with, and thus a better idea of where you might need to investigate further.

Look at the Symptoms

Specific hardware symptoms are discussed in the "Hardware" section of this chapter. Before you begin to draw any conclusions on what the problem is, look at all of the symptoms. Quite often, a complaint comes in one of two forms—the first is when someone states what the symptom is with little or no additional information. The second form of complaint is when someone has already drawn a conclusion of what the problem is and attempts to notify you of this conclusion instead of the actual symptom. Both of these situations require that you tactfully and appropriately ask background questions in order to draw out environmental information and symptoms without offending the people who call in.

Currently, the two most frequent complaints about IT people involve attitude and timeliness. Recognize that your customers are the same people who call in with problems and questions. They deserve respect and credit when it is due, and the overall goal is to get up and running as quickly as possible. Asking probing questions about the symptoms and environment will help reduce these two frequent complaints.

Is Anybody Else Having This Problem?

One of the most important questions you can ask when probing for more information is to determine if anyone else is having the same problem. If nobody else is having the problem and others are using their systems in a similar manner, then more than likely the problem does not lie with server hardware, but instead with a desktop configuration or server software (user settings and permissions are often a huge culprit). This is a common guideline to start with, but it does not rule out other possibilities. It just helps to nudge other possibilities out of the "server hardware" radius. One such "other" possibility that comes to mind involves faulty network drop wiring connecting from the desktop cube or office to a hub/switch, bad hub ports, or bad network interface card (NIC). Again, these are not directly related to server issues, but can be perceived as such. Because most users do not know the difference between the "network" and the "server," it is not unusual for them to assume that desktop connectivity is a server issue.

The primary purpose for determining if anyone else is having the same problem goes back to gathering data and information about the problem. Again, determining the scope of the problem can help you correctly focus on exactly where the problem is by determining what it is that all of the affected people have in common.

What Changed?

Server specific problems, as well as single user issues, can quite often be traced to a particular change. Upgrading BIOS, CPU, hard disk drives, NOSs, software settings, and so on can trigger problems or changes that are perceived as problems. (Do not forget that users frequently perceive something out of the ordinary or different as a problem just because they are unaware of a change.) Again, perception is key. For example, a single user regularly (and accidentally) deletes files on the network. She perceives the problem as a server issue where the hard drive is going bad. As a matter of fact, when she calls you about it, she says, "the server drive is going down." This can easily send you into panic mode. Rather than be alarmed, ask a few important questions. What changed? Has this happened before? On one hand, you may find that she changed keyboards a few weeks ago when the problem began and has been mistaking the insert key for the delete key. On the other hand, subsequently asking if someone else is having the problem, and getting a yes for an answer, could definitely point to a server problem. You might also ask if everyone is having similar issues: If the answer is yes, you just might be dealing with a drive problem. If the answer is no, you need to find out what changed on the server, and troubleshoot the problem from that point.

Know Your History, Find a Pattern

One of the reasons troubleshooting is so difficult to teach is because there are many "very important" points to learn that are not tangible and are not rule based. Servers live in complex systems and environments. A single symptom can point to five different problems. Because time is of the essence, it is not appropriate to troubleshoot all five problems. It is better to ask probing questions and use analytical fact and data gathering techniques to systematically rule out candidates.

Probing questions, such as "Is anybody else having this problem?" or "What changed?" are excellent questions to ask, but they are useless if you don't know what the answers mean. The best way to systematically rule out bogus problems while troubleshooting is to find a pattern to the problem. Has this problem been happening every Monday at 9:00 A.M. for the past month? What changed a month ago? Does everybody have this problem at 9:00 A.M. only on Monday? These are all questions that, when asked in the proper order, can point you in the direction of the true solution. Patterns for you to look for include the following:

➤ *People*—Does this problem happen only with this one person? If the problem is isolated, and this person uses a different computer, does the problem continue? What if the person sits at a different desk? If the problem is not isolated to a single person, determine the commonality between all of the affected people. Asking these questions helps determine the exact scope and pattern of how many people the problem affects, which can assist you in determining several things. Isolated user issues can be related to user error, local computer failure, network interface failure, drop failure, hub port failure, user permissions, or any number of other software or hardware issues. Problems affecting multiple users are almost always network based or network related. This is when you really need to determine what they all have in common. Are they all on the same network hub? In the same room? Using the same software? Members of the same user group? The list goes on and on, but you surely get the point.

➤ *Computers*—Does this problem happen only on this computer? If the computer is moved to a different user, does the problem follow the user or the computer? The questions to ask and the thought processes behind them are almost identical to those you would ask in the previous people component. One of the quickest (although sometimes painful) ways to determine if you are dealing with a hardware issue is to remove the affected equipment and replace it with a "known good."

➤ *Frequency*—Does this happen often? Has it happened several times in the past day, week, month, or year? File corruption on servers, for example, occurs occasionally just in the course of existence—users shut off computers, files become garbled during saves, or power outages cause corruption. If file corruption occurs frequently, you may be dealing with a faulty drive or controller.

➤ *Time of day/week/month/year*—Know your history. Does this problem happen every year in the last week of February? Does it happen only once a week, at a certain time of day, on a particular day of the month, or annually? These questions can deal with frequency, but are designed to get you pointed in the direction of whatever it is that triggers the failure or problem. If the network slows down at 8:00 A.M. and 1:00 P.M. every day, it could be because everyone gets into the office or back from lunch at those times, and the network becomes flooded with logon traffic.

➤ *What is happening at time of failure*—What was the server doing when the problem happened? What were you (or the user) doing when you noticed the problem? What applications are running? What is the current memory usage? CPU utilization? Free disk space? How long has the server been running without a reboot?

 When searching for patterns—especially when dealing with problems that appear erratic or random—start asking compound questions and looking for common threads to the answers. Does this happen more often for one person than another? Does it happen on the first floor at 9:00 A.M. and on the third floor at 2:00 P.M.? Is everybody accessing the payroll application at the end of the month when the problem occurs?

Because of the diversity of problems that can occur, troubleshooting by rote or from a script is extremely difficult. If we give you a fish, we feed you for a day, but if we teach you to fish, we feed you for a lifetime. In addition to teaching you some of the rote troubleshooting tips that are covered in the exam, we are also teaching you many of the troubleshooting skills and tactics that Server+ companies are looking for. Asking appropriate questions can be the determining factor in whether or not you need to be involved in an issue from a server perspective, whether the issue is perceived as a server problem, or whether or not it is a server problem at all.

Draw a Conclusion

After you gather information or data about a problem and its symptoms, you need to draw a conclusion as to what the problem is. Remember that when troubleshooting, the conclusion isn't equal to a problem's solution. In just the same manner as problems can be multifaceted, you need to always keep in mind that finding and solving a problem can be a multistep process.

Earlier, we discussed how a single symptom may point to multiple problems. Sometimes even when you ask all of the appropriate questions, you still need other questions answered in order to narrow down the possibilities. Other times, there are questions that cannot be answered immediately without performing tests. This is when you should come up with an interim goal and draw a conclusion based upon it.

Let's say that a problem affecting multiple users exists. All of the affected people are connected to the same server, and they all reside in the same room. For the sake of simplicity, let's say that there are two different problems that can be the culprit: the server is down, or the network connectivity is down. Select one of these problems and attempt to prove it. Neither one of these situations points to the real problem because it does not provide a solution. If you determine that the server is down, you still have not figured out why. The same applies for network connectivity. These are intermediate conclusions for you to test and modify appropriately. It is very important that you have the patience to formulate these intermediate conclusions in such a way that you can narrow down the potential problems. Remember that with so many complex server-related problems, you need to deal with the process of elimination before dealing with the process of fixing in order to save time and money.

Test Your Conclusion

Once you draw a conclusion, you need to know and understand the expected results when it is tested. If at all possible, build a proof or test for your conclusion that eliminates more than one possibility or points to one possibility in particular.

Let's say that in the previous example you conclude that the server is down. To test it, you can look at the server and determine its status. If it is not down, you will need to draw another conclusion and test again.

Use Test Results to Modify Your Conclusion

Let's use the earlier example of the technician and the blank monitor. It is fairly obvious that the technician concluded that there was a power or data cable issue. He proceeded to test that conclusion and was in the process of drawing another conclusion when the solution presented itself. This is a prime example of why it is important to ask the right questions and be thorough. By asking more explicit questions, the technician probably would have drawn a different conclusion and saved a lot of time and money in doing so.

In the example where you had a choice of the server being down versus network connectivity having problems, you determined that the server was up and running, so the only other choice was that network connectivity was disrupted. Let's say you go back to test the network connectivity by using the **PING** command to determine if the server is available from one of the affected systems. You then determine that network connectivity is okay as well. The results from both of these tests first lead to the conclusion that there must be another possibility. This is when you begin to look outside the area of your involvement in the process. If you are responsible for the software piece of the server, there may be problems with security permissions, group membership, or other NOS-related configuration issues that are truly out of the scope of this exam. If you are not in charge of software, you certainly have enough information at this point to reasonably prove that this is not a server hardware issue.

Know When It Is Not Your Problem

Using the monitor scenario described earlier, let's modify it a bit. Let's say that you are dealing with a server, and you are on site attempting to fix the problem. Of course, you would instantly know when the power went out, and you would power down your servers before the UPS batteries died. But is this problem related to you? Maybe. If power in the entire city or block is down, you don't need to worry any further. If, instead, only the building or suite is affected, you may need to investigate further.

We once had a situation where all connectivity to the network would go down around 9:00 A.M. each day. After asking a few questions (Is anybody else having this problem? Is anything else not working?), we found that everyone could access the printer, which was located in the same room, but could not access data on the server, which was located on a different floor. we found that the remote networking hub had lost power because the circuit breaker had tripped. Again, this particular situation was not directly related to a server issue, but it was perceived as a server issue. Simply resetting the circuit breaker was a temporary fix, yet it still remained squarely on my shoulders to fix. As a stopgap measure, we purchased a UPS for the hub and plugged it into a separate circuit. It turned out that every morning the sales staff would turn on three coffee machines and frequently used two microwaves located in the kitchen, which was on the same circuit as the network hub. Once we determined that the true issue was centered around circuit load, we could reasonably step back and hand off the issue to management.

Ockham's Razor

In the fourteenth century, a philosopher named William of Ockham made the following observation: "When you have two competing theories that make exactly the same predictions, the one that is simpler is the better." His original statement was in Latin, and somewhat more difficult to understand, as his point was not science oriented. Subsequent scientists from Newton to Einstein used this principle to eliminate bogus or unwarranted conclusions from complex formulae and scientific principles.

Ockham's razor can be applied to troubleshooting in a similar manner. When drawing your conclusions, begin with the simple, and work your way to the complex. You have a greater chance of success (not to mention reducing your embarrassment) when you eliminate the obvious rather than jumping to a complex conclusion that does not provide enough test data for you to draw a more focused conclusion.

Again, the monitor technician situation provides a perfect example of how asking the right questions could allow Ockham's razor to eliminate all complex possibilities in favor of the simple and obvious: The monitor was blank because the power in the entire building was out.

The Hunt

The methodologies we have described can apply towards troubleshooting and solving nearly any complex or technical problem. As IT administrators and managers, we have often found ourselves using these techniques to tackle problems with telephones, copy machines, and even minor injuries. Quite a bit of the Server+ exam is devoted to troubleshooting. We have already covered many of the "what can go wrong" topics throughout this book. However, we still need to specifically discuss troubleshooting from the point of view of addressing a new problem.

Consider for a moment that you are troubleshooting a server environment. It is important to keep in mind that server problems, by their very nature, should always be considered mission critical. Desktop issues and failures are critical to the single user who currently uses the desktop, or the few users who may be affected by that particular system's faults in a peer-to-peer network. Servers are different because they hold data and provide services to many people. A downed server can negatively affect the function of an entire corporation, so you should approach server problems with a sense of seriousness and gravity.

Just as important as this serious demeanor toward server problems is the necessity for you to keep a clear head. When a server is down, it is not unusual for employees and management alike to become somewhat panicked. Although it may be easy to succumb to the environment of urgent desperation to get back up and running, you need to remain calm and maintain some semblance of control over the situation. They will look to you and your colleagues for reassurance and progress. Communication is paramount, and the key to that communication is your own attitude of competence and progress. When you communicate with others in the midst of a problem, avoid "pointing fingers" at someone or something, and instead focus on solving the problem. Report to management and others about your progress as you are troubleshooting, and document everything. Even if you do not have concrete answers, always be prepared to tell the truth about your current status and how you plan to resolve the issue. Although not always immediately valuable, documentation is important in order to determine exactly how a problem was ultimately solved and what steps were taken to solve it. Documentation can also play a key role in a post-mortem process when a problem has been solved, but when you still need to determine how it started and prevent it from happening again.

Your personal, internal attitude while troubleshooting, however, should be that of a detective or hunter. As previously mentioned, symptoms do not always lead to problems, and you need to stay focused by systematically following tracks, trails, and other symptoms of the troublemaker.

Troubleshooting Tool Belt

As mentioned earlier in the "Troubleshooting 101" section of this chapter, much of your "troubleshooting tool belt" exists in methodology. In addition to this methodology, specific tools and utilities can be used in troubleshooting server and perceived server problems in order to, for the most part, "prove beyond a reasonable doubt," the exact nature of a problem and how to solve it.

Server Troubleshooters

Many well-equipped servers come with management tools that detect current or pending problems, such as temperature, hard disk failure, or memory failure. Once these configured thresholds are defined within the management application, the application can create logs, send messages to network computers or pagers, or even shut down the server. If these triggers have been configured for the affected server, you can check for any logs or messages. This particularly applies in situations where the server reboots itself in an apparently random manner.

Many servers are equipped with Wake-on-LAN features. Advanced features may include a remote administration capability that allows you to remotely perform management functions. Even when a server is "locked up" or "frozen," it is possible to perform limited management tasks on a server through this same Wake-on-LAN connection.

System logs exist for all NOSs covered on the exam. Check the system logs for any unusual events. This is where it is particularly important to know your system and how it behaves under normal operations, as we discussed in Chapter 7.

In the event that the server is completely down or failed, reboot it, and watch it carefully. Take note of any unusual beeps or messages that appear as the server initializes. The BIOS will beep with any failures occurring in memory, hard drives, the keyboard, or other major systems (depending on the type and complexity of the BIOS application).

Network Troubleshooters

Once a server has been configured and placed into production, many corporations establish a de facto policy that the server is in a state of being "lockeddown." This type of "lockdown" status basically means that system and configuration changes are not made directly to a server without going through some sort of testing and implementation process that is usually highly documented. Quite often in a lockdown environment, server and server-related issues are more likely to be related to network connectivity, configuration, or application software because lockdown helps prevent NOS and hardware-related problems.

Troubleshooting network connectivity, which includes access to both local and remote or Internet resources, can quickly begin by using the PING utility. The PING utility, originally a Unix program, is a surprisingly powerful tool that can be used to determine network connectivity in networks that utilize TCP/IP.

PING can be run on server and desktop systems running Microsoft OSs, NOSs, or Unix. PING can also be run on client systems running Microsoft operating systems, Unix, and OS/2. Similar to a submarine, PING is used to determine whether another system is on the network. Instead of emitting a sound into water, however, the **PING** command uses the TCP/IP protocol to basically "tap" a specific computer or server on the network to determine if it responds. Both systems must be running the TCP/IP protocol in order for the utility to function. Pinging a system is the equivalent of knocking on someone's door and asking, "Are you there?" In order to execute the **PING** command, at the command prompt, type "PING" followed by the IP address or server name of the system to which you want to determine connectivity status. PING can be used to determine the IP address of a server by simply running PING against the server name. As shown in Figure 10.1, the utility will always respond (if connectivity is positive) by displaying network response statistics of the server in terms of its IP address. In order to determine IP configuration functionality, you can also ping the address 127.0.0.1. This address is a local loopback address for a local computer. Any time you ping 127.0.0.1, you are essentially pinging yourself to determine if the current IP configuration is installed properly.

IPCONFIG/IFCONFIG is a dual network configuration and diagnostic utility that is used to determine the current IP address. IPCONFIG can be used for Microsoft OS and NOS systems, and IFCONFIG applies to Unix servers and desktop boxes. IPCONFIG is particularly useful for quickly determining the current IP address on systems that are Dynamic Host Configuration Protocol (DHCP) clients. DHCP is a network service that dynamically assigns IP addresses and other IP related configuration information to network clients. When a network client boots, it will find and query the local DHCP server for an IP address (if the client is set up to do so). Using the IPCONFIG (or IFCONFIG) /**RELEASE** and /**RENEW** switches will erase the current IP address configuration

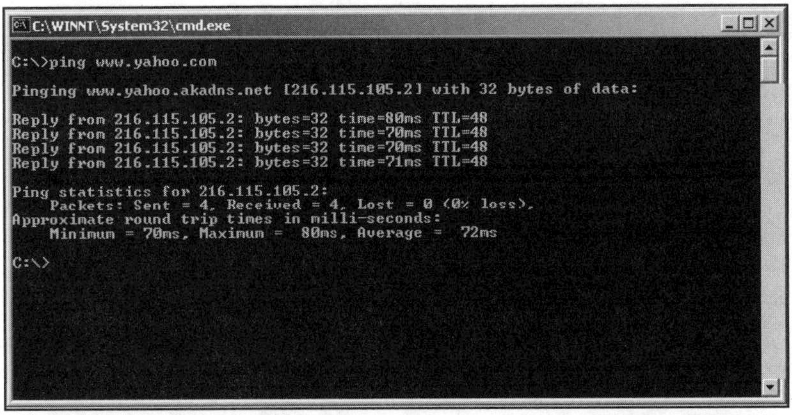

Figure 10.1   The PING utility.

and requery the local DHCP server for another IP address. This is particularly useful to determine if the DHCP server is functional and to eliminate address conflicts. In the event that the DHCP server reconfigures the client with the same conflicting IP address, you will immediately know that there is something wrong with the DHCP server configuration.

TRACERT is a utility that is used in more complex situations where a portion of the network may be down or nonfunctional. Let's say that you attempt to ping an Internet server, and the server is unavailable. You will need to subsequently ping the internal router address, external router addresses, and perhaps the IP address of your ISP or service provider. Rather than run through this process, TRACERT will do this for you without all of the research. Similar in syntax, the TRACERT utility primarily works the same as PING: TRACERT is followed by the IP address or server name (including fully qualified domain names [FQDNs]) of the server. As shown in Figure 10.2, TRACERT shows the IP addresses of every server that routes the request until the ultimate destination is reached. TRACERT can tell you where a network breakdown has occurred, thus allowing you to focus more closely on specifics, such as determining whether a network device is malfunctioning or if it is the network circuit.

In addition to these low-level utilities, you can also check SNMP and RMON for network server functionality. RMON can provide more detailed information about network traffic and devices and RMON supported switches, hubs, and routers, which will increase your knowledge on whether a network device has failed as opposed to a server. When someone cannot establish connectivity or reach data located on a server, it is easy to conclude that the server is down rather than consider the possibility that a portion of the network or wide area network (WAN) might be nonfunctional due to a cable, circuit, hub, or router problem.

```
C:\WINNT\System32\cmd.exe                                    _ □ X

C:\>tracert www.yahoo.com

Tracing route to www.yahoo.akadns.net [64.58.76.179]
over a maximum of 30 hops:

  1   <10 ms    <10 ms    <10 ms  AMDY [192.168.0.1]
  2   <10 ms    <10 ms    <10 ms  10.0.0.1
  3    50 ms     50 ms     50 ms  loop1.phnx-ds1-gw16.phnx.uswest.net [65.101.14.2
54]
  4    50 ms     50 ms     50 ms  104.gig0-0-0.phnx-agw2.phnx.uswest.net [209.181.
135.126]
  5    50 ms     50 ms     50 ms  gig2-0.phnx-gw2.phnx.uswest.net [206.80.192.251]
  6    50 ms     60 ms     60 ms  s1-gw15-ana-1-1.sprintlink.net [144.232.192.21]
  7    60 ms     60 ms     60 ms  s1-exodus-7-0-0.sprintlink.net [144.232.192.38]
  8    60 ms     60 ms     61 ms  bbr02-g6-0.elsg01.exodus.net [216.34.192.36]
  9    60 ms     60 ms     60 ms  bbr01-p1-2.irvn02.exodus.net [216.32.132.113]
 10   110 ms    110 ms    110 ms  bbr01-p1-0.dlls01.exodus.net [206.79.9.34]
 11   110 ms    110 ms    110 ms  bbr02-p0-0.ftwo01.exodus.net [206.79.9.198]
 12   101 ms    110 ms    110 ms  bbr01-p1-0.atln01.exodus.net [206.79.9.189]
 13   100 ms    101 ms    120 ms  bbr02-g2-0.atln01.exodus.net [216.35.162.4]
 14   130 ms    130 ms    131 ms  bbr01-p6-0.hrnd01.exodus.net [206.79.9.50]
 15   120 ms    130 ms    131 ms  bbr02-p6-0.stng01.exodus.net [209.185.249.137]
 16   120 ms    130 ms    130 ms  dcr04-g10-0.stng01.exodus.net [216.33.96.162]
 17   120 ms    130 ms    130 ms  216.33.98.18
 18   120 ms    131 ms    120 ms  216.35.210.122
 19   130 ms    130 ms    130 ms  www10.dcx.yahoo.com [64.58.76.179]
```

Figure 10.2   The TRACERT utility.

Hardware

Now that you are aware of troubleshooting methodologies and some of the basic troubleshooting tools that are covered on the Server+ exam, let's move on to server specifics. In this section, we talk about how specific symptoms equate to component failures.

Hard Drives

Symptoms of hard drive failures come in many shapes and sizes. The most common symptom includes recurring file corruption that is more frequent than the norm. This will appear to you and your users as files and data that is missing, incomplete, garbled, or just trashed. Unfortunately, file corruption is one of those symptoms that can be the result of several different problems. In the "Software" section of this chapter, we discuss software based or related file corruption and how to recognize its symptoms.

Unfortunately, when file corruption occurs, the problem can be related to drive cables, the disk controller, or the drive itself.

Hard drive cables rarely fail simply because they have no moving parts, and there is no embedded logic that can go wrong. It is possible to fry the wires in the cable by applying too much current, which can occur during an electrical discharge. In such situations, you are far more likely to have larger problems than just a fried cable: Anything that is powerful enough to fry wires is likely to severely damage other electrical parts in your server or desktop. If a cable does fail, you are more inclined to encounter problems with the hard drive or controller, because cables transfer not only data, but also electrical current.

Hard drive data cables are ribbon cables and usually have a red stripe on one side or another. Any time you are working with these cables, you need to make a note of which side the stripe should be in relation to the cable plug. Most plugs nowadays are "keyed" with a groove that prevents you from plugging the cable in backwards or off center. But older systems don't have this feature. When a hard drive cable is plugged in backwards, the system usually fails to boot completely. Remember that during Power On Self Test (POST), the hard drive is started and checked to ensure that it exists so that the BIOS can later pass functionality to the on board NOS or OS. If the data cable is unplugged, the system will eventually display a message that a bootable operating system cannot be found. If the cable is plugged in backwards, the system completely stops with a blank screen and, with some BIOSs, a beep code. Any time either of these symptoms occur, check the hard drive data cable.

Hard drives also have power cables. The power cable is comprised of a group of four or five colored wires attached to a white plug that is keyed in such a manner that it cannot be plugged in incorrectly. If the power cable is unplugged, any of the previous symptoms can occur, so you need to check all cables.

Note: The phrase "Check yer cables" is often called the number 1 rule of troubleshooting.

Hard drive controller failure does not happen often. When it does, it is usually a result of either misconfiguration or electrical discharge, such as a lightning storm (another reason to keep your servers connected to a UPS). Electrical discharge that occurs from lightning storms or even electrostatic discharge (ESD) events can lead to somewhat erratic symptoms. Most often, you will see the system lock up or hang erratically with no apparent trigger, stimulus, or reason. You may also experience situations where the system spontaneously reboots. Any time a system experiences electrical damage, be aware that more system components may be damaged than you first perceive. Service technicians will often replace an entire motherboard and often hard drive(s) in order to eliminate most electrically damaged components.

SCSI controllers, however, are a completely different story. Most non-SCSI disk controllers rely on the CPU to handle controller and drive processing. Most SCSI controllers, on the other hand, are computers in their own right, as they have their own processor chip, memory, and BIOS functionality. This enables SCSI drives—particularly RAID arrays—to be configured and managed in a complex manner separate from the server's BIOS. In turn, this exposes a SCSI RAID controller to more potential failures. If a controller has completely failed, the server is likely to stop with a blank screen and some beeps during POST because the hard drive will not be available. If a SCSI controller (or SCSI drive) is installed incorrectly, error messages may occur indicating that the hard drive cannot be read, but you are more likely to encounter random hangs during boot. Any time these types of erratic events occur, make sure that the SCSI channel is properly terminated and that all drives are plugged in properly. If a SCSI controller is misconfigured, however, you will see an error message after POST but before the NOS initializes. Most of these error messages are very rudimentary, but still provide some clue as to the nature of the problem. As discussed in Chapter 3, each device in a SCSI will have a logical unit number (LUN) assigned to it via the SCSI configuration interface. If, during boot, the controller expects a particular drive to have a certain LUN and it doesn't, error messages can appear indicating a configuration error.

If a SCSI RAID array hangs during boot, the problem is most likely related to proper termination. If the array displays an error message, the problem is usually related to configuration.

SCSI error messages that mention the BIOS usually require a BIOS upgrade in order to properly support the SCSI controller card. Other messages mentioning configuration usually deal with the physical placement of the devices in the SCSI channel or chain. Again, you need to check that the LUNs are correct and that the chain is properly terminated as well.

If you happen to notice or hear a hard drive making a lot of noise and file corruption occurs frequently, the problem is most likely a drive failure. Hard drives are made of several metal platters or disks coated with magnetic material. These physical platters look much like small record albums. As with a record, there is data on both sides of the disk. In order to read this data quickly, a single rocker arm extends to each side of the disk so that the disk can be read without flipping it over. The hard drive arm has devices on the end called heads. Drive heads read information from the platter magnetically. Information is written to the platter in the same way. Magnetically charged electrons do not live forever, and it is possible for a hard drive to wear out after much usage. Occasionally, the alignment between a hard disk platter and the drive heads becomes misaligned, and the drive heads press harder on the platter than they should. If you consider that these platters spin at thousands of revolutions per minute, you might understand how quickly one of these heads can wear a mark in the platter, completely destroying not just the platter, also but the entire hard drive.

Most hard drives have minute variations on the surface of the drive platter that makes it impossible to safely store a piece of magnetic information at that location. These types of flaws are normal and are nothing to be concerned about.

Most NOSs today automatically recognize these "blips" when they trip across them. Upon recognition, the OS flags the spot as bad, and writes the data elsewhere. NetWare has had this feature since version 3.x. Microsoft did not begin this type of disk maintenance until Windows NT 4.0.

Drives will often make a lot of noise when the bearings are wearing out. Remember that hard drive platters spin at great speeds, and the ability to spin is directly related to small round metal balls that are encased in the center of the platters. If these balls are not lubricated properly, are worn out, or simply will not spin, a hard drive will begin to fail by first producing a high-pitched squeak, and then by emitting a groaning or grinding sound. The hard drive will usually function during these times, but you need to be aware that the drive may be failing, and retrieve data appropriately. Eventually, the bearings will fall apart from heat friction, stress, or age, and the platters will no longer turn. This action is called *seizing*. When the bearings seize, the drive is toast, and the data is irretrievable. You can usually tell when a drive has seized when it first gets power during server POST. You will actually hear the motors slam against the gears in an attempt to engage the platters to make them spin. There is no basic remediation to prevent a drive from going bad when its bearings are failing. The best thing you can do is to be proactive about it and make regular backups of the data until you can replace the drive—preferably before the bearings seize. However, when a hard drive squeaks, it doesn't necessarily mean that there is something wrong with the bearings. Quite often it does, and you need to be very aware of the situation. Sometimes lubrication within the bearing case has become off balance and the bearings will squeak only part of the time. Unfortunately, because drive platters spin so quickly, the squeaking is often heard as a solid tone. If you hear this tone, keep an eye on the system. If the squeaking goes away in a day or two, the drive is okay.

Also, keep an eye on any management tools and disk tools that will monitor the number of physical corruptions and write failures. These tools will definitely be able to proactively tell you when a hard drive is in a downward spiral. If you have these management tools in place and have either disregarded or not configured them for notification, check the logs and statistics for the application as soon as you can.

Network Interface

Troubleshooting network-related hardware problems can be quite hairy sometimes because quite often the handful of symptoms are the same for cables, network cards, or hubs. Add in software factors, and troubleshooting networks in general can be downright annoying.

NIC failures are few and far between. As with most other hardware components, the primary cause of failure is related to ESD and electrical events that overload the wiring or circuitry.

In any suspected NIC failure, you should first check the lights at the back of the card. Most NICs (with the possible exception of coax connectors) have two lights on the back. One light represents data being received, and the other represents data being sent. If one of these lights is on when the NOS boots, it is unlikely that the NIC has failed.

Unlike most hard drives, NICs require drivers to be present in order to truly function. NIC drivers are NOS and OS specific, which places them squarely within the software realm of troubleshooting. Unfortunately, because these drivers act as interfaces between the NOS/OS and the hardware, the point of view can be taken that drivers fall within the hardware realm. As such, we will discuss NIC drivers in this section and leave pure software issues covered on the exam for the section entitled "Network Issues" in the "Software" section of this chapter.

As mentioned earlier, NIC drivers are NOS and OS specific and usually will not initialize until the OS begins to boot. Once a driver initializes, that is the point when you will see the lights on the back of the card. If the network cable is not connected, the NIC will not initialize, and the lights will not be lit. One of the two lights (which are rarely labeled) will occasionally flicker as the server attempts to communicate with other devices on the network. If both lights flicker, you can be relatively sure that the hardware is not damaged. In addition, you will need to resort to commands like **PING** and **TRACERT** to determine what the connectivity on the network looks like and how far it goes. This is, of course, assuming that you are running the TCP/IP protocol stack on the server. Start by pinging 127.0.0.1 to determine if the driver and IP configuration are functioning properly. It might also be beneficial to use another computer to ping the server's IP address to determine if the server is reachable on the network. If you are starting with a single complaint of "I cannot access my files," try pinging from the affected client machine and maybe one or two others in the area just to determine if the problem is widespread or not. If other clients can connect to the server and one cannot, it is definitely not a server problem. Instead, it is a specific workstation issue dealing with connectivity. Methodologies and troubleshooting tactics still apply, however, and surprisingly, client connectivity is covered somewhat on the exam. This is definitely when you will want to keep your thinking cap on because gathering the appropriate information can be the difference between a server problem and a workstation problem. Once you have checked the lights on the NIC and have also run PING to check that the protocol stack and the driver is functioning appropriately, you can safely say that the problem is not with the NIC.

Newer BIOS and NIC features seem to allow systems to literally boot to the network. In reality, this particular type of configuration does not boot to the network. Instead, the BIOS allows the NIC to query the network for a proper boot device that can replace the boot process, which would normally occur when the BIOS handed off to the hard drive for OS initialization. This particular technology is called Pre-eXEcution (PXE), which is pronounced "pixie"; and it is gaining usage within the Windows 2000 world for automated OS installations. In addition to this particular functionality, PXE boot network cards are also being used for thin client technologies where a system basically boots to a Terminal or Citrix server. Although you need to be aware of the technology, it is unlikely that you will encounter any exam questions dealing specifically with PXE type environments.

The number one problem with cable failures is related to actually plugging them in. If the cable is plugged in, most NIC drivers will fully initialize, and one of the two lights on the back of the NIC will be lit. If neither light is on, either there is a problem with the cable not being plugged in, or the cable is damaged or assembled improperly.

There are several types of networking cables available; however, the two most frequently used are coax and 10Base-T. Figure 10.3 shows a diagram of coax cable.

The cable is attached to a connector that conducts current along both the wire mesh shielding and the center conductor. Data is transmitted via the center conductor, and current is conducted through the wire mesh shielding, which serves two purposes. The wire mesh shielding acts as a faraday cage that completely

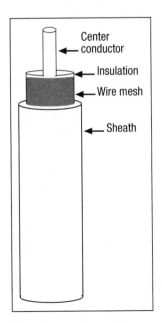

Figure 10.3   Diagram of a coax cable.

prevents RF and electrical interference from penetrating to the center conductor and impacting the data flow. The mesh shielding also acts as a ground to provide a path for unnecessary current to flow out of the system. Any grounded circuit carries electrical circuit.

In addition to physical damage, there are three types of problems that occur with coax cables. If the center conductor does not make a good connection to the center conductor on the connector, the cable will fail because data will not be transmitted. If you have ever made cables of this type, it is not easy, and it is definitely possible to accidentally bend or break the center conductor. The wire mesh must also maintain a good connection to the connector in order to ensure that the ground circuit is maintained. When making coax cables, it is challenging to make these mesh connections because the mesh unravels. The third type of problem that can occur with coax cabling—and by far the most frequent—happens when a terminator is not placed appropriately at each end of the network. Computers that are networked via coax cable are essentially daisy chained together using a T-connector, which connects computers linearly. Each end of the cable line must be terminated in order to prevent data from echoing back across the wire. The primary symptom of improper termination is an excessive number of network collisions on the network. If you have a coax hub, a blinking collision light will indicate when collisions occur. Occasional collisions occur on any Ethernet network, so it is important that you have a good idea of what the norm looks like when all is running well. NetWare will also report excessive network collisions.

One more note about coax cabling: The wire mesh shielding provides a distinct advantage over 10Base-T cables in environments where electrical interference is a problem. Of course, the first symptom of an electrical interference problem will occur on your monitor. If the monitor displays variable wavy lines or one section in particular that is rainbow-like or discolored, you have an interference problem. Temporary and solvable interference usually comes from magnets or motorized machines located near the computer, such as electric fans that make white noise. Move the fan away from the computer, and the problem will be eliminated. Major interference usually comes from nearby transformers or heavy electric current that is close enough to radiate and interfere with the computer. Coax cabling can be used as part of an overall plan to eliminate this type of interference in these environments, but it will do nothing towards fixing your monitor or other server components. As shown in Figure 10.4, 10Base-T cables come in two varieties: straight and crossover.

With 10Base-T cables, two wires are used for sending data, and two other wires are used for receiving data. Network hubs and switches literally take incoming computer "speech" from computers and transmit it along the "listening" wires to waiting computers on the network. In order to connect two computers to each

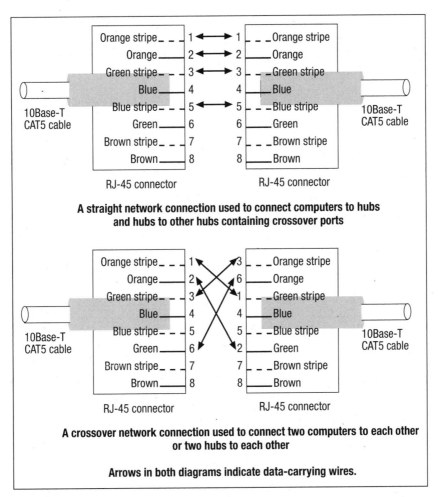

Figure 10.4   Diagrams of straight and crossover 10Base-T cables.

other, it is necessary that the cable be crossed over so that the speech from one computer transmits to the ears of the other. Straight cables are used to connect between a computer and a hub or switch. Crossover cables are used to connect two computers together. Crossover cables are usually not marked as such, and you will need to be able to distinguish the difference when looking at the connectors. The easiest way to do this is to take both ends of the connector and line them up. If all of the wire colors match on both sides, the cable is straight. If the colors are flipped as shown in Figure 10.4, it is a crossover cable.

Another 10Base-T cable failure can simply occur in the connections. If you look at any telephone or 10Base-T cable, you will see that these small wires are placed into the connector along little rails that guide the wire to a small sliver of metal that literally bites into the wire to make the connection. Sometimes the metal does not connect very firmly, and the wire can work its way loose. Symptoms of this type of problem range from outright network connectivity failure to erratic connectivity that seems to function randomly.

Hubs and switches are just as susceptible to electrical interference, surges, and ESD events as any other server or computer component. Many UPSs and power strips provide surge and power protection for a hub or switch. Keep in mind that it does no good to put a server on a UPS if a power surge travels along the network and kills the server through its network connection.

Other than susceptibility to being electrically damaged, hubs and switches can also fail on individual ports. Although it seems unlikely that a single port can go bad and not the entire device, it is possible. This is because of the internal circuitry that is designed to eliminate "bleed" between ports. Bleeding (also called crosstalk) occurs when the signals from one cable are so strong that they are partially transmitted along neighboring wires. You will not see crosstalk with coax cable due to the wire mesh that shields most electromagnetic radiation. Hubs and switches are designed to reduce and eliminate crosstalk, and to some extent, they will also isolate electrical problems.

Most hubs are electrically powered, so you need to make sure that the unit is plugged in, especially if you are seeing failures in several client systems. Once you have determined that the NIC is functioning, make sure that you always leave a single port open on every hub so that you can move a connection to another port in order to determine if the problem is hub related or a cable issue. If the connection works after moving the port, you will need to label the bad port so you do not use it again. If the connection does not work, you probably have a bad cable.

CPU

CPU issues can be heinous to track down because they often behave erratically and can be misconstrued as undocumented or undetected viruses. Outright CPU failure does not occur often. When it does occur, it is usually associated with heat, humidity, or ESD events. Your best tool for troubleshooting potential CPU problems exists with management software. Management software can detect and report impending or existing CPU failure as well as many of the contributing factors that can lead to it.

Even in multi-CPU servers, the BIOS still utilizes only one CPU during boot. If that CPU fails, the system will instantly hang or reboot. Some management tools can be configured to automatically detect when the "primary" CPU has failed and shunt BIOS activity to the secondary CPU, which will help alleviate the immediate urgency that a failed CPU causes. If the BIOS supports the option, you can manually switch primary CPU functionality to accomplish the same goal more slowly.

Again, imminently failing CPUs are difficult to detect because the symptoms can be wide and varied. A CPU that is simply not performing up to par can be tracked using monitoring tools such as Performance Monitor or Event Viewer. Be careful because a slow system can be the symptom of problems with RAM, hard drives, or a CPU. Be sure to monitor and check CPU faults and efficiency. This is another situation where it is valuable to know how the CPU behaves under normal circumstances in order to come to an appropriate conclusion.

Other CPU problems most often include frequent system lockups. In such cases, there are many other more likely culprits, so you will need to systematically remove them all before concluding that the CPU is bad. Make sure that an antivirus program is installed on the server. Many viruses behave destructively by corrupting data and hanging a server. If an antivirus program is already installed on a server, update it. Also consider temporarily disabling it because antivirus programs can cause some disruption and system hangs. Also disable or remove any unnecessary applications, NetWare Loadable Modules (NLMs), or services from the system. This will help you to track down the true issue.

Memory

Server memory can create problems in a number of different ways, ranging from installation to simple failure. When you install RAM and the system simply does not see it, it can be due to one of three problems. When purchasing and installing RAM, you need to ensure that the clock speed is compatible with the speed of the front-side bus (FSB) on the chipset. Most higher speed FSBs will support lower speed RAM chips, but this is not always the case. Another problem can occur with the supported amount of RAM that the chipset or motherboard will support. If you install 512MB of RAM on a system that is designed to handle only 256MB, the system will recognize only 256MB of RAM—even less depending upon the configuration of the RAM cards installed. One additional configuration type issue is more frequent with older servers. System RAM is plugged into slots on a motherboard that the system recognizes as banks. A bank of RAM can consist of two to eight slots. Not too long ago, a motherboard's chipset and BIOS would fit even if different capacities and speeds of RAM cards were installed in the same bank. It was possible to have separate speeds and capacities within the same system as long as they were installed on different banks on the motherboard. Newer servers do not really care if RAM is mixed and matched. Of course there are some optimization issues that are likely to occur, but nothing that you need to troubleshoot. When you do happen upon these newer servers, they will usually beep during POST. Depending upon the number of beeps, you should be able to research and determine what is going on.

Many BIOS applications have an option to bypass time-consuming memory tests during boot. If you think you might have a memory problem, turn this option on.

This will cause the system to thoroughly test the RAM during POST and, as a result, bad RAM will be detected and reported either via a message on the screen or a series of beeps. These beeps can be the same as the ones you would encounter with different RAM capacities and speeds as described previously. The difference is that a system that will not accept different RAM cards on the same bank will not boot—not even once—after installation.

BIOS

BIOS issues rarely occur as a result of a BIOS fault in and of itself. Because the BIOS is such a central authority for server hardware, issues occur more often when hardware changes and the BIOS is not notified or upgraded appropriately. This, in turn, points to most BIOS issues not really being BIOS problems, but instead hardware and peripheral upgrade and installation issues.

The only true "BIOS" issue that you are likely to encounter at least once in your career is battery failure. In order to better understand the nature of BIOS and the battery, we need to talk about the differences between RAM and a hard drive.

A hard drive stores data. It is that simple. RAM stores data too, but it is the additional "features" that come with each one that becomes the deciding factor between choosing a hard drive or RAM to store data. RAM is fast because it stores data electrically. If you remove the electrical current from a RAM card or chip, the memory being stored will disappear. Hard drives, on the other hand, are much slower because they contain moving parts, but the trade-off lies in the fact that the data is stored magnetically on drive platters. If you remove the electrical current from the hard drive, the platters stop spinning, but the data remains intact.

The unique role of the BIOS requires the stability of a hard drive while maintaining the speed of RAM. The compromise between the two is to place a lithium battery on the BIOS chipset that will provide enough of a trickle charge to the BIOS memory to maintain current BIOS settings. If this battery dies, the BIOS will not hold its settings. Many BIOS features are automated, such as hard drive detection, and it could be awhile before you notice that the battery has died. This is especially true of servers whose very nature precludes them from rebooting often enough for you to notice these changes. Realistically, a server's battery could die, and you wouldn't notice it for months. Older servers do not have as many automatic features, and a dead system battery could cause serious problems, such as no longer being able to use the hard drives. This is why it is important to document all BIOS settings at a point in time when the system is alive, healthy, and stable.

System time is also maintained with the help of the same battery. If you consider any server or PC, it is reasonable to conclude that the only active component that needs to be alive at all times, even when the system is turned off, is the system time. The time is controlled by the BIOS chip; however, it is the battery that maintains the time as well. If the battery dies, the correct time and date will not be maintained.

Battery replacement can be somewhat tricky as many older systems have battery leads directly soldered to the motherboard. In such cases, you will need to contact the manufacturer and either have the battery replaced or replace the motherboard, which essentially means replacing your server. Newer servers are not as tricky, as the lithium batteries are housed in a standard battery compartment. Replacement simply means that you will need to determine the type and model of the battery, obtain a replacement, and replace the battery. Ensure that the server is powered down, yet plugged in prior to removing the battery. This should ensure that an adequate electrical charge is maintained for the BIOS and allow you to change the battery.

Any major upgrade or configuration change should be preceded by a tape backup.

As mentioned in Chapter 5, the POST process that is triggered by the BIOS will emit beeps when something goes wrong. It is essential that you track down the beep codes that apply to your server, and place that information in a book or log close to the server. Many manufacturers provide this information online.

As discussed earlier, most BIOS issues result from hardware or features that either are not fully supported by the BIOS or require a BIOS upgrade in order to allow full server support. Upgrading the BIOS is a dangerous operation for many reasons. Many BIOS flash operations require user feedback in order to do what needs to be done. You see this quite often when a manufacturer has packaged multiple BIOS updates for separate machines all in the same flash program. Whatever you do, make sure that you are familiar with the manufacturer's instructions on how to flash the BIOS. My intent is not to scare you, but to instill in you the proper respect for this particular process. Make sure that if something goes wrong, it is not because of you. Quite often, if something does go wrong, your server suddenly becomes more valuable as a boat anchor than a server. Remember that the BIOS is the source of many processes, and without it, the system cannot boot. If the wrong BIOS is installed, or (worse yet) there is a failure midway through a BIOS flash, you could have the same boat anchor issue mentioned previously. Many server manufacturers provide additional safety measures to prevent this from happening (in addition to user error).

One method of preventing a flash failure from becoming permanent has been drawn from the software world in the form of a temporary data storage location. What happens during flash (and this is manufacturer specific, so be sure to check for this feature) is that a copy of the BIOS information is compressed and stored in a separate memory location. In the event that the process fails, the flash program will restore the original data to its rightful place.

You also need to be aware that many server management tools have pieces that are often tightly integrated with the BIOS. If you are new to your server, this applies in situations where internal hardware sensors have been configured within the server management tools. Because these sensors function independently of the NOS or OS, it is important that they be alive and running as soon as the BIOS wakes up. This requires that they be coupled somewhat with the BIOS.

Many server management tools integrate BIOS configuration and flashing with their own applications (i.e., Compaq's SmartStart program). For industrial strength servers such as those from Compaq, Intel, Dell, or IBM, you need to do some research. Make sure that when you upgrade the management tools, you do not need to upgrade the BIOS as well—and vice versa. Many features in the management tools may require a BIOS upgrade, and a BIOS upgrade may not work properly if the management tools are not updated properly. Also be mindful of the order of execution when dealing with upgrades and flashes at this level.

Software

Although the Server+ exam is platform independent, it is still difficult to separate software from hardware when many hardware symptoms appear in the software world. The Server+ exam covers potential hardware issues that are evinced through software, and you will be expected to determine when a problem that appears to be a hardware issue is, in reality, a software problem.

File Corruption

File corruption can occur with single events, such as when a server or desktop computer locks up, loses power abruptly, experiences a power surge or brownout, or is shut down inappropriately. This specific type of file corruption occurs in relation to files that were open at the time of the particular event. When an OS opens a file for use, it is flagged as being open and, depending upon the application, is often periodically updated as well. Many applications will clone a file, open the clone for update, and periodically replicate changes back to the original file. This particular method was designed to reduce the possibilities of corruption. When a system locks up, loses power, experiences a power surge, or is shut down inappropriately, these open files can become corrupt in several different ways. Files might be left flagged as "open." As a result, after fixing the trigger event, the file cannot be opened again because it is flagged as being in use by the original instance of the application or OS. The OS will report the file as being read-only or unavailable for use. This usually happens only with data files located on a server used by network users. Just because a file resides on a server does not mean it is immune from issues or events that can occur on the desktop.

Other corruption issues deal with the actual level of activity that was occurring when the corruption/triggering event took place. If the file is in use by the operating system—constantly being updated and used—corruption can occur by essentially scrambling a file's contents in such a manner that it is unreadable. Recovery from this type of corruption is nearly impossible because many system files can become corrupted without your knowledge. These files are usually not mission critical to basic functionality. In addition, there are few, if any, real ways to fix this type of corruption because the operating system quite often does not recognize or fix corruptions. Symptoms of corruption in system files usually include messages about missing or unreadable files.

Performance Monitor/Event Viewer

Most NOSs have monitoring and tracking utilities included with the NOS. For the most part, these utilities are created for the purpose of tracking specific components within both the server hardware and software services.

In Windows NT/2000, the Event Viewer is a logging application that almost exclusively tracks software events on the server. The Event Viewer automatically logs critical server software events, such as when services start up and fail, and is also configurable to track specific issues such as user login or file auditing. It can also be tuned to log different events, such as specific file access, logons, and application service failures. The Event Viewer application tells you when services such as Domain Name System (DNS) and DHCP fail. Outside of these specifics, you probably will not see Event Viewer on the exam. NetWare has similar utilities embedded within specific NLMs and applications, and also a primary log located within the main console.

Windows NT/2000 also boasts Performance Monitor, which can be manually configured to log certain server activities over a long period of time. Performance Monitor is one of the utilities that can be used to gather baseline information. In particular, you use Performance Monitor to track potential hardware problems in the areas of a hard disk, a CPU, paging, and memory. Basically, the utility behaves in a similar manner to SNMP by logging specific events. Unlike SNMP, Performance Monitor will not alert you to issues once a particular threshold has been met. The following items need to be monitored in order to create a proper baseline and to troubleshoot problems appropriately.

➤ *Hard disk*—Several counters exist under the hard disk heading. In particular, monitoring disk faults allows you to determine (along with a good baseline) how often disk errors occur. You can also determine the percent usage of the hard disk. This particular counter, however, can be a mixed blessing. On one hand, a disk with a high percentage rate can tell you that the drive is low on disk space (which is easily found in several different ways) or if it is being used too often. On the other hand, a highly utilized hard drive can be used for memory paging, which points not to a hard drive problem, but to a potential memory issue.

➤ *CPU*—CPUs behave differently from any other device on a server. When the CPU performs a task, it does it with gusto. What this means is that CPU utilization, for the most part, registers either a high percentage or nearly 0. Cause for concern arises when CPU utilization stays at 100 percent more than 60 percent of the time. CPU faults do occur occasionally, so you can also use this particular counter to help determine if the CPU chip is going bad.

➤ *Paging*—Paging is a process that is tightly linked with both hard disk and memory functions. There are times when the memory required by the NOS or application exceeds the physical memory; there are two different ways to deal with this situation. The first is to purchase and install enough RAM to meet the requirements. Unfortunately, the need for memory is often cost prohibitive, and thus inappropriate. Instead, in order to meet the memory requirements, the system can trick the application into thinking that enough RAM exists by sending some of the data stored in RAM to the hard disk for temporary storage. As applications and services function, these bits of disk stored memory are traded back and forth between the hard drive and RAM. Paging occurs seamlessly to both the user and the application. In fact, many applications today are built to rely upon paging in order to boost sales by requiring less physical RAM in the system requirements. Now that we have discussed paging, let's talk about how paging applies to troubleshooting. Again, this is where a good baseline is essential. Many NOSs (Microsoft, in particular) actively use paging even when it is not strictly necessary. You should have a good baseline on the percent of paging that is occurring on the server. If a server is running slowly, you might notice what is known as *disk thrash*, which is when the hard drive is running constantly. This can be seen when the light flickers continuously for several minutes and is a good sign that paging is going on. Many times, paging happens when an application locks up or hangs, but paging can also be a symptom of failing memory, or not enough memory to begin with. With a proper baseline, excessive paging counters can tell you whether or not there is enough memory on the server. Excessive paging can also point to hard drive failure or memory failure. In both cases, you will need to check disk faults and memory faults in order to conclusively determine if either of the two components need to be replaced.

➤ *Memory*—Memory fault counters can be used to determine if RAM is failing on a server. In the past, percent memory usage was a good counter to use to determine if more RAM was necessary. However, with paging being used so much nowadays, this counter is basically useless, and you need to determine this information by checking whether or not excessive paging is occurring on the server.

Network Issues

Connectivity is the number one software related issue that you will be tested on. Questions will deal with the ability or inability to connect to a particular server, system, or resource. Aside from running PING or TRACERT, the probable solutions are few, but valid.

In the event that you are unable to connect to a server or resource on the network, you need to know about DNS and Windows Internet Naming Service (WINS). DNS is a name resolution service that translates domain names to IP addresses. Because TCP/IP is the predominant networking protocol, computers running the IP protocol stack essentially address each other by using an IP address rather than a computer name. Computer and domain names, however, are easier for humans to remember, so translation servers need to be put into place to help bridge the gap between humans and networked computers. Domain names usually look like www.microsoft.com or www.novell.com and are usually used to refer to resources on the Internet.

WINS is a name resolution service that translates computer NetBIOS names to IP addresses. For the most part, WINS is used within Microsoft networks. Windows 2000 theoretically eliminates the need for WINS servers because all systems are referenced using its FQDNs without inconveniencing the users.

Virus

The only other software related issue you might see on the Server+ exam deals with viruses and antivirus software. Computer viruses are small applications that perform some type of unauthorized task on a server. We say "unauthorized" because many viruses are literally harmless. They simply display messages on boot or otherwise annoy users and administrators. Other viruses can be quite destructive, destroying hard drives and software, and even opening portals for hacker intrusion.

Methods of virus infection are wide and varied. It is important to remember that viruses cannot be transmitted from one computer to another without some sort of application, macro, command, or batch file being executed. Most often, viruses will bind themselves on your network through the innocent acts of your users. In general, NetWare will not see the same types of viruses as Microsoft and OS/2. This is because NetWare is not an OS, but a NOS, whereas OS/2 and the Microsoft products are both. As such, NetWare cannot run a standard application or virus such as those you would see in OS/2 and Windows NT/2000. NetWare viruses either have to be written specifically for NetWare (which is rare) or limited to the OS that it lives on, which is DOS. Windows and OS/2, to the contrary, are capable of running applications that any desktop can run, and thus are much more susceptible to virus infection.

Antivirus programs are the most frequent means of eliminating viruses. Unfortunately, they can cause many problems in and of themselves. By their very nature, they must act as constant bodyguards for the server, monitoring anything and everything that enters and leaves the server. At the least, this can negatively impact the performance of a server, and at the most, it can downright interfere with the function of certain applications and services. Antivirus applications can clean and eliminate most viruses, provided they are equipped with the appropriate and most up-to-date profiles for the viruses in the environment. To date, the only viruses that cannot be "cleaned" by an antivirus program are known as boot sector viruses. Boot sector viruses are heinous little programs that place themselves in the boot sector of a hard drive or floppy. When the BIOS passes control to the hard drive to boot the OS or NOS, the virus is activated, and the system continues to boot. As a result, the virus is always present and capable of propagating itself to other disk drives and any floppy disk that is inserted into the system. Once a boot sector virus is introduced into the system, it is impossible to remove. The OS or NOS is incapable of tampering with such a low-level component of the hard drive. The only other way to eliminate the virus is to boot from a clean disk. Unfortunately, a clean boot disk is immediately infected by the virus as soon as it is accessed. There are two ways to "manually" clean a boot sector virus. Certain applications and utilities can make a backup copy of the boot sector and replace the infected boot sector with the backed up clean one. Unfortunately, if you do not have a backup copy before the boot sector becomes infected, these utilities will be unable to help you. Otherwise, it becomes necessary to completely format and clean the infected hard drive. It is possible to restore server data from tape, but you must be very careful. The initial application that activated the virus may be somewhere on the network, and it must be dealt with. This is where your antivirus application can come in handy. Although the antivirus software cannot clean the virus once it has been activated, it can deal with the virus in its dormant state.

Practice Questions

Question 1

> Which method of troubleshooting involves the testing of a conclusion?
>
> ○ a. Ockham's razor
>
> ○ b. Scientific method
>
> ○ c. What changed
>
> ○ d. Gathering data

Answer b is correct. The scientific method can be described as the process of drawing a conclusion, testing that conclusion, using the test data to draw a new conclusion, and retesting the conclusion until the test result fits the conclusion. Answer a is incorrect because Ockham's razor describes the simplest answer as often being correct. Answer c is incorrect because "what changed" is a means of gathering data. Answer d is incorrect because gathering data is a prerequisite to drawing a conclusion.

Question 2

> Which method of troubleshooting advises you to consider the simplest solution first?
>
> ○ a. Ockham's razor
>
> ○ b. Scientific method
>
> ○ c. What changed
>
> ○ d. Gathering data

Answer a is correct. Ockham's razor indicates that the simplest possible solution quite often is the correct solution. Answer b is incorrect because the scientific method involves testing conclusions. Answer c is incorrect because "what changed" is a means of gathering data. Answer d is incorrect because gathering data is a prerequisite to drawing a conclusion.

Question 3

Which of the following can be used to troubleshoot network problems?

    I. PING

    II. PERFMON

    III. Event Viewer

    IV. TRACERT

  ○ a. I and II

  ○ b. III and IV

  ○ c. I and IV

  ○ d. II and III

Answer c is correct. PING and TRACERT can be used to troubleshoot network problems. Answer a is incorrect because PERFMON is the application name for Performance Monitor. Performance Monitor is used to monitor a system's internal processes, not networking. Answers b and d are incorrect because the Event Viewer is used to monitor specific events that occur on a Windows NT/2000 server.

Question 4

BIOS beep codes can notify you of which failures?

    I. OS problems

    II. CPU failure

    III. Memory

    IV. Keyboard

  ○ a. I and II

  ○ b. III and IV

  ○ c. I and IV

  ○ d. II and III

Answer b is correct. Bad RAM and missing keyboard are two beep codes that you are likely to encounter. Answers a and c are incorrect because the BIOS is not active after control is turned over to the hard drive to boot the OS; therefore, the BIOS cannot beep to notify you of OS problems. Answer d is incorrect because a CPU failure precludes BIOS functionality to begin with. If the CPU has failed, the BIOS cannot run.

Question 5

Which of the following will detect temperature, hard drive, and memory failure?

○ a. SNMP

○ b. RMON

○ c. Performance Monitor

○ d. Server management tools

Answer d is correct. Server management tools can detect temperature problems, a failing hard drive, and memory problems. Answers a and b are incorrect because SNMP and RMON are network troubleshooters. Answer c is incorrect because Performance Monitor can be used to detect a failing hard drive or memory problems, but not temperature issues.

Question 6

Which NOS does not support the PING utility from the server?

○ a. Windows NT

○ b. Windows 2000

○ c. Unix

○ d. NetWare

Answer d is correct. The NetWare NOS runs as a console on top of DOS, and the PING command-line utility cannot run from a NetWare server. Answers a and b are incorrect because Windows NT and 2000 support command-line functionality. Answer c is incorrect because Unix is the original NOS that PING was designed for.

Question 7

> When you ping 127.0.0.1, what are you testing?
>
> ○ a. The local IP protocol stack
> ○ b. The default gateway
> ○ c. The local DHCP server
> ○ d. The local DNS server

Answer a is correct. The address 127.0.0.1 is used for a local loopback, which makes the ping go out to the wire and immediately come back. Answers b, c, and d are incorrect because the 127 range of IP addresses are reserved.

Question 8

> Which of the following will detect problems with hubs and switches?
>
> ○ a. SNMP
> ○ b. RMON
> ○ c. Performance Monitor
> ○ d. Server management

Answer b is correct. RMON acts as a network analyzer with the additional ability to detect problems and provide statistics for RMON supported hubs and switches. Answer a is incorrect because SNMP is completely server- and computer-based. Answer c is incorrect because Performance Monitor checks local server activity, not issues on the network. Answer d is similarly incorrect because server management deals with the local server machine and not network devices.

Question 9

> Which of the following will detect page faults?
>
> ○ a. SNMP
> ○ b. RMON
> ○ c. Performance Monitor
> ○ d. Server management

Answer c is correct. Performance Monitor can log paging and page faults. Answers a and b are incorrect because SNMP and RMON are network-based troubleshooters. Answer d is incorrect because server management does not log paging.

Question 10

Which of the following can be symptoms of a hard drive controller failure?

   I. Hanging

   II. Disk thrashing

   III. Power loss

   IV. Error messages

  ○ a. I and II

  ○ b. III and IV

  ○ c. I and IV

  ○ d. II and III

Answer c is correct. A failing controller can hang a server or display error messages during boot. Answer a is incorrect because disk thrashing is a symptom of excessive paging. Answers b and d are incorrect because power loss is an indicator for a failing power supply or a power outage.

Question 11

Your SCSI RAID array is displaying error messages on boot. What do you need to do?

   I. Reconfigure the array

   II. Format the drives

   III. Check the LUNs

   IV. Check termination

  ○ a. I and II

  ○ b. III and IV

  ○ c. I and IV

  ○ d. II and III

Answer b is correct. Because you do not have any information about the error messages, you need to check the LUNs and termination for the channels. Answer a is incorrect because reconfiguring the array and formatting the drives may not be necessary if the LUNs are mis-assigned or if the channel is not properly terminated. In particular, answers a and c are incorrect because reconfiguring the array can cause you to lose your data. Answer d is incorrect because formatting the drive is necessary only when the drives are not formatted appropriately to begin with or when the error message indicates that the drives hold no format.

Question 12

You flash the BIOS on a server, and the system then displays a blank screen. Why?

○ a. The management software was not updated.

○ b. You were not appropriately grounded.

○ c. You flashed the BIOS inappropriately.

○ d. You unplugged the hard drive.

Answer c is correct. Answer a is incorrect because you cannot assume that management software exists on the server. Answer b is incorrect because being grounded has nothing to do with flashing the BIOS. Answer d is similarly incorrect because flashing the BIOS does not require that you manipulate the server hardware.

Question 13

Which of the following can be used to help eliminate interference?

○ a. Coax cable

○ b. 10Base-T cable

○ c. Terminators

○ d. RJ-45 connectors

Answer a is correct. Coax cable has shielding that eliminates electrical and magnetic interference. Answer b is incorrect because 10Base-T is unshielded. Answers c and d are incorrect because they are items that are attached to cables, which means that they cannot truly eliminate interference.

Question 14

> You install 512MB of RAM, and the server will not recognize the additional RAM. Why?
>
> ○ a. The motherboard will not support that much RAM.
>
> ○ b. The new RAM chip is not on the same bay as the others.
>
> ○ c. The RAM is bad.
>
> ○ d. You installed the RAM incorrectly.

Answer a is correct. There is an upper limit to how much RAM a motherboard and chipset can support. Answer b is incorrect because with older servers, using another bay may be the only way you can install a different RAM card. Answers c and d are incorrect because the BIOS would emit beep codes if the RAM was bad or installed incorrectly.

Question 15

> You install 512MB of RAM on a server, and it beeps when you power the server. Why?
>
> ○ a. The motherboard will not support that much RAM.
>
> ○ b. The new RAM chip is not on the same bay as the others.
>
> ○ c. The RAM is bad.
>
> ○ d. A cable is loose.

Answer c is correct. If the RAM is bad, the BIOS will beep. Answer a is incorrect because the BIOS will not recognize the RAM at all—bad or good—if it is not supported. Answer b is incorrect because older servers often require a different RAM card on a different bay in order to function. However, newer servers do not require that the RAM card be in a specific location. Answer d is incorrect because a loose cable will not cause BIOS beep codes—unless it is a loose hard drive cable.

Question 16

> Your server BIOS beeps a code indicating that there is no hard drive. You
> check to ensure that everything is plugged in and that the drive is receiving
> power. What is the problem?
>
> ○ a. The hard drive cable is loose.
>
> ○ b. The BIOS needs to be updated.
>
> ○ c. The BIOS battery has failed.
>
> ○ d. The OS does not exist on the hard drive.

Answer c is correct. Older servers are unable to dynamically configure the hard
drive information. As a result, when the BIOS battery fails, the hard drive information is lost, and the system does not know how to boot to the drive. Answer a
is incorrect because you have already checked that the cables are intact. Answer b
is incorrect because hard drive information is a configuration issue, not a BIOS
version issue. Answer d is incorrect because an unformatted hard drive will display a different error.

Need To Know More?

 Craft, Melissa, Mark A. Poplar, David V. Watts, and Will Willis. *Network+ Exam Prep*. Scottsdale, AZ: The Coriolis Group, 1999. ISBN 1-57610-412-5. This book contains in-depth information on RAID.

 Minasi, Mark, Christa Anderson and Elizabeth Creegan. *Mastering Windows NT Server, 4th ed*. Alameda, CA: Sybex Network Press, 1997. ISBN 0-78212067-9. This book is an ideal administrator's companion for Windows NT 4, covering mostly basic to intermediate content with several advanced topics included as well. Microsoft RAID support and installation is also included.

 Reeves, Scott, Kalinda Reeves, Stephen Weese, and Christopher S. Geyer. *A+ Exam Prep, 3d ed*. The Coriolis Group, LLC, Scottsdale, AZ, 2001. ISBN 1-57610-699-3. This book contains specifics on RAID and SCSI topics.

 Zacker, Craig and Paul Doyle. *Upgrading and Repairing Networks*. Indianapolis, IN: Que Corporation, 1996. ISBN 0-78970181-2. This book is an exceptional reference for specifics and how-tos on RAID and SCSI technologies.

 www.adaptec.com, Adaptec Corporation's Web site, contains an article called "Let's talk about RAID" that contains in-depth information about RAID.

 www.novell.com includes an article, "SFT III for NetWare," that contains information about the NetWare equivalent to clustering and load balancing. Software fault tolerance (SFT) is a complete system mirroring solution and does not currently span more than two systems.

 www.pcguide.com, developed by Charles M. Kozierok and similar to TechRepublic, contains a wealth of information on many IT topics.

 www.storage-area-networks.com contains an excellent article by Kevin Trotman called "Reducing Enterprise Backup Windows," which provides details about the ins and outs of Storage Area Network (SAN) purchase and configuration.

www.support.intel.com is a noteworthy reference for server hardware information.

 www.techrepublic.com contains a wealth of information on any and every IT topic imaginable—everything from hardware and component level information to management decisions and political trends. An extraordinary source for up-to-date definitions and information ranging from the novice to the expert.

Disaster Recovery

Terms you'll need to understand:

✓ Disaster Recovery
✓ Hot site
✓ Cold site
✓ RAID
✓ Hot spare
✓ Hot swap
✓ Hot plug
✓ GFS
✓ Backup
✓ Restore
✓ Cloning
✓ Clustering

Techniques you'll need to master:

✓ Recovering from data loss
✓ Recovering from a power failure
✓ Recovering from a hard disk failure
✓ Recovering from a system failure
✓ Recovering from an entire site going down

Disaster recovery is rarely considered within an organization until something mission critical fails. Then the boss kindly requests a meeting in which he wants to know what went wrong, why you did not see it coming, and how you are going to make sure that it will never happen again.

As we discussed in Chapter 1, the Server+ exam was sponsored by several large corporations that have been down the disaster recovery road. These are the same employers who want to be assured that:

➤ You know what to do in an emergency

➤ You know how to handle nearly any type of computer, system, or software failure involving a mission-critical system

➤ You know how to prevent these types of failures from happening

➤ You know how to minimize the negative impact of failures when they occur

As you can see, disaster recovery is not just recovery; it is also disaster prevention and damage control. In this chapter, we will discuss all of the relevant techniques and strategies that can apply to environments both large and small.

Power Failure

It is highly likely that as an administrator, you will encounter a power failure sometime in your career—a guaranteed bad day. As such, power outages can be uniquely interesting situations depending upon your office and power grid. While most power outages seem to occur in the evening, many do occur during standard working hours and result from construction, storms, traffic accidents, and tripped circuit breakers. By no means does this lessen the importance of systems recovery in power outages at any time of day because, as you are probably aware, many companies require systems functionality seven days a week, 24 hours per day.

Any given power failure can basically be counted as either a short-term or an indefinite power loss. Like many things in this world, you cannot predict which one will happen, and either way, you need to plan for both while maintaining a contingency budget.

By definition, computers do not like sudden power loss, as it usually leads to data corruption and potential hardware damage. The only real way to recover from power failure is to provide alternative power sources to mission-critical equipment. The key is to provide this replacement power only to those systems:

➤ Whose downtime costs the company money

➤ Whose sudden shutdown causes damage

➤ Whose immediate user downtime costs the company money

This is a difficult explanation, as every system in the enterprise could easily fit within one of these categories. The best way to target systems for power replacement is by choosing those systems within these criteria that ultimately cost the company the most money. A server, by definition, usually fits into this category, and usually justifies the cost of power replacement, which typically begins with a battery backup, or UPS system. Exceptions to this rule include test servers and servers whose purpose does not directly affect the bottom line, such as QA and monitoring servers.

Short-Term Power Loss

Short-term power loss can be defined as a loss of power that spans anywhere from a few seconds to a few hours. A good sliding rule of thumb defines a short-term power loss as something your UPS or battery backup device can handle while still maintaining mission-critical systems availability.

Quite often (especially in smaller offices), when the power goes out, the entire community is without power, including all of the clients who are served by the systems in the computer room. In such situations, the priority becomes to simply (and safely) shut down the servers before battery backup fails and data corruption occurs.

Planning a Graceful Shutdown

When you are planning different ways to handle corporate-wide short-term power loss, consider different methods of server shutdown and purchase your UPS system accordingly. In situations like these, the purpose of the UPS purpose is to simply hang around until the computers can be safely shut down. Considering this, there are basically three different ways of accomplishing this type of graceful shutdown:

➤ Put yourself on-call and purchase a UPS whose battery life extends beyond a reasonable amount of time needed for you to get there.

➤ Ensure that there is always someone on site who is adequately trained to shut down the servers safely.

➤ Many UPS manufacturers provide UPS management software that can be configured to shut down safely any PC system via a serial connection to the UPS battery backup system.

In general, putting yourself on-call for power outages is a good idea, in the event that other IT-related issues occur, or that the situation evolves into another situation requiring further disaster control measures. However, putting the integrity of your servers on par with the functionality of your vehicle can be risky and is not recommended.

In a large corporate environment you will more than likely have a 24/7 person onsite for other IT systems maintenance, such as mainframe or mini-computer operations. It is certainly reasonable to add operational functionality such as microcomputer server shutdown to this person's task list. However, be aware that this person will most likely be in charge of several different aspects of damage control during a power outage, and your server shutdown might not get the attention and priority it needs. Additionally, such environments usually have alternative methods of power replacement (discussed below) that can help resolve or alleviate the immediate concern of server shutdown.

UPS management software is the methodology of choice for graceful systems shutdown. Higher-end systems come with additional slots for serial connections, thus enabling multiple-system shutdown from the same battery backup unit.

When considering how to implement automated shutdown procedures, also consider the functionality of the servers in question and other services that might come into play. For example, SQL Server does not like having the system shut down from under it without performing a database shutdown itself. When considering UPS or batterybackup vendors, inquire about application shutdown utilities also.

Overall, an ideal automated graceful shutdown should look like this:

1. Power goes out; battery life has 10 minutes power available for five systems.

2. UPS management software shuts down three less-critical systems at T minus 8 minutes.

3. Battery life recalculates to 30 minutes with only two systems.

4. At T minus 10 minutes, applications on the two remaining systems are shut down.

5. At T minus 5 minutes, one server is shut down.

6. At T minus 2 minute, the remaining server is shut down.

Another way to increase battery life is to get in the habit of powering off monitors. PowerSave monitors are also an option, but quite often risky when ACPI (Advanced Configuration and Power Interface) kicks in, because it takes services and functionality with it. KVM functionality is another plus, because every system that uses a KVM (Keyboard, Video, Mouse) uses one less monitor. Just remember to keep the KVM power on the UPS also; otherwise your servers may be up, but you will not be able to administer them without a working keyboard or mouse.

One important thing to keep in mind with regard to power loss is that even though your computer room might lose power, you might still have mission-critical aspects of the business that are running and functioning fine. This particularly applies for corporations that span multiple physical locations, large businesses, or even Wide Area Networks. If this is the case, it could become necessary to consider the plan of action associated with an indefinite power loss sooner than you otherwise would, because performing a system shutdown would negatively impact the entire organization for what is a merely regional issue.

Indefinite Power Loss

Again, using that same sliding rule of thumb, you can assume that the larger the organization, the more prepared it is to handle an indefinite period of power failure. By definition, we speak of generator backup.

A power generator is basically a diesel engine that has a power feed into the building. Traditionally, this generator is an adjunct to the data center building and is hooked into the main wiring for at least the computer room. Generators are very expensive to purchase, build, and maintain, but quite often it is money well spent when the cost of downtime is measured in the millions of dollars.

Unlike household generators, business generators are usually fed through an additional bank of batteries located in the computer room. This is because computers will burp on any power that is not smooth and constant (for example, brownouts and spikes). Battery backup systems are designed to output specifically to computers, while generators are not. Thus, a corporation with a generator out the back door is more likely to use it earlier in the power-out game than would other companies just to be safer about the whole power loss situation.

Companies that do not have the benefit of a power generator need to consider one of two options...or both. They can purchase enough battery power to allow time to (a) rent a generator and feed the batteries with it or (b) consider another operations site that will have adequate power (hot or cold site).

Again, this is where a UPS management program comes in handy. Configuring an immediate shutdown of less-critical servers will result in a longer battery life for mission-critical systems. It is during this extended period that many difficult decisions might need to be made. A generator might not become available. Even if it does, it has not been tested with your setup. The costs involved can be substantial. However, this is a known method of providing additional extended power in the event of an extended power outage.

If a generator is neither available nor feasible, the option of moving to another operations site is one that we will cover in the "Data Center Relocation" section of this chapter.

Data Recovery

Data loss can occur in any number of ways. Most frequent and annoying is when a user deletes a file. In NetWare environments, a deleted file can usually be recovered by using the **salvage** command. Windows-based environments, however, are more difficult in situations where a file is deleted across the network. Utilities are available for purchase that will recovery network-deleted files, but in all other cases, a restore becomes necessary.

Data Backup/Restore

Data backup is a necessity in business for many reasons. Many companies refuse to acknowledge the possibility that a true disaster will occur. However, most companies will acknowledge that data goes bad occasionally, and that the only recourse for recovery is to restore from backup.

Many backup application companies also sell applications that will further assist you in major disaster recovery (or systems recovery) process development. Spending the time and effort in developing a thorough disaster recovery process can be worthwhile, because with the exception of disk imaging applications, it is necessary to install the operating system and backup application prior to restoring the data from tape. This can be very time consuming and adds to the time required to recover fully from a system failure—something you do not want to deal with in an emergency situation.

 Disk imaging applications do not really function well as backup or restore methods, but they do have their place in the greater scheme of things. Imaging applications require complete and quick access to the hard drive in order to function properly. This is because they take a snapshot of the entire hard disk and its partitions and store the contents in a single image file. Most imagers require that the application be available on a DOS boot disk, and that the backup media (hard drive space or network space) be accessible at the time. This is by no means an automated process. It is not reasonable to perform daily or even weekly backups based on this process. Yet tape drives run slowly, and restoring a base OS image from an image file (with the backup application already installed) can save much time and anguish when compared with installing the operating system and backup program from scratch.

Backup Media

Backup media is the target for backup data. While this might not seem very important, it is necessary to take the following factors into consideration when choosing a backup media type:

➤ The backup media should have sufficient capacity for the amount of data that needs to be backed up.

➤ The backup media should work in an automated or unattended backup.

➤ The media should be reliable, as your company might one day rely upon this media as its sole lifeline.

➤ The media should be cost effective.

➤ The media should be portable, to facilitate restoring data at any other location.

Backup media comes in all shapes, sizes, and technologies:

➤ Tape

➤ WORM

➤ Hard disk drive/network drive

➤ Removable storage devices

➤ Storage Area Networks (SANs)

Tapes come in three standardized types: DLT (digital linear tape), DAT (digital audio tape), and QIC. DAT capacity ranges from 2GB to 20GB, while DLT tapes range from 20GB to 70GB and run slightly faster. QIC tape capacities range from 40MB to 15GB. Because of these differences, there are variable price ranges for both tapes and drives. Non-standard tapes, or proprietary tapes, are available, but be cautious, because that particular drive type might not be available when the time comes to restore the data. Tape backup and restoration is slower than almost any other backup media type, but it provides the greatest portability combined with capacity. Keep in mind that, if you wish to automate your backup process, you need to tailor the backup data and the tape in such a manner as to backup to a single drive. Alternative hardware, such as jukeboxes or chained tape drives, are available. As a result, tape backup is the number one preferred method for performing backups.

 Travan tapes are based on the QIC tape standards.

The greatest concern with tape, however, is cost, as the number of tapes and tape rotation strategies come into play. Downsides to tape media are many, but relatively minor. While the media itself is portable, the drive that uses it generally is not. You can resolve this by purchasing backup software that allows other networked computers to write to a single tape drive on a tape server. Although tape drive failure does not occur often (because we usually are not aware of failures until we try a restore), failure and destruction do occur sometimes, so it is important to choose a drive and tape media type that are highly available in the industry, so that replacement equipment can be obtained easily.

 QIC tapes are compatible with QIC drives; DAT tapes are compatible with DAT drives; and DLT tapes are compatible with DLT drives.

WORM (Write Once Read Many) drives are also known as backup and archival methods. As the acronym indicates, WORM disks can be written only once, which eliminates the possibility of recycling old media as we would see with other backup methods. This limitation has been a drawback for WORM drives; however, the technology is still quite popular today in the form of CD-R.

Backup to a hard disk or network drive is a common method for backing up data. The plus is that the backed up data is highly available, and the backup itself runs quickly. The downside is usually dependent upon the availability of the network or disk drive and the fact that any situation where a specific system requires a restore runs a risk that the network might be unavailable also. Network or hard disk backups are also not portable, and therefore do not lend themselves to recovery in the event of fire, natural disaster, or other site-destroying factors.

Removable storage devices, commonly known as Zip drive, orb, floppy, CD-ROM, and others, are quite common for smaller backup jobs. They are not often found on servers or in multi-user corporate environments, however. Because the capacity of these backup media is limited (ranging from 1 to 700MB), they are usually restricted to personal or individual usage. While most backup applications will write to these media, direct CD-ROM backup is a rarity. The portability factor and price is a plus, however, as many companies choose to use these media types as a data transfer and backup method for individual systems.

Storage area networks (SANs) are a relatively new and evolving technology. Actually, the concept originated with mainframes, where multiple networked backup drives were available and were then backed up to tape and stored offsite. The technology and network media have evolved since then, allowing access by client/server systems via hubs and switches. Advantages to SANs are their availability to any device on the standard network and their faster speed over tape. The disadvantage is that the storage itself is not portable unless it is backed up to tape, bringing us back to a tape solution. If price is a factor, SANs are not your solution, as initial cost can run into the hundreds of thousands. Mainframe conversion is an option, but still expensive.

Backup Types

You can perform data backup using several different methods. Because the Server+ exam focuses on server data backup, we will eliminate the more pedestrian methods of copying files via Windows or DOS interfaces.

Every file on a disk contains something called an archive bit. This is simply a flag that is set on or off based upon the actions performed on that file. Usually the flag is turned on when the file is changed, modified, or when a new file appears. The flag is turned off by a backup program during one of two backup types. All backup types are listed below, along with how the archive bit plays into the backup process.

➤ *Full backup*—Backs up all selected files and resets the archive bit

➤ *Copy backup*—Backs up all selected files and does not reset the archive bit

➤ *Incremental backup*—Backs up all selected files that have changed (where the archive bit is on) since the last full or incremental backup and resets the archive bit

➤ *Differential backup*—Backs up only files that have changed (where the archive bit is on) since the last full backup and does not reset the archive bit

➤ *Daily backup*—Similar to an incremental backup; backs up all selected files that have changed since the last full or incremental backup, but without resetting the archive bits

 Remember that the archive bit is reset for Full and Incremental backups only.

Copy and daily backups are shadows of full and incremental backups and are used for unscheduled backups that will not interfere with the overall tape rotation scheme. Full with Incremental or Full with Differential backup schemes are usually implemented with a tape rotation strategy to allow for the greatest data integrity and historical value balanced with media and time costs.

Tape Rotation

Tape rotation is the way that full and incremental or differential data backups are stored and rotated in a manner that provides the greatest data security. Choosing a proper tape rotation strategy is directly based upon how many tapes you wish to use, the ease of performing a restoration, and how long you want to store the data.

There are as many tape rotation strategies are there are days in a year. Many companies will require that data be archived several years for legal purposes, and this can be a factor in the tape rotation strategy. For the purposes of the Server+

exam, however, only one strategy will be specifically referenced. GFS (Grandfather, father, son) rotation is patterned after a month, week, and day structure. A full backup is performed every week, and an incremental or differential backup is performed on every other day of the week. Daily backups occur either five or six days a week. Another full backup occurs every month. Daily tapes are reused every week, weekly tapes are reused every month, and monthly tapes are reused every year. Refer to Figure 11.1 to get a better idea of how many tapes are necessary for a full year.

Tape rotation takes on another level of importance when you consider offsite storage options. The reasons for offsite storage are to ensure that tapes are taken care of, archived appropriately, and most importantly, available in the event that the data center, computer room, or primary operations functionality needs to be relocated elsewhere.

Disk Failure

It does no good to restore from tape when the media you restore to has failed. Beyond allowing a system to remain down for several hours while you locate a replacement hard drive of suitable configuration, there are methods of facilitating recovery from a drive failure.

RAID Options

RAID was designed with the aim of either enhancing disk performance and/or providing a better means of recovery in the event of a disk failure. A standard term for this is "fault tolerance," basically any means of recovering from a partial or complete failure. Fault tolerance is not a concept or term specific to hard disk drives and definitely is not new to the IT industry nor within quality assurance circles.

Hot swapping, or hot plugging, is a hardware feature that allows hard drive installation while the computer system is on. Most commonly seen in plug-and-play systems for USB support and also in PCMCIA applications, hot swapping is also a specific feature of RAID. When used appropriately, hot swapping a failed drive in an array will automatically kick off a parity restoration of the missing data.

A hot spare is very similar to a hot swapped drive. The hot spare drive, however, is already located on the drive array so that it will not be used until one of the array's drives fails. When this happens, the spare hard drive will automatically be formatted with data from the failed drive.

When analyzing various hardware- and software-based RAID options, it is important to understand what types of involvement are necessary to maintain continuity when a drive fails. This is called failover—the process whereby a failed activity or function moves to an alternate location to resume function.

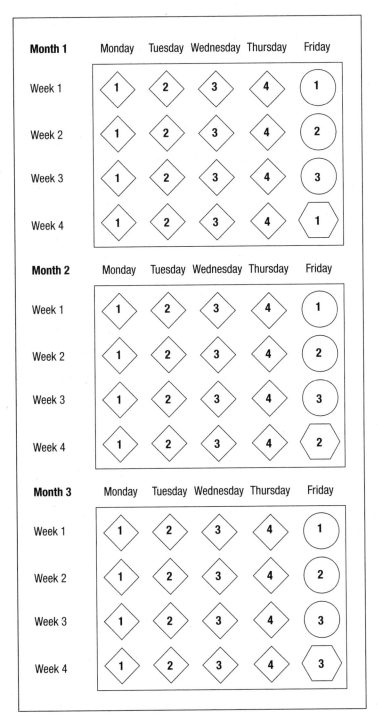

Figure 11.1 GFS five-day tape rotation for a three-month period, providing that a full backup resides on a single tape.

Hardware mirroring and duplexing are also options that help avoid complete tragedy in the event of a disk failure. The reason that hardware-based RAID is required here is that the current software technology does not adequately support automatic failover when a drive goes belly up. No doubt RAID can be expensive (although partial RAID controller support is getting cheaper every day!) and might not be possible for every organization, but the advantage of an automated recovery without human intervention might be worth the expense.

You also need to determine how administrator notification will occur when a drive does fail and automatic failover occurs. If the administrator is not made aware that a drive has failed and the hot spare is now no longer available, the situation could escalate critically when the next drive fails.

System Recovery

Recovery from a partial or full system failure can be a challenging and daunting task, considering that a message stating exactly what the problem is will rarely be available. Troubleshooting can become exponentially difficult because nothing in a computer truly lives on its own. A drive failure might in reality be a controller failure that caused a hard disk to go bad. You might not notice this until the second drive went bad, at which point you would begin considering other issues within the system. Most of these troubleshooting tactics are covered in Chapter 10, "Troubleshooting." For now, however, it is safe to say that when mission-critical components fail, you will know fairly soon. A full system failure can mean that the entire computer got fried, or it can simply mean that it would take longer to target and resolve the issue on the failed system than it would be to move the functionality to another system.

Component Failure

The Server+ exam covers component failure, but you will not be tested on what to do when a mouse fails. The scope of the exam will be limited strictly to mission-critical components and major replaceable parts.

Cables

Cables, in general, have always been the first thing to think of in troubleshooting. Because of their long, stringy nature and sometimes haphazard assembly, they are far more prone to malfunction than we recognize. Be sure to keep at least one spare hard drive, power, parallel, serial (if applicable), and VGA cable on hand.

Controller Failure

Any PC or server has several different controllers on board, including video, serial, parallel, USB, and disk drive. Controllers, by definition, both define the parameters of a given device to the operating system and handle two-way communications between other PC components, the operating system, and the devices. Controller failures are quite often heinous. Symptoms can be erratic or complete, and it quite often appears as though the attached device is bad. Beyond checking for device functionality on another system, the only way to determine whether a controller has failed is to first replace the device, and then replace the controller. This applies to both hard disks and other peripherals on a server.

 RAID level 1 can consist of either mirroring or duplexing, because both drives are mirrored. The only real difference is that duplexed drives run on different controllers.

Many controller functions are handled by on-board motherboard controls. While this is an administrative convenience, it becomes a nightmare if the motherboard requires a full replacement just because the on-board serial ports do not work. Remember that every on-board motherboard controller has an equivalent PCI solution at relatively little cost that could save some money in the long run. In these situations, it might be worthwhile to stock spare serial, parallel, video, disk, and USB controllers in order to reduce the greater downtime (and cost) of replacing a motherboard.

 When you analyze systems that have several different fault tolerant components, consider adding fault tolerance for any components that contain moving parts.

Network Card Failure

Network cards are the first in a chain of devices that are prone to annoying outages. Fortunately, nine times out of ten, the network cable is bad, so stocking a spare cable is worthwhile. While network cards themselves rarely fail, they are susceptible to configuration issues, particularly in older networks. If the lights in the back light up, consider changing the frame type (in Novell networks) or manually configuring the speed. Most network cards will automatically detect speeds without causing damage on the network. However once in a blue moon this functionality fails and requires a manual adjustment.

Also know that multiple network cards can be installed into a system in order to maintain functionality should one of them fail. Having multiple network cards can save time troubleshooting a complex network setup. Be aware, however, that not all systems that are installed with two network cards are configured that way for fault tolerance purposes. Quite often, a second network card is installed to connect two separate TCP/IP subnet networks for the purpose of routing data between the two.

Other Network Equipment Failure

One in every fifty networking problems is a result of a failed hub or switch port, or a faulty network drop. Either one could work erratically or not at all. It is always a good idea to have a spare hub and cables on hand to recover from situations like these while you handle warranty maintenance or repunch the network drop.

Routers, DSL modems, and other higher-priced hardware can be purchased or leased with a service or depot maintenance plan. Service plans will allow emergency on-site service repair for big-ticket items, and depot maintenance calls for equipment to be drop shipped to your site without first returning the current product. Both of these options should be seriously considered, as they are usually mission-critical to the business, and replacements are quite often beyond the immediate capacity for the company to acquire.

Power Supply and CPU Fan

Occasionally, a power supply or CPU fan will fail on a server or mission-critical system, particularly if there are environmental humidity or temperature problems in the room. Power supplies can be easily purchased; however, they can be tricky to install and plug in. Be careful that both you and the computer are grounded appropriately and that you do not touch any open electrical components on the system. Be sure to remember to plug all computer components back into the power supply also. When shopping for a replacement power supply, be sure to get the appropriate AT/ATX power supply with enough plugs and length to handle all devices in the computer.

CPU fan replacements are a good idea, as they will most likely burn out as often if not more often than the power supply—particularly if the server is always on. Most CPU fans come with their own assembly; however, you need to know what CPU type you are running, and make sure you purchase the appropriate spare fan.

Cloning

Cloning is the process of creating a complete duplicate of a given system to use as a fallback or second-string computer. The process of cloning begins with identical hardware and software installed on two separate systems. Once a duplicate system has been created, it is taken offline for storage and safekeeping. Data should occasionally be copied from the host to the target system using either tape restore or disk imaging software. If the data on the system has a high rate of change, cloning is not a reasonable solution for complete system failure due to the frequency.

Partial cloning, however, is gaining in popularity and ease of usage. Partial cloning begins and ends with a set of identical hardware. In the event of a server failure, components such as the hard disk drive (and perhaps RAM) are moved from the damaged system into the new one. Because there are no new hardware components, the transfer should occur easily, and the system can be up and running in a matter of minutes providing that the hard disk and RAM remain undamaged during the transplant process.

Clustering

Battery backup, striping, duplexing, mirroring, and cloning are all methods of recovering from failure of a single device, function, or process that causes an entire system to fail. Clustering (or SFT III in the NetWare world) is an efficient method of assuring that a given server's failure will not negatively impact the processing efficiency of the entire cluster. All clustered servers, by definition, contain the same software and usually the same hardware.

Server clustering is actually a type of multi-processing configuration. Instead of having multiple processors in the same computer case (called parallel processing), clustering involves distributed processing involving multiple computer systems, whereby a complex software application detects CPU utilization and delegates tasks to other CPUs in a server cluster or farm. Server clustering is usually implemented for client/server applications and database applications that receive a high frequency of user requests.

Load Balancing

Load balancing is a natural evolution from clustering. Because clustering is restricted to simple CPU delegation and sharing, load balancing was created to share application functionality as well. Using load balancing, if a server fails, all tasks and functions previously performed by that server will be delegated to other servers in the load balancing team.

Data Center Relocation

There is always the possibility that something tremendously drastic will happen requiring a partial or complete transplant to a different location. Causes for these moves can range from fire to natural disasters to something as simple as an extended power outage. The reasons for relocating your data center usually revolve around the availability or lack of functionality of the data center environment itself. This does not necessarily mean that it becomes necessary to move every time the air conditioning fails. Relocation should be a consideration, though, if the heat in the room climbs over 100 degrees Fahrenheit (far above a safe operating range) and you have no idea when the problem will be resolved or you know that it will not be resolved within two weeks—certainly long enough to disrupt the business longer than simply moving operations to a different location.

Preventing the need for a data center relocation is a pretty broad task; however, there are some things that can be done:

➤ Ensure that adequate fire suppression is available and nearby.

➤ Place the chilling systems on their own circuit.

➤ Reduce the risks of physical injury and electrical damage by installing a raised floor in the data center. This will make everything tidier by allowing cables underfoot, increase air circulation, and keep potentially hazardous electrical connections away from general access.

Unfortunately, preventing natural disasters or extended or unreasonable power outages is not possible. This is when relocating the data center and operations to a different facility becomes a requirement. It is also during times like these that an adequate and properly documented disaster recovery plan becomes a critical tool. Although it is not a happy thought, the possibility remains that certain key personnel might not be available to function in a real disaster, and documentation might be the only key to maintaining a company's business. Disaster training is also important to maintain a core group of people who know what to do and what should happen during emergencies like these.

Hot Sites

Companies requiring as close to 100 percent uptime as possible deal with data center relocation by moving to a facility that already has computers, servers, tape drives, and telephones available for usage. This is called a hot site because for all intents and purposes, it becomes immediately available as soon as the client walks in. Some configuration and customization is necessary to ensure full functionality; however, as far as the Server+ exam is concerned, the data center can be up and running in a matter of a few hours.

Hot sites are usually located on the premises of a specific "business continuity" vendor providing these services to companies. They usually have considerable experience in disaster recovery and planning and can assist you greatly in devising and documenting a complete recovery plan.

Although not specifically covered in the exam, here is how a disaster recovery plan would look like for a call center moving to a hot site:

1. Power goes out for an indefinite period of time.

2. Notify the hot site that you will need the facility.

3. Notify the backup tape storage company that it needs to deliver the latest backup set to the hot site facility.

4. Split the call center representatives in half and send half of them to the new facility.

5. While the call center representatives are en route, the hot site personnel will be in the process of programming the phones to fit your needs and will also be configuring your computers and servers when the backup tapes arrive, depending upon what depth of services you have purchased from the company.

6. As soon as they arrive, call the local phone company and have them transfer the 800- numbers to the new facility.

7. As soon as the phone change is complete, move the remaining personnel and yourself to the facility.

8. As soon as the backup tapes arrive, begin a tape restoration.

Although some details are missing from this particular scenario, you definitely get the idea that disaster plans of this sort need to be practiced, planned, practiced some more, and documented thoroughly. Most of these continuity companies will provide a locker for you to store software, documentation, and other necessities. They also usually provide lounges, TV, and recreational areas in the event that personnel are required to stay at the facility for an extended period of time. Hot sites themselves are well protected against power loss with industrial-grade battery backup and generator systems. In some cases, portable hot sites are available. Choosing a hot site vendor is also critical based upon the facilities and locations they support. This is in the event that a natural disaster should occur in an isolated region.

Cold Sites

Cold sites are usually locations where an office and datacenter can be configured and set up, but not without some work. A good example of a cold site would be a branch office or another building belonging to the same company.

Cold sites require more planning and documentation than hot sites because you need to do everything yourself. In addition, immediate costs involved could be more expensive than with a hot site because of the need for computers, equipment, telephone access, and data connections. By definition, a cold site will take more time to bring up, and work best for companies where a few days' loss can be made up with extra work and time. You can maintain a cold site in same geographic area as your primary site, but the same natural disaster that affected your primary site could also affect your cold site.

When choosing between a hot site and a cold site, consider the urgency requirements of the company involved and the costs involved. A hot site provides a quicker setup but costs you money whether you need it or not. A cold site will cost little to nothing unless it becomes required but will cost you more in down time should you ever need it.

Practice Questions

Question 1

> You need to devise a disaster recovery plan for your organization in the event of a system failure. Your company has several locations throughout the United States, with its corporate headquarters in Scottsdale, Arizona. Each site contains a 24/7 call center that requires near-perfect systems availability. If a disaster occurs in Scottsdale, where should the data center go?
>
> ○ a. A cold site
>
> ○ b. A hot site
>
> ○ c. One of the other call center facilities
>
> ○ d. A business continuity facility

Answer b is correct. Because the business requires 24/7 availability, a hot site is necessary in order to minimize systems downtime. Answer a is incorrect because a cold site would take days to configure appropriately. Answer c is incorrect because moving to one of the other call center facilities would essentially constitute a cold site due to the additional equipment and space required. Finally, answer d is incorrect because although a business continuity facility is a type of hot site, not all hot sites are business continuity vendors.

Question 2

> You need to devise a disaster recovery plan for your organization in the event of a system failure. Your company has several locations throughout the United States with a corporate headquarters in Scottsdale, Arizona. Each site contains a team of programmers that requires systems availability between the hours of 6 A.M. and 6 P.M. If a disaster occurs in Scottsdale, where should the data center go?
>
> ○ a. A cold site
>
> ○ b. A hot site
>
> ○ c. One of the other facilities
>
> ○ d. A business continuity facility

Answer c is correct. The question does not indicate any particular urgency or requirements to reestablishing data services, therefore one of the other facilities should be used as a cold site. Answers a, b, and d are incorrect because the additional cost that they would incur is not required.

Question 3

You are a single administrator responsible for six servers in a call center. You live 45 minutes from the facility. How should you configure the UPS systems at the office for a graceful shutdown?

○ a. Ensure that the UPS system has 45 minutes of power and shut down the servers when you get to the office.

○ b. Train the supervisor to shut down the servers immediately before the battery power runs out.

○ c. Leave the systems alone until the power comes back.

○ d. Set UPS management to shut down the servers.

Answer d is correct. The UPS system should be configured to automatically shut down the servers before the battery power runs out. Answer a is incorrect because you cannot rely on being able to get there on time to shut down the servers yourself, and many UPS batteries will not support 45 minutes on a full load. Answer b is incorrect because training someone to shut down the servers is a possible answer, but not a reasonable one considering the training needed. Answer c is also incorrect, because leaving the systems alone until power comes back could completely drain the backup batteries and cause the computers to shut down ungracefully, resulting in data loss and hardware failure.

Question 4

You are tasked with configuring and installing a backup system for your company. You determine that because of portability and cost, tapes are the best available backup media. After analyzing the mission-critical files and systems, you determine that you will need to implement a GFS five-day tape rotation strategy with a full backup containing approximately 30GB of data. Which type of tape should you choose?

○ a. DLT

○ b. Travan

○ c. DAT

○ d. MD

Answer a is correct. DLT tapes handle between 20GB and 70GB of data. Answer b is incorrect because Travan is a brand name of tape. Answer c is incorrect because DAT tapes only handle between 2GB and 20GB of data. Answer d is incorrect because minidisks (MD) are not used for data storage in the United States.

Question 5

You are consulting for a government contractor that deals with sensitive information. Your manager notifies you that all the Unix servers and several client workstations running Windows NT, Windows 2000, and Linux that contain any sensitive data need to be fully backed up daily to the same location for offsite storage. Which media type should be used?

- ○ a. Tape
- ○ b. Removable storage
- ○ c. Network drive
- ○ d. Storage area network

Answer d is correct. A storage area network would be fast and accessible by all clients on the network. Answer a is incorrect because mounting tape drives on each computer would be cost prohibitive, and tape backup software would not be able to backup so many clients to a single drive in any reasonable amount of time. Answer b is incorrect because removable storage is not reasonable due to capacity issues. Answer c is incorrect because although a network drive might work as a backup solution, it might not be accessible by all client operating systems.

Question 6

You are conducting a meeting with several colleagues to determine an appropriate tape rotation method to back up 60MB of data. You determine that the best method is the one that utilizes the fewest number of tapes. Which one is this?

- ○ a. Back up 60GB of data fully seven days a week, rotate every month onto DAT tapes
- ○ b. Back up 60GB of data fully with a GFS five-day rotation onto DLT tapes
- ○ c. Back up 60GB of data fully seven days a week, rotate every month onto DLT tapes
- ○ d. Back up 60GB of data fully with a GFS six-day rotation onto DLT tapes

Answer b is correct. A GFS 5-day rotation on DLT tapes will require 19 tapes. Answer a is incorrect because DAT tapes, with only 20 GB capacity, would require 3 tapes per day with 31 days per month requiring 93 tapes total. Answer c is incorrect because a 31-day rotation would require 31 DLT tapes. Finally, answer d is incorrect because a GFS 6-day rotation on DLT tapes would require 20 tapes.

Question 7

You need to run a full backup on the servers before a scheduled power outage occurs. Which type of backup should you run?

○ a. Full backup

○ b. Copy backup

○ c. Incremental backup

○ d. Differential backup

○ e. Daily backup

Answer b is correct. A copy backup will fully back up all files without resetting the archive bit, therefore not inadvertently tampering with the current backup scheme. Answer a is incorrect because a full backup will reset the archive bit on the files, which would cause an incomplete backup to occur if the scheduled backup is set to be incremental or differential. Answers c, d, and e are incorrect because an incremental, differential, or daily backup will not contain all files.

Question 8

The terms hot swap and hot plug apply to what technologies? [Choose all that apply]

❑ a. Serial

❑ b. USB

❑ c. RAID

❑ d. PCMCIA

Answers b, c, and d are all correct. USB, RAID, and PCMCIA technologies all support hot swapping and plugging equipment. Answer a is incorrect because serial connections do not support these types of equipment.

Question 9

What is the difference between clustering and load balancing?

- ○ a. Clustering is sharing application load, whereas load balancing is sharing processor load.
- ○ b. Clustering is sharing application and processor load, whereas load balancing is sharing just application load.
- ○ c. Clustering is sharing processor load, whereas load balancing shares application load.
- ○ d. Clustering is sharing processor load, whereas hile load balancing is sharing both processor and application load.

Answer c is correct. Clustering shares processor tasks, and load balancing balances application loads. Answer a is incorrect because clustering is not a form of multiprocessor support. Answer b is incorrect because clustering shares only processor load with other computers. Answer d is also incorrect because load balancing shares application loads.

Need to Know More?

 Craft, Melissa, Mark A. Poplar, David V. Watts, Will Willis. *Network+ Exam Prep*. Scottsdale, AZ: The Coriolis Group, 1999. ISBN 1-57610-412-5. Contains in-depth information on RAID.

 Reeves, Scott, Kalinda Reeves, Stephen Weese, and Christopher S. Geyer. *A+ Exam Prep Third Edition*. Scottsdale, AZ: The Coriolis Group, 2001. ISBN 1-57610-699-3. Great for specifics on backup methods and media.

 Zacker, Craig and Paul Doyle. Upgrading and Repairing Networks. Indianapolis, IN: Que Corporation, 1996. ISBN 0-78970181-2. An awesome reference for specifics and how-tos on RAID, disaster recovery, and backup methodologies.

 www.adaptec.com. "Let's talk about RAID". Adaptec Corporation's in-depth information about RAID.

 www.techrepublic.com. This site contains a wealth of information on any and every IT topic imaginable—everything from hardware and component-level stuff all the way to management decisions and political trends. An awesome source for up-to-date definitions and information ranging from the novice to the expert.

 www.storage-area-networks.com. "Reducing Enterprise Backup Windows". This is a good article by Kevin Trotman about the ins and outs of SAN purchase and configuration.

 www.comdisco.com/Index.cfm/16/3016DFA1-FD83-421A-BC1436837444BF7C/. The "Continuity Glossary" contains many terms and definitions that are important toward disaster prevention and recovery. Always remember that Web sites can change frequently, so if this page is invalid, look for the continuity glossary at www.combidsco.com.

 www.pcguide.com. This site by Charles M. Kozierok and similar to TechRepublic, contains a wealth of information on many IT topics.

www.microsoft.com. "Clustering Architecture". A pretty good overview of clustering technologies and how they apply to Windows NT.

 www.novell.com. "SFTIII for Netware". Information about the NetWare equivalent to clustering and load balancing. SFT is a complete system mirroring solution and does not currently span more than two systems.

Sample Test

Question 1

Your server is backed up to tape every day. A full backup is performed every Friday, and differential backups are done every Saturday through Thursday. The server fails on Tuesday. Which tapes are needed to restore the system?

○ a. Friday, Saturday, Sunday, Monday

○ b. Friday, Saturday, Sunday, Monday, Tuesday

○ c. Friday, Monday

○ d. Friday, Tuesday

Question 2

You receive an alarm stating that the temperature in the server cabinet has reached 100 degrees Fahrenheit. Each server has a cooling fan on the CPU and on the server itself, and the cabinet also has a cooling fan. What can you do to decrease the temperature?

○ a. Open the server cases to increase circulation.

○ b. Add another cooling fan to each server.

○ c. Upgrade the fan on the CPU.

○ d. Add another cooling fan to the cabinet.

Question 3

A technician upgraded the system BIOS in a server and rebooted the server. Later, you notice that the tape backup fails. The parallel port tape device has always worked well in the past, but it is not working now. What is the problem?

○ a. The tape drive is bad.

○ b. The BIOS was not upgraded appropriately.

○ c. The tape port needs to be enabled within the BIOS.

○ d. The tape media is bad.

Question 4

You have received a new server with a RAID array that was preconfigured at a vendor's site. The hard drives came in a separate box from the RAID array, which requires that you install the hard drives into the array. Once you turn on the server, you receive an error message indicating that the array configuration has changed and needs to be configured. What do you do?

○ a. Return the server.

○ b. Check the LUN and termination for the SCSI channel.

○ c. Reconfigure the array.

○ d. Replace the hard drives because they are bad.

Question 5

Your server is configured with a backup tape, UPS, SNMP monitoring, and a network card. What can you do to increase reliability and fault tolerance?

    I. Run a backup.

    II. Add a second network card.

    III. Install RAID.

    IV. Replace the server fan.

○ a. I and II

○ b. II and III

○ c. III and IV

○ d. I and IV

Question 6

The SNMP monitor on a server reports network utilization at 5 percent, what should you do?

○ a. Replace the NIC.

○ b. Replace the network cable.

○ c. Create a baseline.

○ d. Change the trap threshold to 60 percent.

Question 7

Your company has decided that it is necessary to protect its data from potential fire on the premises. What is the best thing to do?

○ a. Store backup tapes at an offsite storage facility.

○ b. Store backup tapes in a fireproof cabinet.

○ c. Store backup tapes at an employee's home.

○ d. Store backup tapes in the server room that has a fire control system.

Question 8

You are receiving calls indicating that the network is running slowly. Upon investigation, you notice that one particular server is running slowly. You run some tests, compare the information against the baseline data, and find that the memory pages/second has increased, and CPU utilization has decreased. What is wrong?

○ a. Bad memory

○ b. Bad hard drive

○ c. Not enough memory

○ d. Not enough hard drive space

Question 9

You are installing a PCI 33 MHz card on a 66 MHz PCI bus. What do you need to do in order to make it work?

○ a. Nothing. It will work.

○ b. Install the card on the first slot in the PCI bus.

○ c. Upgrade the BIOS.

○ d. Nothing. It will not work.

Question 10

You receive a call from a user that cannot log in to the server. After investigation, you determine that you cannot ping the server name or the server's IP address. You can, however, ping 127.0.0.1, and you notice that other users are having the same problem. What is the problem?

○ a. The server is down.

○ b. The NIC on the computer is bad.

○ c. The network cable is bad.

○ d. The user's computer is not connected to the network.

Question 11

Your company has built a new data center. Before moving the old data center to the new location, you have a technician check to see whether or not the room is ready. He checks network connections, cabinets, cabling, and the fire suppression system, but decides that the room is not ready. Why not?

    I. The walls are not stable.

    II. The ceiling is not secure.

    III. The temperature and humidity are not appropriate.

    IV. The room does not provide adequate electricity.

○ a. I and II

○ b. II and III

○ c. III and IV

○ d. I and IV

Question 12

Upon investigation, you determine that there are 4U available on your server rack. How much space is this?

- ○ a. 7 inches
- ○ b. 4.4 inches
- ○ c. 6 inches
- ○ d. 3.81 inches

Question 13

You need to create a baseline for your servers. How do you do this?

- ○ a. Generate SNMP monitor logs for one day.
- ○ b. Generate SNMP monitor logs for the same span of time for five days.
- ○ c. Generate Performance Monitor logs for a week.
- ○ d. Generate Performance Monitor logs for high traffic times.

Question 14

Which of the following provides the fastest external connection?

- ○ a. RS-232
- ○ b. USB
- ○ c. SCSI
- ○ d. IEEE 1394

Question 15

You want to attach three different servers to the same KVM that already has four servers attached to it. These servers are brand new and have not been used or previously turned on. What cables will you need?

○ a. 3 monitor cables, 3 keyboard cables, 3 mouse cables, 3 network cables

○ b. 4 monitor cables, 3 keyboard cables, 3 mouse cables

○ c. 4 monitor cables, 3 keyboard cables, 3 mouse cables, 3 network cables, 3 power cords

○ d. 3 monitor cables, 3 keyboard cables, 3 mouse cables, 3 network cables, 3 power cords

Question 16

After installing one of your servers on a UPS and plugging in all of the components, the UPS becomes overloaded and emits an alarm. What overloaded the UPS?

○ a. Tape drive

○ b. Keyboard

○ c. KVM

○ d. Monitor

Question 17

A service on your server fails. What should you do next?

○ a. Install SMS.

○ b. Restart the system.

○ c. Set up monitoring.

○ d. Initiate system recovery.

Question 18

One of the daemons on your server has stopped. What do you do first?

○ a. Manually restart the daemon.

○ b. Check the status of the other services.

○ c. Reboot to start a clean environment.

○ d. Eliminate other services one by one until you find the culprit.

Question 19

One of the services on your server has failed. You manually restarted the service, but it failed again. What should you do?

○ a. Manually restart the daemon.

○ b. Check the status of the other services.

○ c. Reboot to start a clean environment.

○ d. Eliminate the other services one by one until you find the culprit.

Question 20

Your server is backed up to tape every day. A full backup is performed every Friday, and incremental backups are done every Saturday through Thursday. The server fails on Tuesday. Which tapes are needed to restore the system?

○ a. Friday, Saturday, Sunday, Monday

○ b. Friday, Saturday, Sunday, Monday, Tuesday

○ c. Friday, Monday

○ d. Friday, Tuesday

Question 21

The SNMP monitor on a server reports network utilization at 65 percent;
what should you do?

- ○ a. Replace the NIC.
- ○ b. Replace the network cable.
- ○ c. Compare this to the baseline to see if it is acceptable.
- ○ d. Change the trap threshold to 60 percent.

Question 22

You need to protect your company's data against natural disaster. Your boss
has given you the task of determining the best method for ensuring that the
company will be functional in the event of a catastrophe within 48 hours.
What is the best way to do this?

- I.   Establish a hot site.
- II. Store tape backups in an offsite storage facility.
- III. Set up a cold site.
- IV. Store tape backups in a fireproof safe.

- ○ a. I and II
- ○ b. II and III
- ○ c. III and IV
- ○ d. I and IV

Question 23

You are installing a PCI 66 MHz card on a 33 MHz PCI bus. What do you need
to do in order to make it work?

- ○ a. Install the PCI card and do nothing else. It will work.
- ○ b. Install the card on the first slot in the PCI bus.
- ○ c. Upgrade the BIOS.
- ○ d. Nothing. It will not work.

Question 24

You decide to purchase an external hard drive for your server. You find that several different connection methods are available for the device that you need. Which of the following is the fastest?

○ a. RS-232

○ b. USB

○ c. Parallel

○ d. IEEE 1394

Question 25

You update the SNMP software on one member of a server farm. What do you do next to ensure that the update propagates to all other members of the farm?

○ a. Update SNMP on all other members of the server farm.

○ b. Trigger the other servers to propagate changes.

○ c. Nothing—it is only necessary on one server.

○ d. Deploy the update via SMS to the other servers.

Question 26

You need to back up 80GB of data. Which media can you use?

○ a. CDR

○ b. DAT

○ c. WORM

○ d. QIC80

Question 27

During a violent storm, your office building collapsed in the middle of the night. One of your servers was destroyed. The tapes were stored in an offsite location, and you need to restore the data as soon as possible in order to get back up and running. When the DLT tapes are delivered, you find that you only have a Travan tape drive to work with. What do you need to do to restore the data?

○ a. You cannot restore the data.

○ b. Purchase a DLT drive.

○ c. DLT tapes will work in a Travan drive.

○ d. Purchase a DLT to Travan conversion cartridge.

Question 28

You have configured your management software to perform predictive failure analysis on your RAID 5 array. The program notifies you that Drive 2 is failing. What do you do?

○ a. Back up Drive 2 and replace it.

○ b. Image Drive 2 and replace it.

○ c. Use the management software to fail the drive, replace it, and rebuild the stripe set.

○ d. Use the management software to fail the drive, replace it, rebuild the stripe set, and restore from tape.

Question 29

You need to install an Ultra ATA drive on an Ultra 2 channel. How can you do this?

○ a. It is not possible.

○ b. Purchase a 68- to 120-pin connector converter.

○ c. Install a 20 ohm terminator.

○ d. Change the LUN for the Ultra2 controller to match the default ATA LUN.

Question 30

You have upgraded a server that is running 64MB RAM with a 256MB SIMM. The server only recognizes 64MB RAM. There are no errors during POST. Why?

○ a. The speed on the 256MB SIMM is different.

○ b. The 256MB SIMM will not work with the 64MB SIMM.

○ c. The system will not recognize that much RAM.

○ d. You cannot mix registered and nonregistered RAM.

Question 31

You need to perform systems maintenance on your server. What do you do first?

○ a. Power down the system.

○ b. Reboot.

○ c. Run a tape backup and verify.

○ d. Defragment the hard drives.

Question 32

You have placed two servers on the same UPS unit because a single server only uses approximately 30 percent of the battery. While testing both servers on the UPS, you find that there is not enough battery power to last long enough to perform a proper shutdown. How can you increase the battery time?

  I. Buy a new battery.

  II. Install APM on the server.

  III. Install UPS management software.

  IV. Configure the system to do a safe shutdown automatically.

○ a. I and II

○ b. II and III

○ c. III and IV

○ d. I and IV

Question 33

At times tape backups are taking too long to complete, and you are often forced to abort the backup job in order to prevent problems during the day. What can you do?

○ a. Perform a full backup daily.

○ b. Perform an incremental backup daily.

○ c. Perform a differential backup daily.

○ d. Perform a copy backup daily.

Question 34

Your server had a boot sector virus, so you ran fdisk.exe and reformatted the drive. You then reloaded the NOS using a boot disk and the installation CD. Unfortunately, the virus is still present. What happened?

○ a. The CD-ROM was infected with the virus.

○ b. FDISK will not kill a boot sector virus.

○ c. The boot disk was infected with the virus.

○ d. The virus is being stored in RAM.

Question 35

After performing system maintenance, you reboot the server, and an error message appears indicating that there is an error mounting the SYS volume. Which NOS are you using?

○ a. Windows NT

○ b. Linux

○ c. Unix

○ d. NetWare

Question 36

You just installed a tape drive on your server, and as soon as you reboot it, the log fills with confusing errors. What do you do?

○ a. Unplug the tape drive.

○ b. Reboot the server.

○ c. Check the logs.

○ d. Install a tape driver.

Question 37

A service failed on a remote server, and the failure was logged, but nobody noticed. The next day, the service fails again, causing the server to go down in the middle of the day. What can you do to help solve this problem?

○ a. Use remote administration tools to check the server on a regular basis.

○ b. Train someone onsite to check on the server regularly.

○ c. Reboot the server.

○ d. Configure SNMP to notify you via pager or email when the failure occurs.

Question 38

You need to upgrade the CPU on your server. You have managed to locate a CPU that is compatible with the one that is already installed, and you are ready to install it. What else do you need to do?

I.   Update the server drivers.

II. Upgrade the BIOS.

III. Check with the motherboard manufacturer to see if a second CPU is supported.

IV. Replace the CMOS battery.

○ a. I and II

○ b. II and III

○ c. III and IV

○ d. I and IV

Question 39

Before performing a system upgrade, you need to run a tape backup. What is the best way to ensure that if the upgrade fails, you will be able to restore the server data from tape?

○ a. Use the verify option after the tape backup.

○ b. Run a test restore of the data.

○ c. Clean the tape.

○ d. Clean the tape drive.

Question 40

Your server is backed up only on the weekdays, Monday through Friday. A full backup is done every Monday night, and incremental backups are done Tuesday through Friday. A hard drive fails on Saturday. How many tapes will you need for the restore process?

○ a. 5

○ b. 2

○ c. 3

○ d. 4

Question 41

You receive an alarm stating that the server temperature has reached 100 degrees Fahrenheit. The server has a cooling fan on the CPU and on the server itself. What can you do to decrease the temperature?

○ a. Open the server case for increased circulation.

○ b. Add another cooling fan to the server.

○ c. Upgrade the fan on the CPU.

○ d. Add a cooling fan to the room.

Question 42

You have received a new server with a RAID array that was preconfigured at the manufacturer site. The hard drives come in a separate box from the RAID array and require that you install the hard drives into the array. Once you turn on the server, you receive an error message indicating that the array configuration has changed and needs to be configured. What do you do?

- ○ a. Return the server.
- ○ b. Replace the hard drives because they are bad.
- ○ c. Reconfigure the array.
- ○ d. Install the hard drives in the correct slots.

Question 43

Upon investigation, you determine that there are 4U available on your server rack. How much space is this?

- ○ a. 7 cm
- ○ b. 4.4 cm
- ○ c. 17.8 cm
- ○ d. 10 cm

Question 44

A technician wants to upgrade the EISA network card on your server to an ISA network card. You do not agree with this recommendation. Why?

- I. ISA runs faster.
- II. EISA config needs to be run.
- III. Incoming packets will be faster because EISA is faster.
- IV. ISA cards will not fit on an EISA bus.

- ○ a. I and II
- ○ b. II and III
- ○ c. III and IV
- ○ d. I and IV

Question 45

You have received budget approval to implement RAID on your server system. Which fault-tolerant RAID is more cost-efficient?

○ a. RAID 1

○ b. RAID 0

○ c. RAID 10

○ d. RAID 5

Question 46

The magic packet function transmits 16 consecutive MAC addresses in order to accomplish what?

○ a. Wake-on-LAN

○ b. CLC

○ c. SMTP

○ d. SNMP

Question 47

You have configured the antivirus software on your server to automatically perform monthly updates from the manufacturer's FTP site. Unfortunately, this has not worked for the past three months. Regular connectivity to the server works fine. What do you do to fix this problem?

   I. Check the connection to the site.

   II. Ping another local server.

   III. Make sure the antivirus program is running.

   IV. Reboot the server.

○ a. I and II

○ b. III and IV

○ c. I and III

○ d. II and IV

Question 48

You have configured a server with a tape drive, RAID, and a network card, and you have set up GFS tape rotation. What can you do to increase reliability?

   I. Add a UPS battery.

   II. Change the tape rotation.

   III. Add a hard drive to the RAID array.

   IV. Install a second NIC.

   ○ a. I and II

   ○ b. III and IV

   ○ c. I and IV

   ○ d. II and III

Question 49

You implement RAID on your Pentium 1.2 GHz server, which is running 1GB of RAM, and the overall performance of the server slows down. What can you do to increase performance?

   ○ a. Add another hard disk drive.

   ○ b. Add more RAM.

   ○ c. Install hardware RAID.

   ○ d. Install software RAID.

Question 50

You need to reboot your server. What do you do?

   ○ a. Power off

   ○ b. Ctrl+Alt+Del

   ○ c. Type "down", then exit

   ○ d. Type "shutdown", then exit

Question 51

You have an Ultra3 SCSI controller installed in your computer and have been given an Ultra2 SCSI external hard drive to install. What do you do?

○ a. You purchase a 50-pin to 68-pin adapter and install a 132 ohm terminator.

○ b. You install a 110 ohm terminator.

○ c. You purchase a 50-pin-to-68-pin adapter and install a 110 ohm terminator.

○ d. You tell the person who assigned you this task that these devices are not compatible and you cannot install the hard drive.

Question 52

You are replacing a failed HVD Fast SCSI CD-ROM with an LVD Ultra3 SCSI CD-ROM. What do you do?

○ a. Purchase a 50-pin-to-68-pin adapter and install a 110 ohm terminator for active termination.

○ b. Install a 132 ohm terminator.

○ c. Purchase a 50-pin-to-80-pin adapter and install a 132 ohm terminator for passive termination.

○ d. It will not work.

Answer Key

1. c	19. c	37. d
2. d	20. a	38. b
3. c	21. c	39. b
4. b	22. a	40. a
5. b	23. a	41. d
6. d	24. d	42. d
7. b	25. a	43. c
8. c	26. d	44. c
9. d	27. b	45. d
10. a	28. c	46. a
11. c	29. a	47. c
12. a	30. c	48. c
13. c	31. c	49. c
14. c	32. c	50. c
15. d	33. b	51. c
16. d	34. c	52. d
17. b	35. d	
18. a	36. d	

Question 1

Answer c is correct. A differential backup backs up all data that has changed since the last full backup, thus requiring the full backup tape from Friday and also the differential backup that occurred on Monday. Answer a would be correct if incremental backups were being performed. Answers b and d are incorrect because the Tuesday backup has not occurred yet.

Question 2

Answer d is correct. Most cabinets are equipped to handle more than one fan. Answer a is incorrect because server cases are designed for optimal internal circulation. Answer b is incorrect because most servers are already equipped with the appropriate number of fans to handle circulation in the optimal external environment. Answer c is incorrect because upgrading the fan on the CPU will not decrease the temperature in the server.

Question 3

Answer c is correct. While troubleshooting this problem, you should ask yourself, "What changed?" In this case, the BIOS was upgraded, so you must assume that the problem is somehow related to the BIOS problem. Answers b and c both deal with BIOS, but answer b cannot be correct because all of the other functions on the server work okay, so the only reasonable answer is answer c. Answer a is incorrect because the tape drive worked before the BIOS upgrade. The same applies to answer d. Because the BIOS upgrade should not have an impact on the functionality of the tape drive or media, there is no reason that these items should not work.

Question 4

Answer b is correct. One of the first things you can do when there is something wrong with a SCSI channel or array is check the logical unit number (LUN) and termination for each device in the array. More than likely, the drives were installed incorrectly in the array and checking the LUNs and termination will point you in the right direction. Answer a is incorrect because returning the server is a bit premature. The same applies for answer d. Answer c is incorrect because if you reconfigure the array, you will lose all data that is currently on those hard drives.

Question 5

Answer b is correct. Adding a second network card and installing RAID will add fault tolerance to the overall system. Answers a and d are incorrect because running a backup should be standard operating procedure. There is no reason to replace the server fan. Answer c is also incorrect because there is no reason to replace the server fan.

Question 6

Answer d is correct. If your network is running at 5 percent, be grateful, and change the threshold to 60 percent, because at 60 percent you might have a real reason to worry. Answers a, b, and c are incorrect because a 5 percent network utilization does not indicate that anything is wrong.

Question 7

Answer b is correct. Storing the tapes in a fireproof cabinet onsite will provide adequate fire protection. However, it may not provide protection against water damage. Answer a is incorrect. In this case, where fire protection is the only requirement, offsite storage is overkill. Offsite storage is adequate for protection against fire, but most professional offsite storage facilities also protect against security threats, flooding, and other natural disasters. Answer c is incorrect because storing tapes at someone's home will not necessarily ensure fire protection. Although a fire suppression system in a server room may stop a fire after it has begun, there is no guarantee that it will stop a fire before any data is destroyed. Therefore, answer d is incorrect.

Question 8

Answer c is correct. This is a troubleshooting question. The first thing to do is break down the information you have and look at it in pieces. Low CPU utilization is probably an indicator that the bus mastering hard disk controller is doing all the work, and that there is not enough memory on-board. Anytime paging increases beyond normal baselines, it is a good indicator that either your RAM is going bad, or you need to upgrade your RAM. If memory was going bad, you would probably see an error message during POST, so you must assume that answer a is incorrect. Answers b and d are incorrect because paging is not symptomatic of any hard drive problems.

Question 9

Answer d is correct. It is important to remember that PCI bus and card speeds work much like a freeway. If you put a high-speed card on a low-speed freeway, the card can always slow down to match the speed of the freeway. On the other hand, if you put a low-speed card on a high-speed freeway, the freeway will not slow down for the card, and a traffic jam will occur. Answer a is incorrect because the 33 MHz card will not work on the 66 MHz bus. Changing the slot that the card is installed on will only bring it closer to or further away from the CPU. It will not change how the card behaves, so answer b is incorrect. Answer c is incorrect because the BIOS does not have control over the external bus.

Question 10

Answer a is correct. The server is down. Because other users are having the same problem, you can assume that answers b, c, and d are incorrect.

Question 11

Answer c is correct. Temperature, humidity, and electricity, are viable reasons for postponing or stopping the datacenter relocation. Issues with the walls or the ceiling would be handled by construction people, not your technician. This eliminates answers a, b, and d.

Question 12

Answer a is correct. 1U on a server rack or cabinet is 1.75 inches.

Question 13

Answer c is correct. Generating logs consistently for a full week will give you an adequate baseline. Creating a baseline involves gathering "standard" or "normal" data from your server over a period of time. Although it is possible to gather information for a short period of time, you cannot get a good idea of normal performance without looking at a server over a longer period of time. Therefore, answer a is incorrect. Answers b and d are incorrect because gathering data during specific periods of time does not give you a good overall idea of when the server is being used, and to what extent.

Question 14

Answer c is correct. SCSI connections are by far faster than any other connection speed to date. RS-232 is a connector type for serial connections, which makes answer a incorrect. Answer b, although similar to IEEE 1394, is much slower than both SCSI and IEEE 1394. In this list, IEEE 1394 is faster than all other choices except SCSI, so answer d is incorrect.

Question 15

Answer d is correct. Answer c is incorrect because you are only dealing with three monitors. Because these servers are brand new, you will need all the necessary cables for the servers, not just those required for KVM connection. Immediately, you will need three power cords for the CPUs, which eliminates answers a and b. Because there are only 3 devices, you will need only 3 monitor cables, 3 keyboard cables, and 3 network cables.

Question 16

Answer d is correct. The monitor has overloaded the UPS. In the same way that your house circuits may trip when overloaded, your UPS battery can do the same. Just like at home, you should look for a single item that uses the most power. Answer b is incorrect because it receives its power from the KVM or the server itself. Answer c is incorrect because there are no high power capacitors or moving parts in a KVM. Answer a is incorrect because, although there are moving parts, the capacitors in a monitor use more power than anything else on the system including the server.

Question 17

Answer b is correct. Restart the system. Ideally, you should restart the service and watch to see whether it goes back down immediately. Because this is not an option, you need to restart the system to get a "clean" environment and watch the service and the server to see whether the problem occurs again. Answer a is incorrect because software deployment has nothing to do with this problem. Answer c is incorrect because configuring monitoring may not be necessary at this stage. Answer d is incorrect because you have not determined whether anything has changed or become corrupted.

Question 18

Answer a is correct. Similar to question 17, the first thing you should do is restart the daemon and watch to see whether the problem happens again. Answer b is incorrect because checking the status of other daemons or services will not help solve or eliminate the problem. Answer c would be correct if the daemon was restarted and it failed again. Once you have manually restarted the daemon and have rebooted to start a clean environment, you then need to eliminate other services one by one until you find the culprit. At this stage, however, answer a is correct.

Question 19

Answer c is correct. You need to start with a clean "normal" working environment in order to monitor the service. If the service still fails after answer c has been performed, answer d should be done. At this point, however, answer d is incorrect. This question is similar to questions 17 and 18. Again, once the service stops, you need to manually restart it. Because you have already done this, and it failed again, answer a is incorrect. Answer b is incorrect because checking the status of other services does not help diagnose or eliminate the problem.

Question 20

Answer a is correct. Incremental tape backups will back up data that has changed since the last incremental or full backup. Answers b and d are incorrect because the backup has not yet occurred for Tuesday. Answer c would be correct if differential backups were being performed.

Question 21

Answer c is correct. With the information that you are given in this question, comparing to a baseline is the only single reasonable thing that can be done. Answers a and b are incorrect because, although they are both legitimate trouble-shooting tasks, you do not have enough information in the question to lead you towards replacing the NIC or the network cable. Answer d is incorrect because setting the threshold to something less than it currently is will not eliminate the message, and it will not help solve the problem either.

Question 22

Answer a is correct. A hot site allows you to be up and running in hours, and storing data in an offsite facility ensures with the highest degree of probability that the data will not be damaged in any way during a given catastrophe or disaster. Answers b and c are incorrect because a cold site requires acquisition of equipment, wiring, and furniture. A cold site would not be available for use within two days. Answer d is incorrect because storing tapes in a fireproof safe will not even remotely ensure the safety of the data if the building is flooded.

Question 23

Answer a is correct. A 66 MHz PCI card will slow down to match the speed of the bus. The opposite does not apply. Answer b is incorrect because installing a card on the first slot has no impact on the card speed or functionality. Answer c is incorrect because the BIOS does not control PCI bus speeds or functionality. Answer d is incorrect because a 66 MHz PCI card will work just fine on a 33 MHz bus.

Question 24

Answer d is correct. If SCSI were on this list, it would be the fastest option. Because it is not, IEEE 1392 is the fastest external connection method given. Answer a is incorrect because RS-232 indicates a serial connection, which is slower than IEEE 1392. Answer b is incorrect because although USB is a close cousin to IEEE 1392, it is much slower. Answer c is incorrect because parallel ports are slower than IEEE 1392.

Question 25

Answer a is correct. Update SNMP on all other members of the server farm. A server farm is a buzzword for a set of clustered or load balanced servers. In clustering, CPU functionality is shared across several different servers. In load balancing, a specific application is shared across different servers as well as CPU functionality. In both situations, this does not mean that other applications and data are also shared across other servers. Answer b is incorrect because there are no built-in triggers to propagate data from one member of a server farm to another. Answer c is incorrect because each server still maintains its own identity for other tasks and must be monitored and maintained as such in order to reduce overall server and server farm downtime. Answer d is incorrect because there is no mention of SMS being installed on any of the servers within the question.

Question 26

Answer d is correct. A QIC80 tape will back up 80GB of data. Answer a is incorrect because a CDR will only hold 700MB of data Answer b is incorrect because DAT will hold a maximum of 24GB of data. Answer c is incorrect for the same reasons answer a is because CDR is a variety of WORM.

Question 27

Answer b is correct. Purchase a DLT drive. The key to this question—and many others on the exam—is to remember that you are working in the server world, which means that you *must* find a way to make things work if at all possible, and often, money is no object. Answer a is incorrect because you absolutely need to restore the data in order to get things working. Answer c is incorrect because DLT tapes will not work in a Travan drive. Answer d is incorrect because a DLT to Travan converter does not exist.

Question 28

Answer c is correct. Use the management software to fail the drive, replace it, and rebuild the stripe set. Because this is RAID 5, you are unable to back up or image a specific drive. Therefore, answers a, b, and d are incorrect.

Question 29

Answer a is correct. It is not possible. In many ways, this is a trick question because most network administrators know that IDE cannot be mixed with SCSI. Unfortunately, it is easy to get confused because both types of drives can use the word "ultra" in their name, and many people do not realize that ATA is the original, formal name of IDE. Answer b is incorrect because there are no connectors or converters between SCSI and IDE. Answer c is incorrect because IDE does not require termination. Answer d is incorrect because there are no LUNs in the ATA world.

Question 30

Answer c is correct. The system will not recognize that much RAM. The key to this question lies in the statement that there are no errors during POST. If the speed on two SIMMs were different, an error would occur on POST, thus eliminating answer a. If the installed SIMM was incompatible with other installed SIMMs, an error would also occur on POST (answer b), and certainly the same would occur if the SIMM were bad altogether (answer d).

Question 31

Answer c is correct. Before performing any major tasks, including systems maintenance, you need to run a tape backup and verify that the backup will restore data appropriately. Answers a and b are incorrect because rebooting or powering the system down are not standard systems maintenance functions. Answer d is incorrect because before defragmenting the hard drive, you still need to perform a backup.

Question 32

Answer c is correct. You need to install the management software and configure it accordingly. You can increase battery time by configuring management software to power down one or both of the servers after a certain period of battery time has elapsed. Answers a and d are incorrect because purchasing a new battery will not increase battery life. Answer b is tricky because installing APM and UPS management software are both good steps toward increasing battery life, but unfortunately, individually they do nothing, and together, they still do nothing until you configure them to shut down automatically. Answer b is therefore incorrect.

Question 33

Answer b is correct. Perform an incremental backup daily. The question states that this is only a problem "at times," which indicates that differential backups are occurring. This makes sense because later in the week the system will back up more data than it did earlier in the week, and that backup might take longer than usual. Answer a is incorrect because running a full backup usually takes longer than a partial backup. Answer c is incorrect because the system is currently performing a differential backup daily. Answer d is incorrect because a copy backup takes just as long as a full backup.

Question 34

Answer c is correct. The boot disk was infected with the virus. Floppy disks can be overwritten by viruses. Answer a is incorrect because a CD-ROM is read-only and therefore cannot have a virus. Answer b is incorrect because FDISK will kill a boot sector virus. Answer d is incorrect. Viruses cannot write themselves to RAM without risking their own death the next time the system is rebooted.

Question 35

Answer d is correct. Windows 2000 now has a SYSVOL folder, which is also called the system volume, but it is different from the SYS volume used in NetWare. Answers a, b, and c are all incorrect because Windows NT, Linux, and Unix do not utilize volumes for data storage.

Question 36

Answer d is correct. This is because you might receive error messages if the driver is missing, installed incorrectly, or corrupt. This is a potentially confusing question because each option is a viable troubleshooting step. Answer a is incorrect because unplugging the tape drive will have no effect on how the system reacts to the device when it is not being actively used. If a service or daemon were actively using it and it had problems, you might see some changes. Answer b is incorrect because the server has already been rebooted. Answer c is incorrect because the question stated that the logs filled with confusing messages, which is an indicator that the logs have already been checked. You have to assume that during the installation the tape's driver was installed correctly, because none of the answers offered the possibility that the installation was incorrect. Installing the driver again probably will not do any good; therefore, answer d is incorrect.

Question 37

Answer d is correct. Configure SNMP to notify you via pager or email when the failure occurs. If you are a busy administrator, you really do not have time to drop everything and check on a remote server every few minutes, so answer a is incorrect. Answer b is incorrect for the same reason—nobody has time to babysit a remote server. Answer c is incorrect because rebooting the server already occurred when the server went down.

Question 38

Answer b is correct. You will most likely need to check with the motherboard manufacturer to determine whether the motherboard supports multiple CPUs and retrieve the BIOS update from the manufacturer. Answers a and d are incorrect because CPUs do not require drivers. Answer c is incorrect because replacing the CMOS battery will risk the BIOS information and not change the status of the CPU configuration.

Question 39

Answer b is correct. There is no better way to ensure that the data can be restored than to actually restore it. Running a verify is a way of ensuring that the data has been placed on the tape, but it does not ensure that a restore will work, so answer a is incorrect. Answers c and d are incorrect because cleaning the tape or tape drive will not ensure that the restore will work. This is another one of those questions where all answers are viable, but you need to choose the best answer.

Question 40

Answer a is correct. Because the question talks about incremental backups, you will need a tape for every day until the day the server fails. Answer b is incorrect because two tapes would be necessary if a differential backup were being performed. Answers c and d are also incorrect.

Question 41

Answer d is correct. Add a cooling fan to the room. Answer a is incorrect because server cases are designed for optimal circulation within the compartment. Answer b is incorrect because you do not know for sure that adding another cooling fan is possible on this server. Answer c is incorrect because it is not possible to upgrade fans.

Question 42

Answer d is correct. Install the hard drives in the correct slots. Answer a is incorrect because returning the server might be a bit premature in this situation. Answer b is incorrect because if the hard drives were bad, a different message would appear. Answer c is incorrect because reconfiguring the array would cause all data on those drives to be lost.

Question 43

Answer c is correct. 1U on a server rack is 1.75 inches. Because there is 2.54 cm per inch, you can safely calculate that 1U is 4.45 cm. Answer a is incorrect because 7 inches would be 4U, not centimeters. Answer b is incorrect because this is the space of 1U on a rack.

Question 44

Answer c is correct. EISA is faster and ISA cards will not fit on the EISA bus extension. Answers a and d are incorrect because ISA is not faster than EISA. Answer b is incorrect because EISA config does not need to be run when dealing with ISA.

Question 45

Answer d is correct. RAID 5 provides the most efficient use of disk space because as the number of installed disks increases, more disk space becomes available for usage rather than for parity information. Three RAID 5 drives have an equivalent of two drives available, which represents 66 percent available for usage. Four

RAID 5 drives have an equivalent of three drives available, which represents 75 percent available for usage. Answer a is incorrect because 50 percent of all disk space is lost in fault tolerance. Answer b is incorrect because RAID 0 is not fault tolerant. Answer c is incorrect because although RAID10 provides the greatest performance efficiency due to the implementation of RAID 0, it essentially mirrors striped drives, which will require twice as many drives as RAID 5.

Question 46

Answer a is correct. The word "packet" indicates that the question deals with networking, which eliminates answer b. Answer c is incorrect because Simple Mail Transport Protocol (SMTP) is not covered in the exam. SNMP deals with remote management and logging, and is used primarily within the TCP/IP protocol, which does not have a "magic packet."

Question 47

Answer c is correct. The update may be failing if the manufacturer's FTP site is down or if the antivirus update program is not running. Answers a and d are incorrect because regular connectivity to the server works fine and really has nothing to do with how clients connect to the server. Answer b is incorrect because rebooting the server will not ensure that the automatic update function of the antivirus program will work.

Question 48

Answer c is correct. Adding a UPS and a NIC are both viable fault-tolerant measures and will increase reliability. Answers a and d are incorrect because changing the tape rotation will not increase reliability. Answer b is incorrect because adding a drive to the RAID array will not guarantee reliability.

Question 49

Answer c is correct. A RAID installation of some sort occurred, and because it slowed down performance significantly, you can assume that the question is talking about software RAID rather than hardware RAID, which means that the

CPU is overloaded. The best solution to completely eliminate the problem is therefore to install hardware RAID. Answer a is incorrect because adding another hard disk drive will just aggravate the problem, not solve it. Answer b is incorrect because adding more RAM will not fix a CPU problem. Answer d is incorrect because software RAID has already been installed.

Question 50

Answer c is correct. This is the only complete and accurate reboot process listed, and it happens to be for NetWare. This is a trick question because it does not indicate which type of server is being rebooted. Answer a is incorrect because powering off any server is detrimental to its health. Answer b is incorrect because this key sequence will either force a hard reboot of a NetWare, Unix, or Linux server or begin the shutdown process for Windows NT and 2000. Answer d is incorrect because there is no shutdown command for any of these operating systems.

Question 51

Answer c is correct. The Ultra3 SCSI controller has a 68-to-68-pin connector, and the Ultra2 hard drive has a 50-to-50-pin connector. To make the connection you will need an adapter. Answer b is incorrect because although the correct termination is 110 ohm for active termination, allowing both of the devices to operate in LVD mode, a 110 ohm terminator alone will not solve the problem. Answer a is incorrect because if you use the 132 ohm terminator, you will be using passive termination, and the bus will revert to SE mode and limit the bus speed. Answer d is incorrect because it is possible to attach an Ultra2 SCSI drive to an Ultra3 SCSI controller.

Question 52

Answer d is correct. HVD and LVD are not compatible. The old HVD CD-ROM had to be installed on an HVD controller. The LVD CD-ROM is not going to work with the controller. Answer a would be correct if both devices were HVD or LVD, but they are not. Answers b and c are incorrect because a 132-ohm terminator is only required for SCSI 1.

Glossary

10Base-T

10Base-T is one variety of the Ethernet standard known as IEEE 802.3. 10Base-T is specific to twisted-pair cabling using RJ-45 connectors similar in nature to telephone cable. The maximum speed is 10Mbps.

100Base-T

Also known as IEEE 802.3u, 100Base-T is an Ethernet standard that allows network transmission at speeds of up to 100Mbps, which is the equivalent of 12.5Mbps. 100Base-T can be accomplished with twisted-pair or fiber-optic cables, but not coaxial cables.

Accelerated Graphics Port (AGP)

AGP is a PCI-based bus standard specifically designed for graphics needs. AGP is often considered a bus type, but technically it is a port not a bus because of its singular nature. An AGP port is 32 bits wide and runs at 66 MHz.

Active Directory Services

Active Directory Services is the directory service exclusive to Windows 2000. ADS is LDAP-based using logical objects to create a tree and forest structure where all objects are interrelated. ADS also handles everything in a Windows 2000 domain from user accounts to multidomain site replication.

AGP

See Accelerated Graphics Port.

ambient

Generally used as a nontechnical term, ambient refers to the environment or surroundings. Ambient temperature refers to the average temperature existing in the open spaces of a computer room (as opposed to inside server cases or cabinets).

AT attachment (ATA)

Also known as IDE, ATA drives integrate parts of the hard disk controller with the device. Several ATA flavors exist: ATA 2, ATA 3, Ultra ATA, and ATA 66.

ATA

See AT attachment.

authentication

The process whereby a user receives access to network resources. Authentication usually requires a username, password, and an authentication authority (such as a server).

backside bus

A bus internal to the CPU chip that connects the CPU circuitry to the L2 cache.

backup

A copy or clone of something that contributes to an overall disaster recovery or fault-tolerance plan. The term often refers to data backups that can be placed on separate media and transported or placed in different types of storage in order to ensure full recovery and prevent data loss; it can, however, refer to copied computers or computer images as well.

backup domain controller (BDC)

Exclusive to Windows NT, a BDC is a server that stores a read-only copy of the domain's SAM database. This backup copy is regularly replicated to the BDC by the primary domain controller (PDC).

baseline

A set of standard or average performance metrics based on a server or computer that can be used for comparison. Baselines should include performance data for hard disk, memory, paging, and CPU utilization. A baseline should also cover a period of time sufficient enough to determine when the system is used during what points of the day, week, and sometimes even month.

basic input output system (BIOS)

A chip or processor that contains basic information about a computer or computing device. The BIOS contains programs that usually enable the device to initialize without accessing an alternative memory source.

BDC

See backup domain controller.

BEDO RAM

See Burst EDO RAM.

BIOS

See basic input output system.

bit

The smallest unit of data that can exist, in the same way that an atom is the smallest unit of matter. Technically, a bit is also the space taken up by a single piece of data. This single piece of data can be either a 1 or a 0.

bridge

A device or server that makes a data translation from one format or platform to another. A bridging device usually translates different types of media such as Ethernet and Token Ring, or fiber and Ethernet. A bridging server usually translates data between different servers of a particular type, such as email (Lotus and Exchange) or database (Oracle and SQL) servers.

Burst EDO RAM (BEDO RAM)

A specific type of RAM that sends data in bursts in order to speed up data transfer rates. The advantage is that the RAM does not need to remain in sync with the CPU constantly; the disadvantage is that it requires bus speeds of 66 MHz or less.

bus

An electronic highway of sorts that enables data to travel from point a to point b. Advanced internal buses, such as PCI, allow data to travel to and from multiple points. Buses also can exist externally between computers or devices in the form of data or network cablesThese types of external data buses can be serial, USB or IEEE 1394, among a host of other connection types.

bus controller

An authoritative device that ensures proper bus utilization. As covered in this book, the bus controller is usually the CPU, but it can also be a bus master.

bus mastering device

A device that has the ability to become the bus controller for short periods of time. A bus mastering device (usually a hard drive controller) is distinct from the standard bus controller, which is usually the CPU.

byte

Eight bits of data.

cache

A term that refers to a physical device as well as a process. As a process, caching takes frequently used information and stores it in higher priority memory. This higher priority memory is called the cache. Caching is similar to book marking a page in a book for easy reference. Rather than searching through the entire book for a given word or definition, caching not only bookmarks the page, but also copies it into a smaller book that is easily readable and faster to use. Caching usually occurs with memory and hard drives.

cache bus

A bus that communicates between a device and a cache. The buses between RAM and the RAM cache, the hard drive and conventional RAM cache, and the CPU and the L1 cache are all examples of cache buses.

CAT3

A type of unshielded twisted-pair cable that can support data transfer speeds of up to 10Mbps. The cable resembles telephone cable and contains four pair of wires in twisted pairs. Traditionally used for networks, only two pairs of the available four pairs are used for data transmission.

CAT5

A type of unshielded twisted-pair cable that can support data transfer speeds of up to 100Mbps. The cable resembles telephone cable, and contains four pair of wires in twisted pairs. Traditionally used for networks, only two pairs of the available four pairs are used for data transmission.

central processing unit (CPU)

A computer chip that processes instructions and information from all systems on the computer. Nothing occurs on the server or system without the CPU being involved and either delegating or delivering instructions or data.

Certified NetWare Engineer (CNE)

A Novell NetWare certification that requires passing six exams. More advanced certifications exist as well, such as Master CNE (MCNE) and Certified NetWare Instructor (CNI).

client/server

A networked application model according to which application processing is split between the server and the client, thus theoretically producing a faster and more efficient networked application. Client/server applications often are database applications where the user interface processing is handled by the client computer, and the data processing is handled by the server. Parts of the processing that is between the user interface and data processing is split between the two systems.

cloning

The process of making an exact copy of a computer, system, or data. Cloning a computer does not occur frequently, however hard disk cloning is an effective means of data backup and also computer deployment.

clustering

A process whereby multiple computers or servers are networked together for the purpose of sharing CPU utilization.

CNE

See Certified NetWare Engineer.

cold site

An offsite disaster recovery facility that can become functional in a matter of days or weeks. Cold site facilities usually consist of separate offices or branch locations and may not include equipment, wiring, or electricity.

controller

A device that manages data transfer between the computer and a designated device, such as hard drive or printer.

copy backup

A data backup where the selected files are copied but the archive bit is not reset.

CPU
See central processing unit.

crosstalk
The process whereby data or information from one unshielded cable can bleed into another unshielded cable.

daily backup
A data backup in which all files that have changed since the last incremental or full backup are copied, yet the archive bit is not reset.

DAT
See digital audio tape.

data center
A large computer room that can contain many different types of computers, such as mainframes and minicomputers as well as microcomputer servers. A data center is to a computer room what a computer room is to a server closet.

database
A specific type of memory storage method or a server that is dedicated to this type of storage. A database stores information in a logical and sometimes relational format in such a manner that a database application can easily and quickly gather different types of data for presentation and analysis by a user or client program.

DDR SDRAM
See Double Data Rate SDRAM.

DHCP
See Dynamic Host Configuration Protocol.

diagnostic
A method or tool used to determine specific status on a computer or server.

DIB
See Dual Independent Bus.

differential
A data backup that copies all data that has changed since the last full backup. A differential backup does not reset the archive bit.

digital audio tape (DAT)
A type of data backup media that can store anywhere from 2GB to 24GB of data.

digital linear tape (DLT)
A backup media that can store from 20GB to 40GB of data.

DIMM
See Dual Inline Memory Module.

Direct Rambus DRAM (DRD RAM)
A proprietary type of memory that uses the full frequency to transmit data across a narrow bus that effectively increases speeds. DRD RAM uses a specific module called a Rambus Inline Memory Module (RIMM).

directory services

The service or daemon that controls and maintains network and resource access. All network resources, including shares, drives, data, users, groups, and scripts, are stored in a directory service. Novell NetWare uses NDS, Windows NT uses SAM, and Windows 2000 uses ADS.

disaster recovery

The process of recovering partially or completely from a failure. Disaster recovery often refers to complete destruction, but it should more properly be considered on a granular level. Disaster recovery should include planning for any system or component that is mission critical to the business.

DLT

See digital linear tape.

DNS

See Domain Name System.

domain

A logical grouping of objects, such as computers, servers, resources, and devices, within a logical security boundary living under a single authentication authority.

Domain Name System (DNS)

A name resolution service that traditionally runs on Unix servers; however, Microsoft is offering an equivalent within the Windows NT and 2000 platforms. DNS resolves domain names to TCP/IP addresses.

For example, when you ping **www.microsoft.com**, it is DNS that makes the translation to 207.46.197.100.

Double Data Rate SDRAM (DDR SDRAM)

A type of standard SDRAM that transfers data only on the upward half of the transmit frequency. DDR SDRAM transmits data on the complete frequency, thus allowing twice as much data to be transmitted.

DRAM

See Dynamic RAM.

DRD RAM

See Direct Rambus DRAM.

Dual Independent Bus (DIB)

A bus architecture that uses one bus from the processor to main memory and another bus to the L2 Cache. These buses are also known as the backside and frontside buses. DIB architecture is unique because the processor can use both buses at the same time, which increases speeds. DIB is available only on Pentium II and Pro systems.

Dual Inline Memory Module (DIMM)

A type of 168-pin memory module that offers no pin redundancy as seen in SIMMs. DIMM RAM is faster than SIMM RAM. DIMM modules are used in DRAM and SDRAM.

Dynamic Host Configuration Protocol (DHCP)

A protocol designed for dynamically assigning TCP/IP configuration information to client computers. Any server running this protocol can be termed a DHCP server. The implementation of DHCP eliminates the need to manually document and maintain unique TCP/IP addresses across clients on the network.

Dynamic RAM (DRAM)

An older and nearly obsolete type of RAM that sends data one address line at a time.

ECC RAM

See Error Correcting Code RAM.

EDO RAM

See Extended Data Out RAM.

EISA

See Extended Industry Standard Architecture.

electrostatic discharge (ESD)

An event in which a difference in electrostatic current is discharged by way of contact with something that both conducts electricity and has a different charge than the original object.

Error Correcting Code RAM (ECC RAM)

A type of memory that tests and corrects memory.

ESD

See electrostatic discharge.

Ethernet

A type of LAN (also known as IEEE 802.3) that defines physical and certain software layers of the OSI model. Ethernet's uniqueness lies in the fact that it uses collision detection to allow multiple simultaneous communications to occur.

Explorer

The trade name for several different software packages within the Microsoft stable. Windows Explorer is the current operating shell that is used in the Windows 95, 98, NT, and 2000 operating systems. Unfortunately, Windows Explorer is also the name of the file manager program. Internet Explorer is the interface for the Web browser, and there is also a hardware mouse available bearing this name. For the purposes of the Server+ exam, the term Explorer refers to the file manager program.

Extended Data Out RAM (EDO RAM)

A type of RAM that is slightly faster than FPM RAM.

Extended Industry Standard Architecture (EISA)

A PC bus architecture that is faster than ISA and supports multiprocessing.

failover

A fault tolerance concept where functionality of a device or component will, upon failure, shunt over to another device or component automatically. The device that receives the functionality is called a failover device.

Fast Ethernet

A marketing term for 100Base-T, which is an Ethernet standard that transmits data across a LAN at up to 100Mbps.

Fast Page Mode RAM (FPM RAM)

A type of RAM that is faster than standard DRAM and slower than EDO RAM.

FAT

See file allocation table.

FAT32

A drive format that supports hard drives larger than 2GB, available only with certain versions of Windows 95 and 98.

fault tolerance

A concept that involves plans, means, and methodologies used to recover from systems and device failures. The term usually refers to immediate or near immediate recovery methods.

file allocation table (FAT)

The original disk format that also describes the method of file location on a hard drive. In this particular format, a hard drive's table of contents is stored in a file allocation table.

File and Print Services

A type of server that serves network clients by providing files and printer accessibility to network clients.

File Transfer Protocol (FTP)

A protocol and a server type that allows remote clients to access, modify, and create files. FTP has

been used with Unix and minicomputers for many years.

firewall

A type of server or network device that assists in the prevention of unauthorized access from outside the LAN.

FPM RAM

See Fast Page Mode RAM.

frontside bus

The bus that connects the CPU to main memory.

FTP

See File Transfer Protocol.

full backup

A copy of all available data on the system where the archive bit is reset.

gateway

A server or device type through which all clients must pass in order to reach resources or data on the other side. Typically, a "default gateway" is a router or server that must be crossed in order to access the Internet.

generator

A machine that typically runs on diesel fuel, which generates power suitable for usage within any number of different situations. Generators can be used to sustain computer rooms or data centers. These types of generators range from mobile devices on trailers to large engines placed on a pad outside of a building.

GFS
See Grandfather Father Son.

gigabit Ethernet
A variation of the 802.3 standard that allows up to 1000Mbps transmission speeds. Newer technologies are being developed; however, current media for gigabit Ethernet is restricted to fiber optics.

Grandfather Father Son (GFS)
A tape rotation scheme where one tape is used for a single backup every month, four to five other tapes are used for a weekly backup, and six additional tapes are used for daily backups.

graphical user interface (GUI)
An interface that communicates functionality and receives user input that is graphically based, as opposed to text-based. GUI interfaces are common with recent versions of NetWare, Unix, and Linux. The only NOSs that sport a full GUI are Windows NT and 2000.

group
A logical grouping of users or computers that is used to assign resource permissions and scripts.

GUI
See graphical user interface.

High Performance File System (HPFS)
The default file system used in OS/2. Support for HPFS is available with Windows NT, but not Windows 2000.

Hot Plug PCI
A specialized form of PCI bus that allows devices to be installed and removed without shutting down the server.

hot site
An offsite facility that is equipped with computers, wiring, electricity, and servers. A hot site should be fully functioning for your company within two or three days of a disaster situation.

hot spare
An additional device that is installed and available for immediate failover in the event of a similar device's failure.

hot swap
The functional ability to install and remove a device without shutting down the server. Hot Plug PCI is a form of hot swapping, yet not all hot swap devices are Hot Plug PCI devices. Hot swapping can also be used for server fans, power supplies, and hard drives.

HPFS
See High Performance File System.

hub
A network communications device specific for Ethernet that connects multiple systems together.

IEEE 1394
A standard that allows data I/O speeds of up to 40Mbps. Also known as FireWire. IEEE 1394 is the fastest external connection outside of SCSI.

IEEE 1394 devices can include a hard drive, keyboard, mouse, modem, CD drive, or any other peripheral available externally.

IFCONFIG.EXE
A Unix/Linux utility that allows you to configure TCP/IP address information. Other network information is also available.

incremental backup
A partial backup scheme where only data that has changed is backed up, and all data that is backed up resets the archive bit.

Industry Standard Architecture (ISA)
The I/O bus type that was standard when PCs were first created.

I/O bus
Any bus that is used to connect peripherals. Types of I/O buses include ISA, EISA, MCI, and PCI.

IPCONFIG.EXE
A utility that is used to view and configure TCP/IP address information. The /release and /renew switches allow the system to erase all TCP/IP configuration information and request new information from a DHCP server.

IPX/SPX
The default protocol used in Novell NetWare systems.

ISA
See Industry Standard Architecture.

Kerberos v5
A key-based authentication system that allows secure communications on a very insecure network. Kerberos is named after the three-headed dog that guarded the gates of Hades in Greek mythology, and is intended to indicate the strength and stability of the product.

KVM (keyboard, video, mouse)
A device that allows multiple computers or servers to use a single keyboard, monitor, and mouse. KVM switches can also be combined to allow up to 64 devices to use the same keyboard, monitor, and mouse.

L2 cache bus
The data path between the CPU and the L2 cache, which is located on the CPU chip. Also known as the backside bus.

LAN
See local area network.

LIF
See low insertion force.

Linux
An NOS that uses an open standard that is based on Unix. Linux started out as a free operating system whose source code was available on the Internet. Tremendous popularity and demands have enabled several companies to create specific versions of Linux to meet more corporate demands. The cost of these specialized versions, such as Red Hat and Caldera, is still minimal compared to the equivalent versions in Unix, NetWare, and Windows.

load balancing

The process where several computers or servers are networked together for the purpose of sharing CPU utilization and application processing.

local area network (LAN)

A group of computers connected via a network interface that allows network communications to occur without the use of a router or gateway.

local I/O Bus

Synonymous with the PC or I/O bus, the local I/O bus is the bus that connects peripherals on a PC or server. ISA, EISA, and PCI are all local I/O bus types.

low insertion force (LIF)

A socket type that allows circuit chips to be inserted and removed without using soldering tools.

mainframe

A large computer that can support thousands of simultaneous connections and processes. Mainframe processing is true multiple application processing, but does not support a user interface that is graphically based.

Management Information Base (MIB)

A list of objects that can be monitored by SNMP or RMON.

math coprocessor

A computer chip designed to perform complex mathematical calculations. The math coprocessor is similar to the AGP port or a RAID controller in that it is a processor designed to alleviate certain complex processes from the main CPU. Unlike AGP or RAID, the math coprocessor is located inside the CPU chip.

MAU

See Multiple Access Unit.

MCI

See Micro Channel Interface.

MCSE

See Microsoft Certified Systems Engineer.

MEM.EXE

A DOS-based utility that is still used in Windows NT and 2000. MEM displays current memory usage and availability.

memory bus

The bus that intermediates between the CPU and the memory. It is also known as the frontside bus.

MIB

See Management Information Base.

Micro Channel Interface (MCI)

A proprietary I/O bus developed by IBM for its PC computers. MCI buses are faster than ISA, but not backward compatible or the industry standard.

microcomputer

An IBM-compatible PC or server.

microprocessor

A type of central processor unit that resides on one computer chip rather than on a series of printed circuit boards.

Microsoft Certified Systems Engineer (MCSE)

A premier-level Microsoft certification. MCSE exams and courseware are NOS-based and currently exist for Windows NT and Windows 2000. The Windows NT certification consists of four core exams and two electives. Windows 2000 MCSE certification requires five core exams and two electives. The Windows NT MCSE certification expires in December 2001.

minicomputer

A scaled-down mainframe computer. Minicomputers use central processors that reside on printed circuit boards.

mission critical

An industry term that indicates any system, process, or function which, upon failure, could result in severe negative consequences or the downfall of the corporation or company.

MMX

See multimedia instructions.

modem

A peripheral device that uses a telephone line to connect a computer to a host system with the purpose of performing data transfers.

MSD.EXE

A Microsoft diagnostic utility that gathers information about a given computer. Information gathered includes peripherals, memory addresses, IRQ addresses, DMA memory addresses, and other system specific data. MSD.EXE comes with Windows 3.x, 9x, and NT.

multimedia instructions (MMX)

Specialized multimedia algorithms that are embedded in several types of Intel CPU chips.

Multiple Access Unit (MAU)

A device similar to a hub that acts as a hub for Token-Ring networks.

NAS

See Network Attached Storage.

NDS

See Novell Directory Services.

NetBEUI

The Microsoft flavor of the NetBIOS protocol.

NetBIOS

See Network Basic Input Output System.

NETSTAT.EXE

A utility common to DOS, Windows, and Unix that shows the status of network connections. It can also show specific protocols and routing tables.

NetWare

A network operating system that primarily acts as a file and print server.

NetWare Loadable Module (NLM)
The NetWare equivalent of a daemon or service.

Network Attached Storage (NAS)
NAS devices are literally hard drives that are attached to the network without being directly attached to a server. In many ways, they are similar to network attached printers in that they are plugged into a network in the same way a printer is plugged in. NAS devices are self-configured to work with several different NOS systems to make their resources and data available to one or more NOSs.

Network Basic Input Output System (NetBIOS)
NetBIOS is a connectionless protocol that communicates with systems by a given computer name.

network interface card (NIC)
A peripheral that allows network connectivity.

Network Monitor
A utility that monitors network activity on a single server.

network operating system (NOS)
An operating system that allows a server to operate as an authentication server and also a directory service server. A base-level NOS provides file and print services on the network.

New Technology File System (NTFS)
An advanced file system available with Windows NT and 2000 that allows additional security and permissions features. NTFS also reduces file fragmentation and increases efficiency.

NIC
See network interface card.

NLM
See NetWare Loadable Module.

NOS
See network operating system.

Novell Directory Services (NDS)
The directory service for Novell NetWare. NDS utilizes an LDAP architecture. LDAP is a standard that allows data transfer and interoperability between NOSs that use LDAP.

NTFS
See New Technology File System.

Ockham's razor
An observation loosely stating that the most obvious solution is quite often correct.

Oracle
A type of database server that often runs on a proprietary computer. Oracle is also available to run on Unix, Linux, and minicomputers.

operating system (OS)
The programming and instructional operations set that provides an interface between the user and the computer; it also handles communications between the two.

OS/2

An IBM OS/NOS that was the first true 32-bit operating system on the market.

over clocking

The process of configuring a CPU to run at speeds greater than it was designed for. Over clocking is not recommended because it is possible to literally burn up the CPU.

paging

A process whereby selcted data that is stored in RAM is placed on the hard drive and moved back to RAM as needed.

parity

A process whereby two pieces of data are compared, and if they are identical, a parity bit of 0 is assigned. If they are not identical, a parity bit of 1 is assigned. Parity is used in error correction and also when reconstructing failed drives in a RAID array.

PCI

See peripheral component interconnect.

PDC

See primary domain controller.

peer-to-peer

A type of networking where all computers on the network serve as both workstations and servers. Peer-to-peer networking has its advantages in the fact that dedicated IT personnel are rarely required to administer and maintain the network. A peer-to-peer network has few disadvantages; however, the most prominent is the fact that every user on the network requires some network administration skills and time in order to administer their own "server."

Performance Monitor

A Windows NT/2000 utility that measures the performance metrics of the local server. Performance Monitor can monitor CPU, hard drive usage, paging, and memory utilization.

peripheral component interconnect (PCI)

An I/O bus that is faster than ISA and EISA. PCI is the current standard for both servers and workstation computers.

plenum

A type of cable housing that is fire resistant. U.S. fire code requires that any cables that are run across the ceiling be coated in plenum.

port

A connector or connection to or from a server or PC. Hardware ports come in all shapes and sizes, and are usually used to connect external peripherals to the system. Software ports are usually communications channels that are used for network data transfer.

power on self test (POST)

The process whereby all major server components are powered on and checked to ensure functionality. The POST process is controlled by the BIOS.

power supply

An electrical device that converts the incoming AC (alternating current) electricity to the DC (direct current) that is used by the system.

primary domain controller (PDC)

A type of Windows NT server that contains a read/write copy of the SAM database, which is the directory service for Windows NT. There can be only one PDC in any given domain.

protocol

A specific communications language utilized for network data transfer. The most widely used protocol today is TCP/IP.

proxy

A type of server that accesses the Internet on behalf of a client computer. Proxy servers usually store frequently used Web sites locally in order to reduce Internet bandwidth. Proxy servers can also act as reverse firewalls by preventing users from accessing certain Web sites based on configured lists or published content.

RAID

See redundant array of inexpensive disks.

RAID 0

A specific type of RAID that has data being laid onto multiple drives in a striped manner. RAID 0 has no fault tolerance.

RAID 1

A standard of backup implementation whereby two disk drives are attached to one drive controller that dynamically maintains a cloned copy of data across two separate hard drives. This process is also known as mirroring. Another variety of RAID 1 is called duplexing, which is the same process with an additional hard disk controller.

RAID 5

A standard of backup implementation that uses an array of disk drives where data is striped across multiple drives, with parity data being laid onto a separate drive. Also known as striping with parity, RAID 5 does not include a dedicated parity drive, so the parity information is evenly stored across all drives in the array.

RAID array

A group of three or more hard drives configured as a RAID unit.

random access memory (RAM)

Another term for the volatile memory that is used in PCs and servers. RAM requires a constant electrical charge in order to maintain the data it stores. Thus, when the system is shut down, all data in memory must either be written to the hard drive or lost.

read-only memory (ROM)

Nonvolatile memory that is not changeable; therefore, it does not require that an electrical charge be maintained in order to maintain its memory. ROM is found in memory modules that will not change.

redundant array of inexpensive disks (RAID)

A general term for multiple drives configured in such a manner as to provide increased performance and/or fault tolerance. RAID functions can be performed using either software or installed hardware. Software RAID is cheaper, yet has a severe negative impact on CPU utilization and overall server efficiency. Hardware RAID does not have this impact and also offers additional features, such as hot swap and hot spare, which are unavailable with software RAID.

remote access

A type of server that allows a user to remotely access network resources. Remote access servers are usually modem servers. However, with the advent of virtual private networking (VPN), many remote access servers are simply VPN servers.

Remote Monitor (RMON)

An application that monitors network events as well as specific server events. RMON is a logical enhancement to SNMP, whose standards were delayed by the committees that created it.

repeater

A networking device that copies and amplifies an electrical (and in this case, transmitted network data) signal from one portion of a network to another.

restore

The process of reading and implementing data contained in a backup.

ribbon cable

A type of cable containing several wires laid flat and parallel to each other, and covered with a plastic sheath. One of the end wires is usually colored red or some other different color so as to ensure that the proper connections are made. Ribbon cables are usually data cables and are often seen connecting hard drives.

RMON

See Remote Monitor.

ROM

See read-only memory.

router

A server or network device that acts as a specialized bridge between two network segments. A network segment is defined as a TCP/IP subnet. A router is most often used to connect a company to the Internet.

SAM

See Security Access Manager.

SAN

See Storage Area Network.

scientific method

A problem-solving method where a theory is tested and modified based on the test results until the theory is proven by the test.

SCSI

See Small Computer Systems Interface.

SDRAM
See synchronous DRAM.

Security Access Manager (SAM)
The Windows NT directory service. The SAM database required that a PDC be designated to hold the SAM. Additional BDCs could be created for fault tolerance and redundancy purposes, but these BDCs contained read-only copies of the SAM.

server
Technically, any computer that provides a service on a network. Logically, however, a server can also contain advanced hardware, software, and services that you will not see on any other types of computers. Additional emphasis is placed on server downtime due to their multi-user functionality and general higher profile within a corporation.

Server Fault Tolerance (SFT III)
The Novell NetWare software RAID solution. SFT provides solutions for RAID 0, 1, and 5.

Server Management
A utility or tool that is often shipped with systems that are designed to be servers.

Simple Mail Transfer Protocol (SMTP)
A protocol and type of server that runs this protocol that basically transmits mail. SMTP is an industry standard that is used for most Internet email applications running Unix.

Simple Network Management Protocol (SNMP)
A basic suite of protocolsthat allows the transmission of certain performance data (known as traps) from an SNMP client machine to an SNMP server. SNMP clients can be other types of servers. The performance data is gathered and analyzed by a management application program that also uses SNMP.

single inline memory module (SIMM)
Similar to DIMMs, SIMMs are memory circuit cards that are either 30 or 72 pins wide and offer redundant connector paths. Both SIMMs and DIMMs have memory chips mounted on them.

single inline pin package (SIPP)
A memory module very similar to SIMMs and DIMMs. The difference is that although SIMMs and DIMMs refer to pins, they are not literally pins. The "pins" on SIMMs and DIMMs are flat metal contact pads that come into contact terminals on the connector that they are plugged into. SIPPs, however, are literally pins that stick out from the circuit board and look like a comb. SIPPs predate both SIMMs and DIMMs and were replaced by SIMMs because the pins were easily bent and broken.

single point of failure (SPOF)
A single device, computer, or component that does not have an alternate device that can perform its functionality and whose failure can cause the entire system to fail.

Small Computer Systems Interface (SCSI)

A specific type of hard drive that allows faster data transmission speeds and also supports separate processing in order to lessen CPU utilization. This type of processing also allows for RAID implementation.

SMTP

See Simple Mail Transfer Protocol.

SNA

See Systems Network Architecture.

SNMP

See Simple Network Management Protocol.

SPOF

See Single Point of Failure.

stacked RAID

Compound RAID where two separate types of RAID are combined to reduce the disadvantages and increase the advantages. An example would be RAID 10, which combines the speed of RAID 0 with the fault tolerance of RAID 1.

storage area network (SAN)

A high-speed network that contains various devices designed for high-speed data access and retrieval. SAN networks are very expensive, as bridges are required to get data from the SAN to the "normal" network where users and computers are. Most SANs use fiber-optic cable as the transmission media.

switch

A networking device that acts in much the same way that a hub does. However, additional logic is included to eliminate unnecessary traffic from one switch to another.

synchronous DRAM (SDRAM)

A type of RAM that ties itself to the CPU bus in order to achieve faster throughput.

systems network architecture (SNA)

A connectivity protocol used to allow PCs to act as mainframe terminals. SNA is also the name of a Microsoft server that performs this same task.

tape drive

A backup device that requires specialized software in order to function. A tape backup is the most common method of data backup due to the portability and cost of the media.

TCP/IP

See Transfer Control Protocol/Internet Protocol.

thicknet

A thick coaxial cable used as a backbone for network transmission. Almost extinct and barely a memory for most administrators, thicknet was once used for most network environments due to its speeds and usability. It quickly fell out of favor due to maintenance costs and the sheer fact that building a thicknet network required connector assembly.

thinnet
A network comprised of thin coaxial cable.

throughput
The amount of data that manages to successfully get from point a to point b.

Token Ring
A type of computer network that uses collision avoidance by allowing data along the wire via a single token. Data on Token-Ring networks travels at a maximum of 16Mbps, which was the fastest speed available until 100Base-T was introduced. Today, Token-Ring networks are virtually extinct.

TRACERT.EXE
A utility running under DOS, Windows, and Unix that traces the path that a test packet takes between the source and destination computers.

Transmission Control Protocol/Internet Protocol (TCP/IP)
An industry-standard protocol suite that is used to access the Internet. TCP/IP usage requires a unique TCP/IP address consisting of four binary octets. These octets, when converted to standard decimal, are what appear to us as standard TCP/IP addresses.

uninterruptible power supply (UPS)
An external battery that is used to support the function of one or more servers during a full or partial power outage. A UPS also protects against power spikes and brownouts.

universal serial bus (USB)
An external bus with a flat connector that allows up to 12Mbps data transfer speeds.

Unix
A multiuser multitasking OS/NOS that predates PCs and was designed as a programming platform. Unix is the only OS/NOS that can run on mainframes, minicomputers, and microcomputers. The Unix NOS server is primarily text-based; however, more recent advances have enabled the development of GUIs including the X Windows and MOTIF interfaces, which you are more likely to encounter in the Unix OS workstations.

video electronics standards association (VESA)
A local bus type that was completely backward compatible with ISA, yet faster than ISA.

Wake-on-LAN
A feature of many servers that enables the server to go into suspend mode when not in use and automatically wake itself up when it receives a network request.

WAN
See wide area network.

WFM
See wired for management.

wide area network (WAN)
A group of LANs connected via WAN connections and routers.

Windows 2000

An OS/NOS that is produced by Microsoft. Windows 2000 contains more features and improvements over Windows NT. It uses Active Directory Services.

Windows Internet Naming Service (WINS)

A service and server type that provides name resolution services to translate between NetBIOS computer names and TCP/IP addresses.

Windows NT

An OS/NOS that is produced by Microsoft. Windows NT relies on the SAM for directory services and is a 32-bit NOS.

wired for management (WFM)

A standard that allows internal server devices to be monitored for specific management purposes, such as predictive failure analysis.

Index